EVERYONE
CAN WIN

EVERYONE CAN WIN

Responding to Conflict Constructively

HELENA CORNELIUS
and SHOSHANA FAIRE
with ESTELLA CORNELIUS

SIMON & SCHUSTER
AUSTRALIA

First published in Australia in 1989, reprinted 1989, 1990 (three times) 1991 (three times), 1992, 1993 (twice), 1994 (four times), 1995, 1996 (twice), 1998, 2000, 2001, 2003, 2011, 2020, 2021, 2023 by Simon & Schuster (Australia) Pty Limited
Suite 19a, Level 1, Building C
450 Miller Street,
Cammeray, NSW 2062
Sydney New York London Toronto
Visit our website at www.simonsaysaustralia.com
Second Edition published in 2006
© 1989, 2006 Helena Cornelius and Shoshana Faire

Cataloguing-in-Publication data:
Cornelius, Helena.
Everyone can win : responding to conflict constructively.

2nd ed.
Includes index.
ISBN 9780 7318 1298 1.

1. Conflict management. 2. Interpersonal conflict.
I. Faire, Shoshana. II. Title.

303.69

Illustrations by Roger Roberts
Cover design by Darian Causby
Internal design by Lore Foye
Typeset in 12 on 14pt Minion by Kirby Jones
Printed in Australia by Griffin Press

10 9 8 7 6

Dedicated to
Dr Stella Cornelius, AO, OBE,
peace and conflict resolution activist,
whose wisdom and compassion
continue to inspire us

HELENA CORNELIUS is a psychologist, workshop leader and mediator. She is a founding director of the Conflict Resolution Network. She has authored, produced and co-authored twelve other major works in the area of Conflict Resolution, including *The Gentle Revolution* (Australia: Simon & Schuster, 1998). Her techniques and manuals are widely used in corporate organisations, government departments, schools and the wider community.

website: www.crnhq.org
email: hc@crnhq.org

SHOSHANA FAIRE is a workshop leader, facilitator, mediator and coach and is well regarded as an expert in the field of Conflict Resolution. Her company, Professional Facilitators International, conducts a range of programs on building collaborative workplace relationships for corporations and government departments. She facilitates meetings and teams and mediates conflicts. Over twenty years she has influenced many thousands of people to build constructive and productive relationships in all areas of their lives.

website: www.facilitators.net
email: shoshana@facilitators.net

FOREWORD
TO THE SECOND EDITION

The secret's out! Conflict resolution is an approach with heart. It's based on wanting the best for all concerned and being committed to examining our motives whenever we fall out of compassion. We find these guidelines are compatible with all the great spiritual and philosophical theories. It has become increasingly obvious that these are the skills needed for a peaceful world. We ignore anyone's needs, including our own, at our peril. When all societies turn to skill, instead of violence, to solve problems, world peace becomes a real option. There is a major education job still to be done, so that all people understand how far, with persistence, a collaborative approach that recognises everyone's needs can take us. Perhaps more than anyone else, our leaders must become experts in this field.

Since first writing *Everyone Can Win* nearly twenty years ago, thousands of people have taken training courses in the skills we have developed at the Conflict Resolution Network. The book itself has been read by thousands more — and they have spread the word! We represented the leading edge in 1989; now these earlier concepts form a standard skill set on the training agenda for organisational leadership and management, universities and schools. Out of this wealth of experience — our own and that of many, many others — we have been able to include in this second edition more skills and more refined ways of explaining them.

Those familiar with our first edition and other training materials will see some changes in the order of presentation. We now open with *Responding to Conflict* which roughly equates with our other materials on *Creative Response*. *Partners not Opponents* is our update on the previous topic *The Win/Win Approach*. In this edition we have moved from using the term win/win approach to collaborative approach on most occasions. Some workshop leaders now favour the phrase constructive approach — emphasising the difference between it and a destructive or do-nothing attitude. Some prefer to use the collaborative or cooperative approach, emphasising the importance of joint problem-solving when conflict arises. Some stay with win/win because it clearly directs attention to equality and fairness for all the parties concerned. Others say that in personal relationships they don't think of winning or losing, just: 'Am I listened to or am I ignored? I would only think of winning if I were playing a sport.' Some Aboriginal people with a clearer focus on community and group say 'One win is enough! We all win when conflict is resolved.' These are all fair comments and at times you'll find we do use constructive or cooperative, as well as collaborative and win/win, as the context dictates. If you find a spot where you wouldn't have used our preferred word, mentally replace it with your own alternative.

Over the years we have often had to emphasise that this is an *approach*: it does not always mean we will get perfect *solutions*. We've heard in workshops: 'But the pie is only so big! And half is just not enough!' We love stimulating the conflict resolver's creativity with 'How will you increase the size of the pie?' or, if that pie was apple and there's no apple pie left, 'How will you create one more that is apricot?' This is not idealistic, it's commonsense!

To be gender neutral, we have chosen to follow spoken conventions in this book and use 'they', 'them' and 'their' for the singular as well as the plural.

The fresh ideas from many experts in the field are included in this revised and expanded second edition. We — Helena, Shoshana and Estella — have swept our energy and attention through every nook and cranny of these wonderful skills and once again the material shines like a new pin. Enjoy!

Helena Cornelius and
Shoshana Faire
May 2006

CONTENTS

Acknowledgments   *xiii*

Introduction   *xv*

1. Responding to Conflict   1

2. Partners Not Opponents   24

3. Empathy
   Part I   40
   Part II   57

4. Appropriate Assertiveness   73

5. Cooperative Power   97

6. Managing Emotions   122

7. Willingness to Resolve   141

8. Mapping the Conflict   160

9. Designing Options   179

10. Negotiation   189

11. Introduction to Mediation   211

12. Broadening Perspectives   233

Appendix I — *Conflict clues: what to do about them*   243

Appendix II — *Confronting people in authority*   244

Index   246

ACKNOWLEDGMENTS

We would like to thank the many thousands of participants of conflict resolution skills programs and the many course leaders who trialled, polished and expanded each of the skills in this book and then fed the information back to us so that we could continually improve what Conflict Resolution Network has to offer. These skills have now been refined over twenty years of continuous application in an enormous variety of contexts.

What a joy to have on the writing team for this second edition Estella Cornelius, without whose updates, new stories and section contributions we would never have met our deadline. That makes three generations of Cornelius women at work for a more peaceful planet! Special thanks for suggestions and many hours of careful editing to Malcolm Turnbull and Stella Cornelius, and for contributions to this edition from Christine James, who shares our passion for the power of questions, and to Caroline Butler, who is on the leading edge of 'through the body' approaches to change.

It has been a wonderful exercise to contact many of the most experienced workshop leaders we know to discuss how they have developed the materials for their organisations. This second edition includes many of these developments.

Deepest thanks for support in producing this new edition to Alan Bassal, Robyn Gaspari, Gill Goater, Phillip Hart, Fiona Hollier, Susan Kroening, Kerrie Murray, Janet Sernak, Nancy Shearer, Lynette Simons, Elke Tunold, Kerry Turnbull and Martin Turnbull. From the bottom of our hearts we thank them for being so dedicated to include parts of Conflict Resolution Network materials in many courses they run and for taking the time to update us, letting us review their teaching notes and inspiring us with their favourite books and concepts gathered over many years.

This book builds on the firm foundation laid down for us by many more people who helped create the first edition of this book. They deserve mention again (in alphabetical order): Dart Braeder, Thomas Crum, Professor Jennifer David, Sonya Hall, Patricia Janssen, Robert Kiyosaki, Kirsty Melville, Mike Minehan, Susan Morris-Yates, Rita Spencer and Dr Greg Tillett.

And, finally, may we acknowledge you, the reader, for your commitment to finding a better way to communicate.

INTRODUCTION

Everyone Can Win is a collaborative approach to arguments and difficult relationships. When we have the skills to handle these well, everyone can win in the transaction. The image of victory and defeat is replaced by a partnership in problem-solving.

After you've read the book, we hope you'll be dedicated to this approach — because it works. It's the stuff of community, good will and good skill. It's a better way to play. You get more of what you want more of the time — and so will the people around you. Of course, there will be times when you won't appear to win, but you'll be making every situation into an opportunity for positive change — somehow.

The field of conflict resolution is now immense. Over the last twenty years a groundswell of professional practitioners has been coaching and teaching in this area. This is a big shift since the start of the Conflict Resolution Network (CRN) in 1986. That year was the International Year of Peace, and the United Nations Association of Australia founded the beginnings of our organisation as its contribution to the Year and as successor to its Peace and Conflict Resolution Program, which had been established by Stella Cornelius in 1973. CRN's methods and structure have evolved over the years, but its purpose remains the same — to develop, teach, implement and learn the skills of conflict resolution for personal, professional and international effectiveness. World peace starts with well-handled conflict in our daily lives and public policy reflects community skills.

Drawing on fields as diverse as leadership, management, personal development, Buddhism, psychotherapy, psychology, social work, child rearing, critical thinking and the martial arts we — Helena Cornelius and Shoshana Faire — carefully constructed a package of key skills. These became useful filing drawers for classifying a wide range of thought and literature, which could contribute to the developing field of conflict resolution. Many wonderful trainers have since added major contributions. These skills became the substance of CRN's teaching programme. Their significance and relevance in improving people's lives have become abundantly clear over the intervening years. They've become benchmark courses for people in business, government, schools and community organisations.

Visit our website, www.crnhq.org where CRN, now a resource centre, offers high-quality free and low-cost training materials for educational programmes in areas such as business and management, law, town planning, medicine, nursing, social work, schools, psychology, communication studies and many others. These skills move people and systems away from adversarial approaches towards cooperation which is better for workplaces, community action and personal relationships.

Everyone Can Win presents you with practical tools. We've incorporated the theory into everyday language and extracted what makes a difference on the ground when in a difficult conversation or you want to manage your relationships well. Each chapter introduces one of twelve tools or skills for your toolkit. Just as a tool has many uses, so these skills transfer readily to widely differing contexts. The skills you teach a young child are basically the same ones needed by an international diplomat. One morning, you'll pull out a tool for a problem in the kitchen over breakfast and later find yourself needing it in a difficult business meeting in the afternoon. In choosing our examples and stories we've taken care to include a variety of contexts so that you can see how readily the skills transfer.

Here's a brief run-down of the tools in the toolkit and the questions the book is answering:

Chapter 1 **Responding to conflict**
How can I respond, not react?
What opportunities can this situation bring?

Chapter 2 **Partners Not Opponents**
How can we solve this as partners rather than opponents?
What needs underlie our positions on this issue?

Chapter 3 **Empathy:**
Part I
How can I open up the communication?
What are they trying to say?

Part II
What can I do to let go of my judgements about their approach?

Chapter 4 **Appropriate Assertiveness**
How can I express myself so that I'm more likely to be heard?

Chapter 5 **Cooperative Power**
What will steer us to use power 'with' rather than 'over' each other?

Chapter 6 Managing Emotions
What messages are my emotions delivering to me?
How can I use these messages for positive change?
How will I best manage my own and other people's strong emotions?

Chapter 7 Willingness to Resolve
Am I ready to move beyond personal issues towards forgiveness?
What feelings or issues do I need to release?

Chapter 8 Mapping the Conflict
Would a map of needs and fears give us greater clarity?

Chapter 9 Designing Options
Can we explore creative options together?

Chapter 10 Negotiation
How can I be hard on the problem and considerate of others and their needs?
How can we make the best deal possible that is fair for both of us?

Chapter 11 Introduction to Mediation
Can I make a skilful mediating intervention here?
How could I help the process and stay neutral?

Chapter 12 Broadening Perspectives
Can I put this issue into perspective?
Am I including my 'heart' as well as my intellect?

The questions above can be used at any time you are involved in conflict or are challenged. The toolkit is also a great starting point for documents and speeches you want to offer in conflict-resolving mode.

When faced with conflict or a challenging situation, some skills will be more relevant and others will sit in your toolkit waiting to feature in another context. Use the Appendix Conflict clues: what to do about them ... to decide which strategy you need in a given situation. For group work or home study, do the exercises in each chapter and discuss. You can access more training material and checklists on our website.

For those of you already familiar with Daniel Goleman's writings on *emotional intelligence*, you'll find close resemblances between the skills we present here and the five domains of emotional intelligence he describes.[1] We see that our skills of self-management fit his concepts of personal competencies: self-awareness, self-regulation and self-motivation. Our skills of managing relationships align with his concepts of social competencies: empathy and social analysis. The skills in *Everyone Can Win* are the 'how to' of emotional intelligence. This book can raise your score. As Goleman says, *our brains are very plastic. New neural pathways are constantly being built as we learn new responses, new habits and new ways of thinking.*

As you read *Everyone Can Win*, try to associate the skills with your own experiences. You'll learn the skills much faster by relating to them, talking them over and trying them out, rather than merely reading them. The boxed stories, like little case studies, may remind you of similar incidents.

Throughout the book we often focus on skilful questions and reframes of language that take thinking forward. They appear next to the lightbulb icon. We explain the principles behind our examples so that you can craft your own to fit the situation. A good question can shift someone out of closed-off or ineffectual communication patterns. It can be the turning point, the catalyst for change. Practise your skilful questions and reframes as often as you can. Everyone around you will benefit.

Leave *Everyone Can Win* with your bedside reading or with your reference books at work. This is not a book to read once and put away; keep it handy and reach for the relevant chapter any time you sense conflict developing. Copy out and put up somewhere obvious a relevant catchphrase from one of the boxed key points, or run through a chapter summary with someone else. Work with the book until it's part of your life. Love thy neighbour does not come as a gift; it takes skill and practice.

The aim of *Everyone Can Win* is to celebrate conflict, not to squash it. It is designed to help you get what you want for yourself and others, and to see conflict as a creative opportunity. Successful conflict resolution releases energy, joy and a sense of achievement. Homes become sanctuaries for self-esteem and self-discovery, workplaces foster mutual support and growth, and the global community thrives on effective collaboration. Start where it all begins — with you!

Note

1 Daniel Goleman, *Emotional Intelligence* (USA: Bantam Books, 1995) and *Working with Emotional Intelligence* (USA: Bantam Books, 1998)

CHAPTER 1

Responding to Conflict

How can I respond, not react?
What opportunities can this situation bring?

Conflict exists when two or more people see their needs or values as incompatible. It is the stuff of life. It happens to all of us. As individuals with different needs, tastes, views, values and personalities, sooner or later we are bound to clash. Its scale may be small or large. Conflict flares up over back fences or national borders; cleaning up the kitchen or cleaning up the environment. It happens in the briefest interactions with strangers and in our most intimate relationships.

What happens when conflict is handled badly or not handled at all?

- stress
- unresolved problems
- resentment
- illness

- damaged relationships
- low productivity and motivation
- confusion
- tiredness

What else have you experienced or observed?

With these sorts of results, it's not surprising that we want to avoid conflict!

What happens when conflict is handled well?

- relief
- resolution
- empowerment
- positive changes
- vitality

- closer relationships
- high productivity and motivation
- clarity
- more trust
- respect

What else have you experienced or observed?

Conflict can be positive or negative, constructive or destructive, depending on how you handle it. Why do you settle for less than the best possible outcome? Because you lack the skills and therefore the courage to handle and see the process through successfully.

Our ability to transform conflict from being negative to positive forms part of our *emotional intelligence*. Well-known psychologist and writer Daniel Goleman[1] believes that human competencies such as our capacity for managing our emotions, motivations and relationships are of greater consequence than IQ in much of life.

For most people, the idea of embracing conflict requires a complete shift in attitude. Can you come to regard it as dynamic, even exciting? We hope that by reading this book and putting the skills into practice you will open up to conflict and welcome its possibilities. You will come to trust your sharpened emotional intelligence to see you through.

The first step is to shift your mindset so that you say 'Yes!' rather than 'No!' when conflict comes your way. The second step is to immediately look for the opportunities where you can handle it constructively — so that everyone can win. Within each conflict lies the potential to move the relationship, the situation or the system forward. You can come to believe that conflict is the grit in the oyster that produces the pearl!

Conflict is your opportunity for positive change

Conflict Clues

Start small! Conflict does not have to become a crisis before we take charge of the situation. Many serious issues can be prevented by early attention. Managing a potential conflict long before it's a crisis is a sound investment in time and energy. Start by paying attention to the *conflict clues*, which can range from being very subtle to dramatically obvious.

Discomfort

Discomfort is that niggling or 'gut' feeling that indicates something is not quite right about a situation and you're not sure why. At such times your intuition deserves respectful attention. Ask yourself, 'What is really the matter?' and 'Is there something I could do about this now?'

She started just calling out, 'Honey, I'm home', when she got home, instead of finding him wherever he was in the house. He didn't really like that, but was it worth saying anything?

Incidents

The clue that you are experiencing a conflict incident is usually a minor one. Some relatively unimportant thing happens that leaves you feeling upset or irritated for a while — perhaps there's a short sharp exchange that doesn't end well — then you push the problem aside or forget about it.

She's usually running late getting out the door when they're going out together. It irritates him because he is always organised and punctual. He says nothing. She knows he is often a bit cold and a bit short as they go off in the car, but she really doesn't understand why and doesn't ask.

People often do nothing about incidents because they don't know how to sort them out constructively. Rather than doing something they see as destructive, they do nothing at all and the unresolved incident keeps simmering in the back of their minds. In itself an incident may be a simple problem, but if you don't clear it up, the relationship can suffer.

Misunderstanding

People may misunderstand each other because they make false assumptions. It could be that they have misinterpreted the other person's motives or they have confused some facts; their communications don't clarify the problem and they lack rapport. Sometimes misunderstanding arises because the situation raises a touchy issue.

He worries that her wage, rather than his, is the mainstay of the family budget. He fears this might mean she doesn't respect him enough. When this is on his mind he withdraws and she thinks she's done something to annoy him or that he doesn't really love her anymore.

When misunderstandings start we may mull over the situation and exaggerate it with new concerns.

Tension

A build-up of failed communications usually precedes a state of tension. Once there is tension in the relationship the conflict clues are obvious. Emotions run high. The relationship becomes weighed down with negative attitudes and fixed opinions. The way we feel about the other person changes significantly for the worse. The whole relationship is a source of frequent worry. Tension distorts our perception of the other person and most of what they do.

He's cooking the evening meal. She notices him putting oil in the pan and says: 'That's a lot of oil.' He snaps back: 'Well, you can make your own dinner then!' The anxieties and irritations that naturally arise when two people live together are never discussed by this couple. After each 'situation' the gulf between them has widened. The mounting tension started much earlier and is now far more serious than the problem with the oil.

Crisis

A crisis is signalled by extreme behaviour. It's obvious, out in the open, with emotions at boiling point. When someone walks out on a relationship or a job, it's plain there has been conflict that is unresolved. Violence is a sure sign of crisis, as is heated argument where people hurl abuse and become overwhelmed by their feelings. During crises normal behaviour goes out the window. Irrevocable actions are contemplated and sometimes carried out.

He storms out the door, saying nothing more. She doesn't know when or if he'll be home.

Respond early to the conflict clues

Look for conflict clues *before* emotions are running high. Unhandled conflict can easily escalate. The path from discomfort to crisis is often a slippery slope. The message is, don't ignore discomfort and seemingly minor incidents. They're usually much easier to handle at these early stages. Take a moment for self-examination. Is it something you can easily let go of or would it be wiser to get it out in the open? Does it have implications? If so, look for an opportunity to start a constructive conversation.[2] Make this your standard pattern and you will save many small conflicts from growing into serious misunderstandings, tensions or crises.

Think of a current or recent conflict in your life. Can you identify the level it's reached?

Can you trace the development of the conflict by identifying clues at earlier levels?

The intervention you make will depend on the level the conflict has reached. For more on this, consult the Appendix Conflict clues: what to do about them ...

Reacting to Conflict

As you shift how you view conflict, instead of retreating, you become more willing to engage. You'll want to polish your conflict resolution skills, so that you can actually deliver, for yourself and others, the outcomes you believe are possible. When you engage, you'll do one of two things: you'll react or you'll respond. What is the difference?

In this book, we use **react** for when you behave impulsively — your buttons are pushed, you have a knee-jerk reaction, you act in ways you later regret, you've said something you wish you hadn't or you haven't said something you wish you had.

We contrast this with **respond** — consciously choosing your behaviour and what you do or don't say. Afterwards you feel good about the way you handled the situation.

One of the most useful questions you can ask yourself in a moment of conflict or stress is:

-ᵠ- 'Am I reacting or responding?'

There's the stimulus: the conflict; the reply: what we do or say about it and the space in between: that's you! What's going on inside you determines whether you react or respond. If emotions are given free rein, if you're all geared up for a fight and if you are listening only to the conversation in your own head, handling conflict calmly and constructively is not an option — instead, you react, and often overreact, when you can't make an objective assessment about what is going on. You might be overwhelmed or you might intimidate others with only minor provocation.

Between stimulus and response, there is a space. In that space lies our freedom and power to choose our response.
In our response lies our growth and freedom.

Viktor Frankl

Every day we're faced with situations that have the potential to set off under-attack emotions and trigger survival defences. Perhaps someone appears to be taking advantage of you, not respecting your wishes, making you look stupid in front of others or taking the credit for work you have done. Can you recall a recent situation where you felt threatened? How did you handle it?

Fight, Flight and Freeze

EXERCISE: how do you handle conflict?

FIGHT

Behaviour	Rarely	Sometimes	Frequently	People most likely to get this reaction from me
Explode	❑	❑	❑	_____
Shout	❑	❑	❑	_____
Intimidate	❑	❑	❑	_____
Interrupt	❑	❑	❑	_____
Insist I'm right	❑	❑	❑	_____
Keep explaining my point	❑	❑	❑	_____
Tell them how to behave	❑	❑	❑	_____
Nag	❑	❑	❑	_____
Call on others to back me up	❑	❑	❑	_____
Issue ultimatums	❑	❑	❑	_____
Get even	❑	❑	❑	_____
Make sarcastic comments	❑	❑	❑	_____

FLIGHT

Behaviour	Rarely	Sometimes	Frequently	People most likely to get this reaction from me
Run out the door before anything's resolved	❏	❏	❏	_____
Hope the problem will go away if I do nothing	❏	❏	❏	_____
Hold back my opinions to prevent more conflict	❏	❏	❏	_____
Withdraw emotionally until they change their mind	❏	❏	❏	_____
Become cranky, but say nothing about the problem	❏	❏	❏	_____
Tell myself it doesn't matter anyway	❏	❏	❏	_____
Complain — but only behind their back	❏	❏	❏	_____
Act overpolite	❏	❏	❏	_____
Take it out on the wrong person	❏	❏	❏	_____
Give in reluctantly	❏	❏	❏	_____

FREEZE

Behaviour	Rarely	Sometimes	Frequently	People most likely to get this reaction from me
Go silent. Can't even think what to say	❏	❏	❏	_____
Accept physical or verbal abuse and not stand up for myself	❏	❏	❏	_____
Walk on eggshells so as not to arouse their anger	❏	❏	❏	_____
Get depressed or sick	❏	❏	❏	_____
Try not to draw attention to myself	❏	❏	❏	_____
Pretend the attack didn't happen	❏	❏	❏	_____
Become operational again by suppressing my fear	❏	❏	❏	_____
Maintain peace by denying there's a problem	❏	❏	❏	_____

The Role of the Amygdala

The moment we believe we are under attack, our behaviour is likely to be ruled by a primitive brain mechanism in the base of the brain — the amygdala, which consists of two almond-shaped glands. ('Amygdala' comes from the Greek word for almond.) Their lightning-fast response once served our ancestors by triggering action the instant danger was perceived. The amygdala is the survival watchdog, the body's alarm system. It is essential for decoding emotions and, in particular, stimuli that appear threatening. Our emotional memories associated with fear are stored there for speedy retrieval. The amygdala is responsible for asking the important survival question: 'Will I eat it or will it eat me?' — not a question for which you want to wait too long for the answer!

Nowadays we are rarely under physical threat, but often, under perceived psychological threat. Our senses scan the environment for known threats, based on our history of hurts. If anything alarms us, an immediate danger signal is sent to the amygdala which instantly sends messages to the rest of our body to prepare for action. There's an injection of adrenaline hormones and a resulting increase in heart rate, blood pressure, metabolic rate and blood glucose concentration. Over the next few seconds the amygdala receives updates from the slower-to-respond neo-cortex, home to our learning and logical reasoning skills. The hypothalamus which assesses the context and memory of similar situations will also pass on its information to the amygdala. With this extra input the amygdala's initial reaction will be heightened, suppressed or diverted.

In the usual circumstances of our modern lives, we will generally reassess the initial threat, calm ourselves down and take some control of our anger or fear. If these updates do not quickly reassure the amygdala, it may well take control of all brain communication pathways and mobilise a full-on fear/anger reaction. Reason flies out the window! Psychologist Daniel Goleman calls this an *amygdala hijack*.[3] It will activate one of three mechanisms: fight, flight or freeze. Each has its own survival value. Fight can defeat or scare off the attacker. Flight gets you out of there, fast. Freeze may help you to escape the predator's notice. It's not surprising that we rarely achieve positive change from an amygdala hijack.

Warning signs of an amygdala hijack

You can spot these warning signs in your body, emotions and thoughts.

Body

If you move to *fight* mode, you may tense up, raise and broaden your shoulders and tighten your jaw. Your blood pressure goes up, your eyes narrow and you take on a threatening stance.

In *flight* mode your eyes might dart around. You'll look or turn aside and the muscles in your legs are mobilised for movement — away, fast.

In *freeze* mode — you startle, stop breathing and don't move at all.

Emotions

You may be feeling angry, irritated or annoyed (*fight*); hurt, upset or anxious (*flight*); overwhelmed or hypervigilant (*freeze*). Often you may not be able to say exactly what you are feeling — but you know you're really disturbed!

Thoughts

Your thoughts also provide a good clue that you're reacting. In *fight* mode, you may be thinking: 'How dare they! I'll set them straight.' You're so busy thinking what you will say back, that there is little brain power left to consider what is going on for the other person.

In *flight* mode, you may be thinking: 'How can I get out of here?'; 'I don't care what they say, I don't want to continue with this' or 'It really doesn't matter'.

In *freeze* mode you're likely to find it difficult to think at all. Nothing comes into your head: a bit like stage fright!

Are some of these familiar to you? Which ones do you do? Acting out these reactions usually does not serve you well. There is an alternative … if you can calm your amygdala, you can direct its aroused energy towards a more considered response. Of course, you don't have conscious control of your brain's biochemical state, but you can transform beliefs about yourself, which will affect that state. How? You can allow new information to be more important than old programming. You can recognise that you can engage in conflict rather than run away from it. The more you notice this new information, the less your past history has a hold over you.

To free yourself up for *a response that is not driven by the amygdala*, you may also need to examine your underlying motives.

If *fight* is your more frequent reaction, consider:

• Why do I need to be in control?

- What would I feel if I found out I was wrong?

- Do I need to make myself feel good by proving I am better than others?

- Do I feel that everyone should have the same values as me?

- Should I perhaps question some of my own opinions? What's not working for me any more?

We already know that fighting damages relationships. With someone you have to live or work with it will create a very uncomfortable atmosphere. You could lose their support. They may hold a grudge, sometimes for years. Beware the loser if you persist with the win/lose mentality. The company that exploits workers can end up with industrial strife; the nation that suppresses an ethnic group often precipitates revolt; the marriage that oppresses one partner can ultimately fall apart.

When is a fight wise? Not often! But if your rights are being seriously abused, or the other person is about to cause someone physical danger, it may be your only option.

If *flight* has been your standard reaction to conflict, what are you assuming?

- When I'm irritated and don't say anything, do I really think that they won't sense it?

- When I withdraw do I think that has no effect on the relationship?

- Are my feelings not as important as the other person's?

- Am I so angry that nothing I'd say would be appropriate?

- How frightened am I of their anger?

- How frightened am I of damaging the relationship?

You'll have noticed that when you physically or emotionally withdraw from a conflict, perhaps from fear of confrontation or disapproval, you no longer have a say in what happens.

When is flight wise? It is wise to withdraw when the conflict is none of your business and your lack of involvement does not affect what's going on or if you need time to calm down before talking.

If *freeze* is your standard pattern ask yourself:

- What's the worst that can happen if I speak?
- Is it fear or habit that prevents me from speaking?
- Do I suppress my vitality when I try not to be noticed?

Being unable to acknowledge conflict is the habit we resort to when we need peace at any cost. Suppressing a serious conflict means you don't talk about its main issues. If you keep silent, the other person does not know all that is going on with you. Even if they sense something is wrong, they won't really know what the matter is. You may resign yourself to the situation or surrender your own needs in hasty compromise.

When is freeze wise? Suppressing your response is sensible when a confrontation over a small disagreement puts too much pressure on the relationship, or when people are not ready to hear what you have to say. Sometimes you can preserve a relationship by choosing tact over brutal honesty. You may want some time to think through your strategy. Some conflicts dissolve just because you stay friendly.

Now you can use all this information to change what you do. Conflict can stimulate a successful unfolding process, but not if you persist in proving your point, avoiding the person or pretending there's no problem. As you become more aware of your communication patterns you'll notice when you have reacted with fight, flight or freeze inappropriately. The moment you spot these warning signs you can shift gears so that you respond rather than react.

Moving Out of Reaction

Fight, flight and freeze are emergency reactions. You probably have used all of them from time to time. What will prevent them ruling your behaviour? In that brief space between the stimulus and your reply, you need quick strategies to turn yourself around. It's most important that you attend to your inner state: focus on your body, thoughts and emotions. Be aware that you are at risk and begin to modify your reactions. Notice what your body is doing. Perhaps take a deep breath or place your hands on your belly to calm yourself. If you are sensing an emotion, name it for yourself. Put reactive thoughts in perspective with:

- ☼ Is this a mistake?
- ☼ Did they mean this?
- ☼ Remember, conflict is opportunity.

If the other person has lost control of their anger, perhaps your reactions of fight, flight or freeze are taking over. If you find yourself about to attack, you might pull yourself up. Do you need a little space to quieten down your overactive amygdala? You might say: 'I don't think I'm capable of continuing this right now. Let's make another time'. These are tactical withdrawals, not reactive flight. You are not avoiding or rationalising. You'll know the difference between avoidance and appropriate withdrawal by how you feel about it afterwards and whether you do complete the conversation later.

Catching the first moment of reaction, while helpful, is not enough. Each interchange is a potential new trigger. As you engage and deal with conflict you will need ongoing processes that condition your amygdala not to flood your awareness with its reactions. Let's look at a number of techniques to help you respond rather than react to conflict. You can use the three pathways — the body, emotions and thoughts.[4] Different people will favour one pathway over another and different situations will make one pathway more accessible than another.

Body

You might move from reaction to response at any moment by taking a few good deep breaths. The good old count to ten works. It gives the neo-cortex time to kick in with a more considered response. You can also centre, flow, and connect.[5] Using the body pathway helps you change your body/energy state very rapidly.

Centre

Centring is a very powerful technique used in the martial arts. Aikido master, author and seminar leader Thomas Crum explains:

> It occurs when the mind, body and spirit become fully integrated in dynamic balance and connectedness with the world around us. There is heightened awareness and sensitivity, a feeling that everything is perfect the way it is ...
>
> Being centered in conflict provides us with a sense of spaciousness and nonattachment ... We move beyond our

*personal struggles and concerns into a larger perspective ...
When a conflict arises ... miraculously we find ourselves
operating calmly, compassionately and appropriately.*[6]

Centring is about bringing yourself back into balance. The centre
of your body is located a little below the navel — about halfway
between your spine and the skin over your stomach. Centring
means bringing your attention internally to that point. Try it now.
Use your breathing as well — take your breath and attention to
that midway point. It helps to be sitting or standing with your
spine straight. Experience your body relaxing, feel any physical
tension drop away.

Centring begins at body level and then influences thoughts and
emotions. Try it again, noticing this time what is happening at the
level of thought. You will probably feel a sense of calm or lightness
— the mind quietens as if nothing special is going on. Buddhists
might call this a moment of 'no mind'. It's time out; we're non-
attached.

Getting centred is very powerful. In the midst of conflict, it's the
quiet spot in the eye of the storm. From this place you can freely
choose to respond. You are no longer at the mercy of body
reactions, distressing thoughts or runaway emotions. Even though
it provides only a momentary interruption, it's enough to put you
back in charge of yourself. You don't hold onto the feeling of being
centred. Instead you choose to be centred, take a moment to
recapture the feeling and then turn your attention to whatever it is
you are doing.

Work five-second practice sessions into simple, everyday
situations; for example, centre yourself as you walk into a room to
meet people, start a new task, answer the phone, sit in the car at red
lights, sit down and stand up, pass through a door, and arrive at
work and at home. It can become a most enjoyable habit. Centring
feels good. So, practise it often until it becomes second nature.
When difficult situations arise you will turn to it almost
immediately.

Flow

The martial art of Aikido has more to teach us about responding
to conflict. The name 'aikido' is a composition of three Japanese
words: *ai* meaning harmony; *ki* meaning universal energy; and *do*
meaning the way.[7] Altogether: 'the way of harmonising with

universal energy'. It teaches that starting from the state of centredness — a calm mind and body — we are able to openly and powerfully embrace conflict and turn it towards solutions that work better for everyone.

Aikido is based on the principle that a universal force or energy flows through everything. Individuals can align themselves with this force and bring the energy of others into alignment with it too. The purpose of an aikido manoeuvre is not to hurt, as it is in some martial arts, but to disarm or divert the attack. The martial artist directs the energy away from causing harm. Its practice resembles a dance as the attacker's energy is deflected and rendered harmless. An aikido master is very alert and *flows with the energy of his adversary*. The expert canoeist does something similar by flowing with the force of rapids and avoiding boulders in the river.

We can apply this principle to verbal conflict. If you flow with the movement of energy, you won't rigidly oppose the other person. You'll use your strength to direct their energy away from causing harm and towards solution. You can move them to the positive, leading them to say what they want or what would fix the problem. It's a dance. Be open to finding the next step that will keep the dance flowing smoothly and in the right direction. Now you are choosing how you will respond. (For more of these 'dance' steps see Chapter 4, Appropriate Assertiveness, Reactive or Proactive? on page 76.)

What is flow like? Like a river swirling around obstacles, like tree branches swaying in the wind. We're flexible, but relatively effortless, we adapt nimbly to changing circumstances but we stay relaxed. Our concentrated awareness ensures we are present — right here, right now. We're likely to know this state quite well when we're calm and attentive, perhaps involved in a project that fully engages us; however, flow isn't that easy in conflict when our emotions are aroused. It's a learnt skill and it takes practice. Sometimes we'll trip up; everyone does. All we can do is get back on track as quickly as possible.

Flow is not about backing down; it's non-combative. It requires a conscious choice to be flexible and courageous. Courage is needed to trust the *process* of communication and our own ability to steer the conversation around obstacles, sway with the wind of other people's emotions, and respond appropriately at each moment.

Connect

When we find ourselves in a situation we don't like, we tend to withdraw so that we separate from the other person. Take a moment now and imagine yourself talking to someone you love spending time with ... Now imagine that someone you dislike walks into the room and interrupts your conversation. What do you feel as you disguise your irritation? Can you feel your energy contracting? It's an unconscious reaction. You might experience it as a body sensation. Your emotions and thoughts will follow this change. This is a spontaneous reaction, and you can alter it.

Instead of contracting, you can consciously choose to expand your energy to embrace the situation. *Greet* the situation as you would open your arms to a friend. Your energy immediately flows towards and around the other person, making you more connected. Sound and light travel, as does your energy, which is directed by your attention. As you pay attention to the field of energy around your body, you can learn how to expand it consciously, like blowing up a balloon or turning up a dimmer switch on a light.

Will you contract or connect?

Energy, awareness, attention and presence are closely linked. As you connect with other people and situations, you fill the space with your awareness. Your behaviour becomes more appropriate because you're more able to sense what is going on. When you contract, through dislike or fear, you lose contact and you're less aware.

You can move out of reaction by paying careful attention to your energy. First, get centred. Go back to the source: picture your energy feeding from an endless reservoir and then expand your personal energy — fill the space. Take charge of the atmosphere and include the conflict or difficulty in your caring presence and awareness. You'll be amazed how often this one invisible act of yours can turn the whole problem around.

If you are in a meeting that's full of hostility, first, get centred, then energetically *wrap* the whole room in your energy field. No one sees you do it, of course, and it only takes a second. Then, do the next ordinary thing that comes to hand. You might ask a question or find yourself settling back and taking a deep breath. Any strategy you design will be better when you're connected. There's more rapport and more trust.

You feel stung and alienated by something someone has just said to you. You can't help it — you react ... and contract. As soon as you notice, apply the antidote — expand. Pump out your energy to wash over and soothe the other person. You will be soothed as you do it and you'll find yourself giving them the space for their bad day without it affecting you. You might even find that shortly afterwards you're spontaneously able to show some care or concern for whatever is going on for them.

You are alone and fretting about a conflict you can't handle effectively yet. It's beginning to get you down. Expand into it, wash it, hold it, flood it with your energetic presence and the desire that things will work out well for all concerned.

Energy follows attention. Energy creates change

Expand your energy field when it's a great day and you want to enjoy it and be touched by it even more.

Emotions

Don't suppress them and don't embellish them. Ignore or suppress or let emotions run wild at your peril. Another pathway for changing a reaction to a response is through the emotions. Sometimes you'll prefer to start here first — rather than with body — if a strong emotion has flared up. The first questions you can ask yourself as you try to move out of an emotional reaction are:

- Why am I feeling this?
- What could I be doing about it?

Emotions tell you *what* to address, but not *how* best to address it. If they're governing your behaviour you're *reacting* — you are at the mercy of your emotions.[8] As you work to respond, rather than react, you are not trying to strip all emotion from your communication. You are taking charge of *how* your emotion is expressed. For instance, you may let the other person know you are angry, upset or hurt, but you'll take care not to attack them. You take charge when you accept your emotions without denying or fixing them. You don't make yourself or the other person wrong for how you feel nor do you embellish the feeling — 'I am so hopeless!' or 'They are completely heartless!' If you are free to experience your emotions, unadorned with self-talk from your overactive imagination, those emotions deliver their message to you and move on. If you need to contain them during the conversation, and you often do need to, you can allow this cycle to complete itself later when the circumstances are more appropriate. An explanation of how to handle this is covered in detail in Chapter 6, Managing Emotions.

As a difficult discussion unfolds it can be useful to notice shifts in your emotions. These can guide you to greater awareness, sensitivity and insight. Your emotions will signal when there is an opportunity to learn more — about yourself, about why the problem is happening and about new solutions.

Thoughts

Just as you can redirect your body energy, you can use the pathway of thoughts to move from reaction to response. Indeed, if you start by redirecting energy, you'll find your thoughts immediately follow. Your aim is to take charge of your thoughts so that you are no longer being swept away by them. You can choose to reinterpret experiences by:

- Modifying your demand for having things your way.

- Shifting away from judgements.

- Reframing negative thoughts.

The discovery mindset

You can take on an attitude of *discovery*: encourage yourself to be open, aware of what is, and look for all the possibilities of what might be. It means you give up what you think you know, how you think things are or should be, what you think is right or wrong. You genuinely explore how another person sees things and explore new ways of seeing or solving issues. You take on what Zen calls 'Beginner's Mind' — that freshness with which a child views the world. To the young child, a fall can be as interesting as the next step because everything is part of the great experiment.

Here are some invaluable discovery questions:

✓ What can I learn?

✓ I wonder what this is really about?

✓ What else could I explore here?

✓ How else could I see this?

✓ How is the other person seeing it?

✓ Why is this important to them?

✓ How would it be possible for both views to be acceptable?

✓ How will I find a creative way to handle this?

Use them to replace reactive, judgemental thinking such as:

✗ Who's right?

✗ They're just being stupid.

✗ They don't know what they are talking about.

✗ How dare they?

✗ What's the point in trying? I'm not going to get anywhere.

✗ I'm no good at this.

✗ I might fail, so I won't try.

✗ This is a disaster!

Asking questions engages your frontal lobes, which takes you out of your emotional brain (the limbic system) into your thinking brain (the neo-cortex). When you ask and answer a good question for yourself, you stop being swamped by your emotions and bring some sanity into the situation. When you ask someone who is angry a question, encourage them to think, to engage their frontal lobes, and so reduce the negative effects of their emotion on decision-making. Questions lead the mind. Good questions lead the mind in helpful directions.

Becoming fascinated implies you shake yourself free of frustration and choose instead to become deeply curious. When you are frustrated **Turn frustration into fascination** you are frowning, uptight and generally not in a resourceful state. Shifting to being fascinated means being in a more open, light-hearted, relaxed and creative space. You might even have an internal smile — it switches on the best in you. From this resourceful state you can look for the possibilities, not the problems: the upsides, not the downsides. Ask yourself:

💡 How can I find this fascinating?

💡 How can I turn this into something that will be better?

Be fascinated … enjoy the moment!

The proactive mindset

Which playing field are you operating in — a reactive or proactive one? In a reactive playing **Will I be reactive or proactive?**

field, you deny, defend and justify. Your thoughts are concentrated on blaming and complaining, focusing on what's wrong and why things can't work, or who's at fault — 'It's their fault' or 'It's all my fault'. It's a breeding ground for depression, hopelessness, disempowerment and inaction. In a proactive playing field, you take responsibility — that is, *response-ability* — your ability to respond. It's your playground for exploring, learning, understanding, addressing issues and moving forward. In this playing field, you empower yourself and take ownership of problems. Your thoughts are on moving forward and fixing. Take the initiative:

- How can I move this forward?

- How can we use this conflict for new understanding?

- How can we improve this situation?

You can greet conflict like a friend. Embrace and welcome the situation. That's the essence of regarding conflict as opportunity. You've created a doorway, now step through and take the opportunity to make things better.

Ah, conflict! What an opportunity

EXERCISE: responding to conflict

For the next week, make it a particular focus to look for early conflict clues. Is there a discomfort or incident you could handle?

Start catching yourself reacting: does a situation come up that triggers fight, flight or freeze for you? As soon as you notice the reaction, pay attention to your body, thoughts and emotions to move to the more resourceful response state:

- Centre, flow, connect.

- Notice your feelings without suppressing them or letting them run wild. What is their message?

- Reframe doom, gloom or blaming thoughts into 'Ah, how interesting! I wonder what the opportunity is here?'

SUMMARY

Conflict can be positive or negative, constructive or destructive, depending on what you make of it. It is your opportunity for positive change.

It is much easier to handle conflict earlier, so be alert for clues.

As you become more willing to engage in conflict, you need to move out of the knee-jerk reactions of fight, flight or freeze and into considered responses.

You can use three pathways to master reactions and direct your response:

- Body — by centring, flowing and connecting.

- Emotions — by not suppressing them or embroidering them.

- Thoughts — by choosing a discovery or a proactive mindset.

Choosing to respond, rather than react, to conflict is the first step. You can develop the skills and strategies that support you in being proactive — taking responsibility and initiative to resolve the conflict constructively.

Notes

1 Daniel Goleman, *Emotional Intelligence* (USA: Bantam Books, 1995) and *Working with Emotional Intelligence* (USA: Bantam Books, 1998)

2 See Chapter 4, Appropriate Assertiveness

3 Daniel Goleman, *Emotional Intelligence* op. cit.

4 While we could separate out the energy pathway from the body pathway, for simplicity we've chosen not to. Energy is sensed as a 'through the body' sensation though sometimes it is hard to locate, and for many, the distinction might be difficult to make

5 See also Chapter 6, Managing Emotions, Bodymind

6 Thomas F. Crum, *The Magic of Conflict* (USA: Touchstone, 1987) pp 53–4, 61

7 Further reading on the *Aikido* approach to life and conflict:
Thomas F. Crum, *The Magic of Conflict* op. cit.
Koichi Tohei, *Ki in Daily Life* (Japan: Ki No Kenkyukai HQ, 2001)

8 See Chapter 6, Managing Emotions

CHAPTER 2
Partners Not Opponents

How can we solve this as partners rather than opponents?
What needs underlie our positions on this issue?

An Adversarial Approach

When faced with conflict we're likely to want to work out who is right and who is wrong. It quickly becomes 'your way' or 'my way'. This is an adversarial or oppositional approach, which tends to direct the rest of the conflict: 'I'll need to make you or your ideas wrong to prove I'm right', 'I'll need to make sure you understand why I am right'. The other person becomes your opponent and you continue pushing and defending your point.

Sound familiar? We have many models for conflict run this way. We see it in public debate, parliament and our court system. It's a competition. We may want to play this way on the sports field where the person or team who scores the most points wins, and the competitive spirit can be acceptable in the arena of business — depending, of course, on how it is approached. Striving to be better gives us goals to achieve. Striving to destroy a competitor can be vicious and dehumanising.

Cutthroat competition between colleagues in the workplace produces poisonous working atmospheres and promotes mediocrity in decision-making. You may defend your idea and attack theirs, but did you allow space for a better idea to emerge? In the arena of human relations a presumption of *right* versus *wrong, true* versus *false, winner* versus *loser* can make for some very nasty arguments. You may end up right but at what cost? When you see family members, friends or acquaintances as your opponents the results are almost certain — alienation, depression and destroyed relationships.

A Collaborative Approach

If you've been used to an adversarial style you may need to discard your old mindset of who's wrong and who's right. You need a fundamental shift towards a collaborative approach: working together to address differences. With the right skills and premises, the principle of treating the other person as a partner in conflict-solving rather than as an opponent can always apply. Of course, that doesn't mean that a collaborative approach means you give in and accept the other person's point of view. Unless you consider your truth *you* won't feel good about the results. If you haven't taken their perspective into account, *they* won't feel good about it either.

The Challenges

You will start to see the world a little differently when you realise that the collaborative principle applies to *all* occasions. Reality begins to become a little soft around the edges. You start to see the truth of what scientists call 'observer-created reality'.

Conflict is the message that your truth, value or opinion does not represent the only reality. The bigger reality of multiple viewpoints needs your attention. The fact that there's conflict reveals that you need to respectfully and skilfully put across your point of view and respectfully and skilfully listen to the other person's. When you combine viewpoints you have the perspective with which to create something better and more comprehensive than you can achieve alone — better solutions and better relationships. In a problem-solving situation, you will often end up with an outcome that is better than either of the individual solutions. In a situation where values and beliefs are involved, you will end up with a greater understanding and appreciation of another person's reality even if it is not one that you want for yourself.

You may need to think differently to act differently and that may present some challenges

Conditioning

Under pressure you fall right back into attack/defend or other ineffectual behaviours. That's what you are used to, what you know how to do and what you have always done. Once a situation heats up, maintaining a collaborative approach takes skill. In our society the adversarial win/lose way is still much more common. It seems to be expected of us to look for what's wrong in the other person's plan or to see what doesn't work at the expense of what does.

Lack of skill

If you grew up learning an adversarial style of debate at school, you learnt to make your point strongly while exposing the holes in the other team's arguments.[1] Most of us won't have been taught how to use dialogue properly. Dialogue, the free flow of meaning between two or more people, is essential for the style of agreement-building that's needed for a collaborative approach.

Getting defensive under attack

You may start off wanting to be cooperative, but your best intentions get lost when your views are attacked, you are not getting what you want, you don't get the help you need, or your rights are being abused. You jump to defend what is important ... and now you are using an adversarial style even though you hadn't intended to.

The adversarial approach

Collaboration is undoubtedly easier when both people are playing the same game. If the other person doesn't approach conflict with a collaborative approach, particularly when the stakes are high, you will need considerable skill to guide the resolution process. There will be times when the challenge seems too great — see Win/Win Challenges on page 33 for some ways through these situations. You don't need to change your fundamental commitment, but you may need to back away to find a level of caring that's beyond the immediate situation. Without mutual respect it will be a bumpy ride. You'll need very skilful manoeuvres if you're the only one using a collaborative method; however, it is always worth the extra effort in the end.

Compromise

Compromise usually means people get a bit and give a bit. Dividing the desired object equally is often accepted as the fairest thing to do. Compromise employs some negotiation skills so that everyone gains something. It seems fair — 'How much for you? How much for me?', but it presumes that there is not enough for everyone to have everything they'd like.

A risk of compromise is that one side will ask for more than they really want so that they do well when the division takes place. One person therefore may really be giving away far more than the other. Sometimes neither side feels much commitment to a plan that falls short of what they want. Compromise is not always the best solution available. Can we do better than mere compromise?

Could you make a bigger pie?

Taking a Win/Win Approach

Remember the concept of *flow* from Chapter 1, Responding to Conflict, your body's pathway to responding rather than reacting? Can you bring that flexibility and skill to the situation? You'll have more in your repertoire than just compromise. By flowing powerfully with and around conflict you gently but relentlessly steer communication towards 'you *and* me' and away from 'you *or* me', uniting your energy with the other person's to become problem-solving partners. Ask yourself:

> A win/win approach is a starting place not the end result

- ☀ How can I take a win/win approach to this situation?

- ☀ How can we aim for a mutually beneficial outcome in a way that we will all feel is the best possible under the circumstances?

- ☀ How can we turn from being opponents into partners?

To grasp the basic principles, let's take a very simple example: you're in the kitchen with a person you live with, and you both want the one and only orange in the fruit bowl. What should you do? Cut it in half? Toss a coin? Decide who needs it most?

> Move your position

When problems confront us we look for solutions — sometimes far too quickly. If you ask yourself what you want, you will come up with something concrete: 'I want the orange', which is an example of a *position*. Such positions are often the starting place of conflict. The win/win or collaborative approach requires you to find out more about the situation first.

> Explore the needs behind the position

Identify the major needs and concerns of the people involved. Ask why the other person needs what they say they want (their position). Examine why *you* need what you say you want (your position). Have this conversation as soon as you can. Now, let's return to the kitchen.

You: 'I want the orange because I'm thirsty and I want to make juice. What do you want the orange for?'

Other person: 'I'm baking a cake. I want the rind.'

When you consider each person's needs you may find people want the same thing to achieve quite different results. This is not surprising: individual differences in personality and purpose constantly create separate needs, but you'll only notice these if you are looking for them. This inquiry opens up new possibilities. It may not be possible for each of you to obtain your position (having the whole orange), but it may be possible for each of you to satisfy your needs.

Create new options where everyone gets more of what they want. Where one of you wants the juice and the other wants the rind, the answer is obvious as both of you can take what you want from the one orange. Sometimes win/win solutions can be that easy, and sometimes they're not. Back to our example — suppose

Create new options

it isn't so straightforward and you're both after the juice because you're thirsty. What are the options then? Sharing the juice is the obvious compromise. If you take a collaborative approach and you're responding with conscious skill, you'll look further. *You'll aim to work out a way that will satisfy both of you.* Flow with the other person to create ingenious options. Somehow you need more to go around — you could make a smoothie with the orange and add some other fruit; buy more oranges; find one of you something else to drink.

You can, on your own, back off from your stance of wanting the whole orange, analyse your and the other person's underlying

Do it together

needs and then design a new option, but it's much more effective if you collaborate. First, two heads are often better than one when it comes to designing creative solutions. Second, you make it clear that you are treating the other person as a partner, not as an opponent, and they see that the process is fair. When you both agree on the best option, the relationship is at least maintained, at best enhanced.

In our kitchen scenario, let's say you both decide that cutting the orange in half is your best option. This solution may *resemble* a compromise, but the outcome is significantly better. The point of this approach is that, whether or not you achieve a perfect solution, you both collaborated — acknowledging each other's needs and finding a way that works for both of you. If you're both happy that this is the best solution you can come up with, then it is a win/win outcome and a climate of trust and respect develops.

MATT

My two boys, Josh and Daniel (8 and 11), were fighting again! This time it was over who should get to use the PlayStation. I wondered if I should just order Daniel to give Josh his turn or was it time for Daniel to learn to share? They were punching each other. I would have to step in yet again, but right now I didn't feel either boy deserved a go. I felt frustrated and I realised this pattern would keep repeating itself unless we could find some alternative. I needed to teach them to sort out their own fights.

I asked the boys: 'Well, what can we do about this? What do you each want?' I tried to keep my own feelings and opinions to myself.

Of course, each said he wanted a turn with the games, but very quickly Josh said, 'I don't mind if Daniel plays it today as long as I get it to myself tomorrow.' Daniel nodded.

I was impressed by how easily they had come up with a new option. What's more, they both had agreed to it! I had underestimated them. I felt better too, when I wasn't laying down the law. I'd simply steered them in the right direction.

Daniel started using the PlayStation the next day, even though it wasn't his turn, and I watched how they handled it. Would he give it up? Would Josh stick up for his end of the bargain?

Josh just said, 'It's my go today', and Daniel quite happily left it to Josh. For once, they didn't argue about it. Not only had they reached their own solution, they had even stuck to it!

Later that week they came up with a similar solution over television watching. They agreed that one boy could choose the programmes one day, the next day the other boy could. It's so great now not to have the inevitable TV fights every afternoon.

When both people participate and their needs are met, both are committed to the solution. If you're going to deal with a person more than once (and even if you are not) it pays dividends to deal

Create partners not opponents

cooperatively with them. It's the foundation of successful business practice and the approach enriches your personal life as well.

Key Ingredients for a Collaborative Approach

Start with heart

Set your sights on wanting the other person to win and for you to win too. Commit yourself to keeping the interaction going until you are both satisfied you've done the best you can.

💡 Am I coming from the right place inside me?

💡 What do I really want for myself?

💡 What do I really want for the other person (or people)?

💡 What do I really want for our relationship?[2]

If anger or resentment has closed your heart to the other person, then work beyond anything you personally feel towards them right now and commit to wishing them well. Use that higher level of concern for their fundamental well-being to direct your efforts. Also absorb the skills in chapters 6, Managing Emotions, and 7, Willingness to Resolve.

Set the Scene

Be aware that there are three things at stake here:

- The content — *what* are you working out?

- The process — *how* will you work it out?

- The relationship — *did* you respect each other in the process?

Usually in a conflict we jump in and want to address *what* the conflict is about without first agreeing as to *how* we might best go about addressing it. If each of you is willing to agree to address the situation constructively, you are far more likely to get an outcome that everyone is happy with. If you don't want to ambush the other person, you might want to make an appointment to work on the issues. It's often better to deal with difficult issues when other people aren't listening in. This can apply at home as well as at work. You don't get the best out of a tired spouse or a child who's about to leave for school.

Create a safe space. Use a collaborative approach. Check your own mindset. Are you in responding mode? Are you open to taking a win/win approach? If so, invite the other/s to engage in a mutually beneficial conversation. It's good to open with some sort of conversational headline that steers things in the right direction; few people will reject the principle of fairness to your face. For example:

- 'Can we work something out together?'

- 'I'd really like to find a way to address this so that it is better for both of us. Would that be okay with you?'

Note that you are inviting a response. If the other person is hard to budge, you might try 'I'm here to solve problems'. It's unlikely they'll reply: 'Well, I'm not!'

Use Collaborative Language

Using the language of collaboration can turn the conversation around.

Use AND not BUT

Add to rather than dismiss

Turn what seem like opposing ideas into co-existing different ideas:

'I understand/appreciate that you see it this way *and* the way I see it is ...'

'I acknowledge how you see it *and* the way I see it is ...'

Banish 'Yes, *but* ...' from your conflict vocabulary even though it's how we often speak. If a sentence containing *but* is on the tip of your tongue when you're in a conflict, weed it out. If it comes out by mistake, immediately correct it.

Tap the power of AND

Include your doubts — don't dismiss them

I'd like to raise this with him, *but* I'm scared he'll think I'm making a fuss, becomes I'd like to raise it with him *and* I'll need to do it so that it won't look like I'm making a fuss.

I'd say something ... *but* I don't want to do it badly (or ... *but* I'm scared it will cause a fight) becomes I'd like to say something *and* I'll need to find a way to do it well.

Include the other person's doubts

You say: 'I think we should opt for changing suburbs for our workshop. The rent will be much more reasonable.' The other person says: '*But* we'll lose staff if we move out of their area.' Use *and* not *but*. 'Right! We could really do with cheap rent for our workshop *and* we don't want to lose staff.' Using *and* points out the direction for creative problem-solving.

Use non-adversarial language

To reinforce your collaborative mindset, here are some phrases to be aware of as they may expose or generate adversarial thinking.

Beware of saying:	Say instead:
✗ 'I *disagree* with you.'	✓ 'I would like to express a *different* view.'
✗ 'I am on Bill's *side* on this one.'	✓ 'I can see some value in Bill's *view*.'
✗ 'I can *argue* against that.'	✓ 'I see it differently ...'
✗ '*Why* would you think ...?'	✓ 'Tell me more about how you see it ...'
✗ '*But* what about ...?'	✓ 'How would it work if ...?'
✗ 'The *problem* with that is ...?'	✓ 'Let's explore other possibilities ...'
✗ 'It *won't* work because ...'	✓ 'I have difficulty with ...'

To reinforce your collaborative mindset not just for yourself but for others, use 'we both' rather than 'you or I'. Use words such as 'discuss issues' or 'express differing views' rather than 'argue', 'make a point' or 'take sides'.

Consistently using non-adversarial language will mean that your time and energy are spent on exploring issues, promoting understanding and generating alternative solutions instead of creating more conflict. In some relationships, this will be a major shift.

HANNAH

Nina had been working in Hannah's team for two years and was one of the hardest working team members. Hannah really appreciated the quality of her work, but was at her wits' end with how much of her time Nina seemed to need. For a while Hannah had said nothing hoping that it would change over time — it didn't. Then she tried to drop some subtle hints, but knew that had failed when she saw the hurt look on Nina's face. Last Friday afternoon she'd lost it and snapped at Nina.

Hannah needed to find a way to lessen Nina's demands on her time and still keep her happy and productive. Hannah needed to think it through carefully. The last time she'd tried to raise a difficulty with a team member, she'd simply cut to the chase and told him what she was unhappy about and he took it badly and left shortly afterwards.

She didn't want this to happen again. She truly wanted to make it work for both of them. She decided to make time for Nina, to open the conversation by letting her know that she valued her and wanted to find a way to manage the demands on her (Hannah's) time that would work for both of them. Nina responded positively and was happy to find a way to manage her work so that she needed to come to Hannah far less frequently. They agreed on how often and over what things Nina would approach Hannah.

Win/Win Challenges

There are many circumstances which will test your constructive and supportive approach to the limit. The other person's behaviour might be impossible for you to put up with: they may mistrust a mutual approach; they may be too attached to what they want to even listen to you. Nonetheless, continue working for their long-term needs as well as your own, whether or not they cooperate in the process. Here are some extra tools for very difficult circumstances.

A friend who never reciprocates favours or colleagues who don't contribute their share?

Emphasise shared goals

Try telling them: 'I want us to remain friends and I find that hard to manage when I don't feel there's equal give and take' or 'I want to continue working with you and I need to know you're matching me with the work load'.

Be creative in responding to needs

Trading with another business that seems headed for bankruptcy? Should my business continue to supply them with goods to sell?

Try saying to them: 'I realise you are in a tight financial situation right now and my company can't risk not getting paid. I'll need cash on delivery. Would it be easier to pay immediately if you had smaller, more frequent deliveries?'

Redefine what is a positive outcome for you

You are in direct competition with others for the same promotion?

Try to stop worrying about the others and concentrate on yourself. Competition is always an opportunity for accomplishment, whatever the outcome. Getting that promotion may or may not be the best thing for you, but there is always benefit to you in doing your best.

Use competition as an opportunity for achievement

What do you do when the opposition (in business or sport) has more power, skills or strength?

Try strengthening your own game instead of weakening your opponent's play. The following story from *Zen in the Martial Arts*[3] illustrates the point.

In sparring practice, a martial arts student was being constantly frustrated by a more skilful opponent. He had used his entire repertoire of tricky moves, but each had been readily countered. At the end of the match, thoroughly dejected, he went to his teacher for advice. His teacher, seeing him upset, drew a chalk line on the floor about two metres long.

'How can you make this line shorter?' he asked. The student studied the line and made several suggestions, including cutting the line in many pieces. The teacher shook his head and drew a second line, longer than the first.

'Now how does the first line look?'

'Shorter,' the student said.

The teacher nodded. 'It is always better to improve your own line or knowledge than to try and cut your opponent's line.'

Your child's behaviour is unacceptable

You suspect that a number of his friends are into drugs and heavy drinking. There's a party this Saturday night and he wants to go. You're worried. You say the only way your son can go is if you pick him up from the party at 11 pm. He throws a tantrum. 'What is so terrible about that solution?'

you ask as calmly as you can. 'I can't be seen to be collected by my parents', you finally get out of him. 'If I wait for you around the corner, would that solve the problem?' you suggest. Support his dignity even though right now he's behaving like a two-year-old. It could be a moment for making the agreement reciprocal. 'I promise not to show up at the party as long as you meet me on time.'

You can't reach a unanimous decision

Keep communicating even if you have to drop the issue for a while. You might disagree dramatically with a work colleague on whether

Keep communicating

or not the company should enter into a contract on the terms proposed, but maybe you could still have a drink together at the end of the working week. Don't freeze the other person out. Allow some flow between you, however small.

Of course, sometimes the other person refuses to communicate and then there is very little you can do about the situation. You might be able to use situations like a birthday or Christmas for a little normal communication by giving a card or a small gift. It may not in itself do anything to fix the problem, but it indicates that your door is open. If they reach out in any way, try to respond even if the argument is not solved.

Is it time to back off?

If it's a negotiation, it is your right to say: 'No deal in these circumstances'. You may feel the other person is very self-serving, is not playing

Know when to walk away

fair, or is abusing your rights. You certainly need to cut off the relationship if the possibility of violence is involved. Sometimes it takes great strength to walk away. Weigh up your motives first. Does the desire to walk come from excessive pride or is this necessary for self-respect?

Some disagreements do resolve themselves over time. You have to decide if you are willing to cooperate if the other person tries to reopen communication at a later date. If you have the skills to communicate well and the strength to walk away if necessary, you might be able to renegotiate a failed relationship.

Don't give up on a win/win outcome

What about someone who won't cooperate?

Your aunt has died, your brother is disputing the will and wants your share of her possessions. Things have become nasty. No matter how difficult, try to leave a corner for him in your affections. Don't condone bad conduct; just be clear on what support you are willing to offer.

MAYA

My husband, Sunil, recently decided to become a self-employed consultant and needed to share my car until his new business got going. It seemed like a good idea because I started and finished my job early. Our plan was that he would drive me to my work and collect me in the afternoon, then return to his office. That would work for both of us.

One afternoon Sunil was half an hour late. He apologised, 'I'm sorry, but you know I'm trying really hard to make the business a success. I am doing this for both of us. Work is work.' It started becoming a habit. One day he arrived forty-five minutes late. His excuse was that his consulting session had gone over time. 'Anyway, Maya,' he said, 'you didn't have anything planned for tonight.' This time I was really annoyed. I felt he was taking advantage of me and not valuing my time. I snapped at him, 'Actually, I had planned to go to yoga and now it's too late for me get there on time.'

I was very upset. 'Why didn't you say you had a prior commitment?' I asked. 'You could have continued on another day. At least you could have called me!'

Sunil was angry too; 'Obviously my work isn't important to you,' he said. Our original car arrangement had been fine with me, but this didn't feel like a reasonable deal any more.

We were both angry and hurt and I realised our car issues would continue to be a sore spot unless we came up with some solutions together. When I had calmed down I went to Sunil to talk: 'I don't want to fight over the car. I really want to find a way of sharing the car that can work for both of us. I do care about your business and I want to offer my support. I also want to do things with my time and not spend it waiting for you when you are late. Do you have any ideas on how we can make this work?' Sunil softened towards me and we were able to start brainstorming together. Sunil suggested,

'Maybe if I knew I could have the car one day to myself I could schedule my meetings that will go late on that day.' I replied, 'I guess I could arrange a lift or catch a taxi on that day. I would also like one afternoon when I can have the car so I can go to yoga or see my friends after work. How about if each of us has one day a week where we make our own arrangements to get home?' I was still concerned about all the times he was late to collect me. I approached the subject being careful not to sound like I was blaming him: 'I would really appreciate it if you could be aware that I am waiting for you and try to be on time to pick me up.' Sunil scowled, 'I can't always get out of the office. Sometimes I have things to do before I can come for you.' I took a deep breath, 'Okay, Sunil, I will try to be more understanding and it would be great if you could call me if you know you will be late. At least then I can choose whether to wait for you or try to get a lift with someone else.' It wasn't a perfect plan but at least we both felt included in it and hoped we could make it work. We had released the tension around our car troubles and that was a great relief to me.

It takes daily negotiation to come up with a win/win solution, but we're valuing each other's priorities and making it work. I had felt uncomfortable about standing up for my rights, but I know it has improved our relationship because I did.

Wherever possible the task is to continue the win/win approach, to show others the value and benefits of cooperation. Return to win/win skills whenever you waver. Don't make it even harder for the other person to change by putting up a wall between you.

The collaborative approach, used consistently and early in a conflict, should generally keep you away from these extremes; however, resolving conflict is sometimes lengthy and needs perseverance. Of course, the end result is important, but generally it is during the process that the real benefits appear — cooperation, mutual respect, better options, commitment and goodwill.

What Next?

Having set the scene, it's time to get everyone's views clearly, openly and honestly on the table. You'll need to listen to and discover their view; express your view constructively; keep the power balanced and manage the emotions — yours and theirs. You'll want to know about drawing up a map, developing options and negotiating. The moment may come when you need to pull back from the finer details and take in the bigger picture, and then dive back in again with a broader perspective. Remember, conflict is an opportunity! How can you make it better for both of you? Your aim is to move into a creative mode the moment conflict arises. Ideally you will find mutually satisfying outcomes together. No matter what the difficulties, maintain the collaborative approach because it speaks of who you are and your fundamental humanity. Conflict is a journey — a collaborative approach is the best way to travel.

SUMMARY

Shift your mindset to the collaborative approach. Conflict is a message that requires a new combination of viewpoints. It challenges you to think, to be and behave differently. It's different to mere compromise. Even if the material outcome ends up the same, the process has been cooperative and everyone feels more positive about the result. It requires that you:

1. Move off your position.

2. Explore the needs behind the position.

3. Create new options where, ideally, everyone gets more of what they want.

4. Do it together. Make it clear you're partners, not opponents.

The key ingredients for a collaborative approach are:

✓ Start with heart.

✓ Set the scene.

✓ Use collaborative language.

When the situation is very difficult you may need to fortify yourself with one or more of the following:

- Emphasise shared goals.

- Be creative in responding to needs.

- Redefine what a positive outcome is for you.

- Use competition as an opportunity for achievement.

- Support underlying needs even when behaviour is extremely inappropriate.

- Keep communicating.

- Know when to walk away.

- Don't give up on a win/win approach.

EXERCISE: a win/win challenge

Here is the beginning of a story:

Jamie and Pat are workmates in the same department, which they both entered four months ago at the same level of responsibility, receiving the same pay. They learn that their supervisor will be retiring at the end of the year and they are the only two employees likely to be offered this one very well-paid and prestigious position.

With this in mind a competitive atmosphere has arisen between them, which Pat, valuing their friendship greatly, regrets very much.

Read again the eight bullet points listed above and then finish the story by describing what Pat could do to improve the atmosphere, using at least four of those eight points.

Notes

1 There is a debating approach known as the Problem-solving Debate that interests many teachers who want to train students in a collaborative approach. For more information on it, see Conflict Resolution Network's website: www.crnhq.org

2 Kerry Patterson, Joseph Grenny, et al., *Crucial Conversations* (USA: McGraw-Hill, 2002) p 34

3 Joe Hyams, *Zen in the Martial Arts* (USA: Bantam Books, 1979), p 36

CHAPTER 3
Empathy Part I

Empathy is often characterised as the ability to put oneself in another person's shoes. It means we have some understanding of another's situation, feelings, motives and beliefs. The other person experiences the openness of our empathic reaching out. They become more open to us, significantly increasing the chances of a successful conversation.

In this chapter we will look at how we can provoke a negative reaction unintentionally, shutting empathy down. We'll also look at how through empathy we open the door to a deeper level of communication and more flexible responses.

We often shut out someone completely when we really have only one or two specific difficulties with them. In your own mind at least, be specific not only about what's causing the problem but also what is still fine in the relationship. When all shutters close, empathy is lost and resolving conflict under these circumstances is almost impossible. If we meet indifference or dislike, we are likely to protect our tender feelings by shutting down. There are bound to be times when your ideas, wishes, beliefs or actions are challenged. You'll be a lot easier to get along with if you can cope with disagreement or criticism. You don't have to be right all the time to be a worthwhile person!

When a relationship lacks empathy, you can struggle on, drop the relationship or do something about fixing it. You won't want to fix every empathy breakdown. But when you can't avoid the person, or you lose out because the relationship is failing, it is worthwhile trying to re-establish rapport.

EXERCISE: what warms communication?

Can you think of a person you have problems with? Find one benefit to you in establishing a better relationship with them. How might you achieve this?

Who?	Benefit of better relationship	What might I do?
_____	_____	_____
_____	_____	_____
_____	_____	_____

Now consider what makes communication work well. It is empathy — the flow between two people where each can understand the other's feelings and motives. This connection and openness between them is also called rapport. As seminar leader and author Dianne Collins puts it, 'Being in One Conversation occurs when both (all) people are concentrated only on what is being said, regardless of who is speaking. Typically we are in our own conversation about the other's conversation'.[1]

Consider three people you feel open to. Taking each in turn, ask yourself what helps the empathy flow between you? You may think of friendliness; having things in common; they listen to your problems and tell you about theirs; they don't put you down; they understand you; or you really enjoy playing tennis together.

Who?   **What helps the flow of empathy in our relationship?**

1. _____   _____

2. _____   _____

3. _____   _____

In the exercise above you may have considered such factors as: we respect each other; we don't have to be perfect around each other; I don't have to wear a mask or be very formal with them; I can be myself with this person.

Building Bridges

If you have a difficult relationship you may decide to put some effort into sorting it out. There are some tried and true methods you can use.

Work on the Relationship Separately from the Problem

Watch your timing

Don't try for a 'deep and meaningful' conversation when the other person is too rushed or stressed to concentrate or you are somewhere where you will be overheard. Pick your time and place with care.

Share an activity

At work it might be going out together to check a new piece of equipment; brainstorming a complex project together; or having a working bee on reorganising the office. At home, try cooking together, going for a walk or going to the movies.

Find safe conversation topics

Try subjects that don't involve the problems you are having. What are the other person's interests? When do they most come alive? What excites them? Ask them about it. A good chat can be a great empathy opener.

The topic is not the real point: you are establishing a flow, tuning in to each other, listening to the music of each other's voices. Of course if someone is in the middle of telling you their problem or something that matters to them, this is *not* the time to switch to small talk! It is listening time.

Empathy breakdowns with parents are a special case. There's something about parents that can bring out the worst in some of us, perhaps because we're hypersensitive to them and react more emotionally to them than to anyone else. It's not surprising, therefore, that many people are very remote to at least one of their parents.

An advantage of being an adult is that you don't have to take your parents' advice when it doesn't suit you or listen to their criticism without the right of reply. Unfortunately, if you shut out that parent completely, you may also cut off a basic source of emotional support. Even if it is expressed badly, their intention may well be loving and concerned. The aim is to recognise this love without engaging in the dramas. Pleasant conversations on non-sensitive issues help us open up to whatever level of caring the parent is capable of. Hold the rest at bay — protect yourself from discussing highly sensitive issues. If you allow understanding to develop, they may sense that you are less guarded and less judgemental. Any efforts you've put into improving empathy will be rewarded if you do have to discuss major issues.

Communication Killers

Have you ever been in the middle of telling someone about a problem only to be interrupted with 'You think that's bad? Let me tell you about the time when I ...', and they redirect the conversation onto themselves so that you're left feeling ignored and unheard?

Have you ever told someone how angry someone else made you feel only to hear back: 'You're silly to feel like that' or 'It's not that bad. They didn't really mean it'. How do you feel then? Have you told someone how miserable you feel perhaps in your job or in your marriage and then been told you should be feeling grateful instead to have the job or the marriage. And what do you do if the response is: 'There's nothing to be upset about'? It's really quite easy to close off, cool down or divert a conversation. Consciously and unconsciously we do it all the time. If we really don't want to pursue the matter, that's okay, but often that is not our intention.

Perhaps, for instance, you are preoccupied with the scenario of your action plan, and with rehearsals of what you are going to say next. Sometimes there's a whole movie going on inside your head and it's so absorbing you are not tuned in to the other person at all. Another reason for poor communication may lie with your uncertainty about coping with someone else, particularly if they are angry or upset. Therefore, you might decide to say nothing, rather than find you've put your foot in it. These are common communication killers we regularly inflict on each other. Take a few minutes now to answer the questions in the blank columns following. Which communication killers do you use on others? Which ones are used on you? By whom? Consider colleagues, family and friends.

> Does the movie in your head match the real-life situation?

EXERCISE: communication killers

Behaviour	Example	Who does it?	
		SELF	**OTHERS**
Giving solutions or advice (when the person just wants to be heard)	'If you'd just be more organised, you would not be in this panic.' 'Why didn't you do it this way?' 'Have you tried …?' 'Just ignore them.' 'Get over it!'		
Refusing to address the issue	'There's nothing to discuss. I can't see any problems.'		
Telling your story (before giving the other person enough time)	In response to 'I had a dreadful car accident last week …' you say 'Let me tell you about mine.' 'I know just what you mean, when I was with Bob he was even worse …'		
Reassuring	'Don't be nervous.' 'Don't worry, it will all work out.' 'You'll be fine.' 'You look great.' 'There're plenty more fish in the sea.' 'You'll feel better tomorrow.' 'Time heals all wounds.' 'It's not that bad — there are plenty of people worse off.'		
Diagnosing motives	'You're very possessive.' 'You've always had a problem with motivation.'		
Persuading with logic	'There's nothing to be upset about. It's all quite reasonable.'		

Other subtle communication killers include manipulating the other person by praising, withholding relevant information or changing the topic to avoid the uncomfortable issue. Very overt ways of shutting the other person down include threatening, giving orders, telling someone what they should do, putting the other person down, and interrogating them.

It's the response you get to your comment that matters. Although somewhat doubtful, even these communication patterns can work if the context and tone of voice support the person. People communicate on many layers. The words

Your real communication is the response you get

themselves form only one level. From words and tone of voice, people constantly interpret (and sometimes misinterpret) their relationship with you. If the final result is that they feel you don't respect them, then your communication has not been effective. You are responsible for more than the message you give; you are responsible for the communication process and for the message they receive.

Examine your own communication style when you notice you have been cut off or blocked out. You may well have used a communication killer without thinking of its consequences. Check with the other person if something you said didn't seem to go down too well for them. You can always refine your own skills. Did they do or say something that hadn't worked for you? You may want to find ways to fix the problem. Your objective will be to help them get a better response from you. You might start off with something like this: 'When you said I was worrying about nothing, I felt really put off, and I don't think that's what you intended'; 'There are other ways of making your point with which I would feel more comfortable'; or 'When I'm upset I don't need you to fix the problem. I really just want to feel you are listening and trying to understand'. (See Chapter 4, Appropriate Assertiveness.)

Communication killers close down connection and leave the other person feeling that their basic relationship needs are not being met. They'll think you have not taken in what is important for them at that time.

Active Listening

When another person won't listen to you, it may not be just because they are being stubborn. Their problem may be that they don't feel heard by you. This may be the moment for pulling out the active-listening tool. When there is a breakdown in empathy, active listening is often the most effective way to re-establish it.

Active listening implies that for a period of time you tune out from your own point of view and tune in to the other person. You show empathy for what's happening for them and let them know you care — even if you disagree or think their behaviour is unjustified. You reserve your judgement and drop the normal give-and-take of conversation for a while.

It means putting your own agenda aside. If you notice your own thoughts, feelings or reactions, you simply refocus on the other person for this period of time. You postpone judgements and trying to think of what to say on your own behalf. Successful active listening opens the door to conversations, connections and understanding with the other person that otherwise might not evolve.

Are you really listening or just waiting for your turn to speak?

Surprisingly few people practise good listening skills. Most have many ingrained habits of poor listening to break through. Listening well entails some responsibilities. We must take in information from the other person and remain non-judgemental and empathic. We'll need to acknowledge the speaker in ways that invite the communication to continue. We'll do it by providing limited but encouraging responses which help the other person carry their idea another step forward.

Hearing happens, listening is a choice

We may need to listen to more than the words: tone of voice and body language will tell us quite as much, sometimes more, than the words used. When we're listening well, we're listening with the heart as well as the head. We're listening to the whole context in which the communication is happening.

DAVE

Dave's father was in hospital. His mother seemed anxious. Dave had tried several times to reassure her that all would be well when it dawned on him that his words were not reassuring his mum at all. He realised all he was doing was shutting down his communication with her. The next time she mentioned her anxiety, he changed gear into active listening. She began to open up about her concerns for her husband and the real possibility of his death and what that might mean for her and for the family. It was one of the most significant conversations Dave and his mother had ever had together. He was amazed that shifting gears to really listen had given them both this important conversation.

HELPFUL HINTS FOR ACTIVE LISTENING

Things to try	Things to avoid
• Focus your attention totally on the speaker.	• Talking about yourself.
• In your words, reflect back your understanding of the speaker's meaning. Make it sound like a question rather than a statement.	• Introducing your own reactions or well-intentioned comments.
• Feed back feelings, as well as content. Probe, if appropriate eg 'How do you feel about that?' or 'How did that affect you?'	• Advising, diagnosing, reassuring, encouraging, criticising or asking fact-finding questions when a response to the feeling is required.
• Reflect back not only to show you understand, but also so the speaker can hear and understand their own meaning and feelings.	• Thinking ahead about what you will say next.
• Try again if your active-listening statement is not well received.	• Pretending that you have understood if you haven't.
• Be as accurate in the summary of their meaning as you can: 'Are you saying what you want is …'; 'Are you saying you feel you can't handle that much pressure?'	• Allowing the topic to drift to less important matters. If it does, then bring it back on track with a question: 'Is what you are saying …?' or 'I want to understand more about …?'
• Sometimes you can subtly challenge powerlessness and hopelessness, eg if you hear 'It is hopeless', you might reflect back: 'It seems hopeless to you right now'. If you hear, 'There's nothing I can do', try 'You can't find anything that could make it better?'	• Fixing, changing, challenging or improving what the speaker has said while you are in active-listening mode.
• Allow for pauses in the conversation.	• Filling in every space with your talk. Don't change topics.
• Notice body shifts and respond to them by waiting. Then, for example, you might respond to the pause and the change in energy with, 'How does it all seem to you now?'	• Neglecting the non-verbal content of the conversation.

Falling Off the Rails

When active listening is going well it is like a train travelling smoothly on a track. With the best intentions you will sometimes fall off the rails even though you know you should be listening empathically. Sometimes you reach a point where you seem to be unable to keep listening without reacting. It may be because you lack the skills of active listening. Perhaps you've grown up with the bad habit of jumping in whenever a thought arises in your mind. Sometimes your own enthusiasm on the topic pushes you to add your view. You may be using selective listening — only listening for what you want to hear. You may disagree so strongly that you just have to say something. You may think the other person is on the wrong track and should be put right. You may have a strong reaction because something they said pushed your buttons. You may just have had enough. You're bored and need to change the topic. It's not that you should stay in active-listening mode indefinitely, but you may need to quickly assess whether the purpose of listening has been accomplished or whether you should shelve that desire to interject or change topic for a little longer.[2]

Practice

In easy conversations with work colleagues or family members, try to put your thoughts, judgements and feelings aside for a few minutes. Centre yourself and consciously focus on what the other

person is saying and why that is important to them. If you notice a tendency to 'fall off the rails', recover as best you can. When you have practised on easy conversations, try to use the method in more difficult situations, where you are more emotionally involved. A measure of your success in this practice is when you find people telling you about things that matter deeply to them. You may also find yourself involved in fewer conflicts.

TERESA

Some time ago I hired Ralph, a consultant, for what I thought would be a couple of days. He was with us as an apprentice Conflict Resolution teacher. His own company wanted him to run a CR course for them and he needed more training. I was looking for opportunities to involve him. I thought it would be reasonable for his company to pay his normal wage for two days while he assisted us with a workshop. It suited us very well to have him there, as his background was engineering and this workshop was for a large group of engineers. The workshop formed part of a strenuous two-week assignment we had taken on for a large organisation. Ralph agreed it was a splendid opportunity for in-depth training and went off to his boss to negotiate paid leave. He didn't do well. While I was out one afternoon he left a phone message saying, 'My company won't pay. Can you pay me?' My reaction was negative. Was he such a bad negotiator that he couldn't get two days' paid leave for doing something of immediate benefit to his company?

I phoned him back, irritated. I launched right in with, 'Well, the best I can offer you is ...' I stopped myself. Something didn't seem quite right. Why wouldn't his company pay two days of his wages for his training? I shifted gears. I went fishing for the facts. Casting a wide net, I said, 'Tell me about the problem.' In the next few minutes it emerged that he'd asked for two weeks off, not two days. He thought it would be good for him to assist on the whole project, not just the two-day workshop. Then, of course, I understood why his boss wouldn't pay him for so much time off. We went back to the two-day plan. He talked again with his boss and had no trouble getting a 'yes' for the more modest proposal.

I'd saved the remains of my budget for other things and my gearshift to 'information mode' had rapidly cleared up our misunderstanding and prevented frustration all round.

Listening may have different purposes. In conflict situations, there are three distinct uses for active listening skills:

- **to gain information**: there are important facts to be clarified. You are listening so you understand and gain a clear picture from the other person.

- **to give affirmation**: the other person needs to be heard on issues that are troubling them. It will help them feel less alone with the problem. You must take care to avoid using any communication killers.

- **to respond to inflammation**: the other person is furious. You are under attack. You want them to feel heard so they are less likely to continue the attack. At the height of their anger, telling them to calm down or attempting to explain yourself is likely to inflame them further. First, they must believe that you really know how angry they are with you and why.

When you're under attack the instinctive response is to defend yourself. It's so tempting to throw into the arena a piece of information from your own agenda, designed to justify, overwhelm or place blame. If you do, unpleasant interchanges will multiply quickly. The conflict becomes more serious and more difficult to resolve.

Even if you are only moderately successful at acknowledging their feelings, in most situations an angry person will calm down if they feel that you mean it. Keep this active listening going until they've finished. That will be when they believe you've understood exactly what they needed to convey. Then they may be able to move forward and hear your perspective. If they heat up again, go back to active listening.

Sometimes you will need to use active listening quite briefly to move the conversation forward successfully. Sometimes you will need to keep the focus totally on the other person for a long time. Be flexible with how you use active listening and it will serve you often and well. It can be your tool for focusing while the other person is talking, so that you concentrate fully on what their words mean.

SARAH

My husband Paul and I have a really good relationship. It was really tested though, when his business went through a very rough patch — it looked as if it could fail altogether. I knew he was worried. We talked about it every day. It was great to be able to support him like that — I felt we were a real team. One evening he told me that Lauren, an old girlfriend of his, had rung him that day. She was offering to work with him and help build up the business again. He asked me what I thought he should do. I knew Lauren. She was very competent and experienced, but I wasn't at all sure of her motives towards Paul. Was she still after him?

I was feeling very threatened. I'd loved to have said, 'Tell her to go away!' I didn't want Paul employing an old girlfriend, but the whole thing was a very touchy situation. If I demanded that Paul didn't employ Lauren, how would he react? He might do the opposite, or blame my jealousy for his business going further downhill. The one thing I could see was that I dared not give any sort of advice.

I asked Paul: 'What factors would you want to look at before you could make a decision?' He soon realised he needed to know what Lauren's real expectations were. So, he organised a meeting with her. Paul told me about it afterwards. She'd come along to it 'seduction incorporated' — the perfect make-up, the tight dress, the sexy glances. Paul said he could see that work was only an excuse for what was really on her mind. That was exactly what I had suspected, but it seemed a good time to say nothing and keep listening.

Was I relieved when Paul told me he'd rejected Lauren's offer! I was pleased with how I'd handled the situation. I'd left him making all his own decisions. I'd been just the sounding-board. Active listening is certainly a great support to our marriage!

ACTIVE LISTENING FOR DIFFERENT PURPOSES

Purposes	Non-verbal skills
To gain information • To find out the details of what the other person is saying. • To clarify instructions	• Use appropriate body language — nodding, noting, recording, watching. • Focus your concentration, block out distractions.
To give affirmation • To show empathy and give acknowledgment. • To help the speaker hear and understand their own meaning.	• Choose a non-distracting and comfortable place. Is privacy needed? • Ideally, don't have furniture, eg a desk, separating you. Consider moving closer to the speaker. • Adopt an open, encouraging posture with welcoming gestures and appropriate eye contact to show attention and involvement.
To respond to inflammation • To let the speaker know you've heard the complaint or accusation and how strongly they feel about it. • To defuse the strong emotions.	• Avoid defensive or aggressive posture and gestures. • Centre: focus your attention briefly in your belly, breathe calmly. • Use attentive eye contact and an assertive stance.

Following skills	Reflecting skills
• Ask questions to get the facts on needs, instructions, context, timing, cost, etc. • Write notes. • Use memory joggers.	• Confirm your understanding by repeating key points and relevant details. • Be sure you both agree on the facts.
• Use minimal verbal encouragers — such as 'mmm' and 'uh-huh'. • Ask only occasional questions. • Try again if you misunderstand: 'I don't seem to have it quite right. Tell me again'. • Allow attentive silences. • Use skills in the Helpful Hints for Active Listening table (see page 47).	• Reflect back both feelings and content. • Feed back your understanding of the speaker's meaning. • Use a tone of voice that shows warmth and interest. • Summarise their major concerns. • Maintain their privacy.
• Acknowledge how they are feeling and their point of view: 'I can see how much this matters to you', 'No wonder you are so upset if you thought that was my attitude.' • Indicate that you've understood — a clear 'yes', a strong 'okay'. • After acknowledging the feeling, ask questions to understand the basis of the attack.	• Same as for listening to give affirmation (above). • Stay emotionally present. Your responses should not sound like you are unconcerned. • Reflect what they are saying. Don't retaliate or justify. • Almost match the intensity of their tone. If you use a flat voice it will sound patronising.[3]

Shift from Blame to Contributions

Reframe arguments about who's to blame into conversations about making contributions.[4] Considering your own contribution to a difficult situation, even when someone else appears to be at fault, is always worthwhile; for example, you're blaming an employee for not passing on some vital information. Have you contributed to the communication failure by giving the appearance of being too busy to be interrupted?

When it comes to blame, are you more likely to shift it onto others or to absorb it all yourself? Neither style is likely to represent the situation accurately. Conflicts are rarely caused by only one person.

You might start a contributions conversation with something like: 'I can see that I have contributed to this difficulty by ...' As the other person sees you take on some responsibility, the climate between you gets less threatening. Perhaps, then, they can reciprocate and consider their own role in the problem: for example, your client cancels an appointment with you twice at the last minute. You're annoyed, but hold it in check. You take responsibility for any false premise they might be working on and you seek more information: 'I'm thinking that I must have implied that it was easy for me to be flexible. Actually, it's quite challenging for me to organise a day to come and see you. I am wondering what went wrong for you?' They may need to tell you about a sick child or a boss that needed an urgent report. You've created a climate for rebuilding rapport.

> Blame: are you a shifter or an absorber?

As we take responsibility for our contributions, rapport builds and we find we are more forgiving. It will often help a very angry person if they can see that you are willing to acknowledge a role in the problem. Assessing the multiple contributions can help prevent similar problems in the future. You may not always want to tell the other person, perhaps a boss, about your contribution; however, you'll be less affected by the feedback if you are willing to acknowledge your error to yourself — forgive yourself for having made it and plan how you will avoid that issue in the future.

RICK

I was having real problems with my twelve-year-old daughter, Zoë. I had recently divorced and was living with another woman, Deborah. We were also living with Deborah's children from a previous marriage.

Zoë spends every weekend with us and was getting on very badly with Deborah's daughter Jessica, who's ten. There was a lot of jealousy and competition between them.

Another fight had exploded in the girls' bedroom. They were screaming at each other as I came on the scene. When I tried to find out what was going on, Zoë yelled at me, 'You always take Jessica's side. I hate you.' She ran out the front door, slamming it loudly in my face as I followed her. I was so worried, I thought, if I don't do something now I could lose Zoë. I ran down the street after her.

I called out, 'Slow down, if you run off now, we won't be able to sort this out.' It worked; she turned back to me. She was really distressed. She accused me of loving my new family more than her. 'Why should I visit you, Dad? I am just in the way and Jessica is a spoiled brat.' Tears were streaming down her face. I realised there was no point in defending my position, she was too angry to hear me. 'You know, Zoë, I am so sorry. I've been busy trying to make everyone happy. I haven't given enough attention to you and me.' Owning my part in our problems seemed to release some of her tension. I asked, 'What can I do to make it easier for you here?'

'I don't know, Dad, I feel like an outsider.' I felt so sad to have let this distance build between us. 'You are the most important person to me and I haven't been good at making time for you.' Zoë smiled tearfully, 'I guess I could have told you how I was feeling, but you seemed so busy with everyone else.' It was her way of saying she also had played a part.

Gently, I invited her to come back inside so we could have some time together, just the two of us. She knew I'd heard her and she calmed down. Once we were alone, we explored how it could be better for her when she stays with me. We were getting back to how we used to be with each other — able to talk things out.

SUMMARY

- Be willing to do things to improve empathy in a conflict situation. *Avoid communication killers*: giving solutions or advice at the wrong time, refusing to address the issue, changing topics, reassuring, diagnosing and persuading with logic are some of the no-noes that can lead to a communication breakdown. If you find yourself on the receiving end, you may need to explain what is making you withdraw from the conversation.

- *Active Listening* requires that you focus your attention on the other person and ignore, for a while, your own point of view. It is an amazingly successful technique for clarifying information, affirming the other person or letting them know that you have heard their anger.

- There will be times when building up a picture of *what and who has contributed* to a problem situation will be very useful. It takes the conversation away from blame and towards objectivity and problem-solving.

Empathy Part II

When two people are very different it is easy for small incidents to escalate into misunderstandings, tension and crisis. Everything they do and say can seem alien and wrong to the other person. Each might think about the other: it's as though we speak another language, we have a personality clash. No matter what I try I'm just not comfortable with them or somehow I always feel less than them in their company. We're talking about major differences in personality style and values.

Difference in itself is not the problem; judgement, however, is. Of course you are likely to get on most easily with people who have a similar style of relating to your own, but it is not necessarily the best balance for a productive relationship. The person who is good at overviewing a situation does well to team up with someone who will do the number-crunching detail. The person who mainly relates through their intellect may do well to marry someone who is more in touch with their emotional life. Combining different personalities can be just what makes a marriage successful or a work team functional.

If your relationships are to work well, your communication must convey *respect*. The other person must believe that you:

> If both of us thought the same way, one of us would be unnecessary

- Respect them as an equal and won't dominate them.

- Respect their right to their own opinions and won't manipulate them into seeing it your way.

- Respect and value their decisions and won't undermine them.

- Respect their values and experience.

This respect is not always automatic. It may require that we enter the other person's frame of reference — that we have some understanding of how it looks from where they stand. People relate to the world in many different ways because of genetic heredity, upbringing and the culture they grew up in. We need to make space for these factors, be non-judgemental and respectful of them, even if we disagree.

Many models are used in training programmes and personal development literature to help us understand our own tendencies, those of others, and how these differ. They are helpful devices for building rapport and they suggest methods we can use to foster mutual respect in the face of differing styles of behaviour, values and life experience.

DISC Model

Make space for difference

This useful model starts with a fundamental distinction pointed out by psychiatrist and theoretician Carl Jung early last century — the difference between extraversion and introversion.

If one is an extravert and the other an introvert, their different and contradictory standpoints may clash right away, particularly when they are unaware of their own type of personality, or when they are convinced that their own is the only right type.[1]

Let's call this a scale from more outgoing to more reserved.[2] A second continuum measures people on whether they are more people-oriented or more task-oriented.[3] These two intersecting scales make four quadrants and point to four very different styles of operating (see diagram next page).[4] These differing behavioural and communication styles are often a key source of misunderstanding and conflict.

Similar distinctions are presented in many different ways with different names. Here we've used the acronym DISC for Direct Influencing Stabilising Conscientious.

Keep in mind that people may fall anywhere along these two spectrums and that people aren't the same in all circumstances. Different jobs may foster different behaviours. We may also be rather different at home than we are in a social situation or in the workplace. The reserved person at work may be a veritable chatterbox at home. Someone who is unassertive at work may be clearly in charge at home. The person who is very task-focused at work may be very laid back and social in other situations. It doesn't

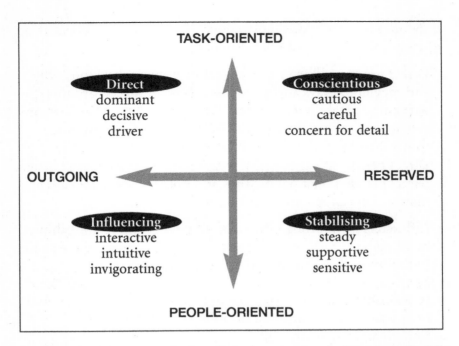

TASK-ORIENTED

Direct
dominant
decisive
driver

Conscientious
cautious
careful
concern for detail

OUTGOING ←————————→ RESERVED

Influencing
interactive
intuitive
invigorating

Stabilising
steady
supportive
sensitive

PEOPLE-ORIENTED

work to categorise people for all circumstances, and few people fall into the extremes. It is useful to notice tendencies that both you and other people have and which ones are showing up at different times. Don't let any labelling system blind you to the individual insights and perspectives of each particular person.

With these provisos, you will often observe that outgoing people tend to say what they think and feel quite easily, whereas those who are more reserved tend to be more reticent. Outgoing people are external thinkers — they think as they talk. Reserved people are internal thinkers — they think things through before they speak. This can lead to risky interpretations of each other's behaviour. For example, a reserved person may well see a very outgoing person as domineering or egotistical. The outgoing person may mistake a reserved person's reticence for a sign of disinterest or agreement.

On the task/people continuum, task-oriented people focus their attention on what needs to be done rather than on relationships. To the people-oriented person this can appear to be very uncaring. To task-oriented people in work mode, the relationship-building preliminaries that a people-oriented person would prefer to spend time on can seem time-wasting and insincere.

All people like to be treated with respect, but different DISC styles have different needs. So it's not surprising that each style values different respectful behaviours. If we can make space for difference in the way we approach people, we can avoid appearing disrespectful when we don't mean to be. In conflict:

- **Direct people** will tend to say what they think quite forcefully and may not always appreciate how difficult this is for others, particularly Stabilisers who may feel bullied. The Direct person can get very impatient with the lack of immediate response from a Stabiliser. If the Stabiliser tries to raise an issue, the Direct person sees them as slow and indecisive, so doesn't listen. Direct people prefer big pictures and bottom lines to details and may regard Conscientious people as too pedantic.

- **Influencers** will probably do a lot of talking and relationship-building before getting to what's difficult, if they get there at all. In the meantime, they're losing credibility with other personality styles, who may see them as too me-focused. Their relationship-building looks like waffle to the Direct person and their lesser interest in detail or order will drive the Conscientious person mad.

- **Stabilisers** will find conflict hard to talk about. They don't like to rock the boat. They're more likely to accommodate the needs of others rather than their own. Unconsciously, they hope for reciprocation. If their needs are not addressed by others in the solution, they can become resentful. They may experience Direct people as uncaring and abrupt and Influencers as insincere.

- **Conscientious people** will be sure to have their facts right and will want to focus on this. Being correct is what the argument is all about for them. They may miss how important relationships and feelings are to others. They may criticise decision-makers who don't plan the fine details. They make careful plans and can get really irritated by Influencers who value their flexibility.

With a list like this, it's a wonder we ever get on with each other at all! Being aware of and appreciating each other's styles brings us one step closer to harmony.

The two tables *Direct and Conscientious* and *Influencing and Stabilising* will help you become familiar with the four styles, understand the needs, fears and behaviours common to each style and judge how best to approach someone given the way they prefer to be treated (see pages 62–3).

When you've got to talk about difficult issues with someone whose style is very different to yours it makes sense to adapt your approach and your way of showing respect to their style. In return, they are more likely to respect what you are saying.

EXERCISE: using the DISC model

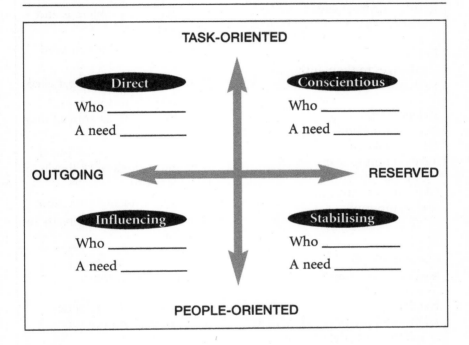

1. Read through the left-hand columns in the tables *Direct and Conscientious* and *Influencing and Stabilising* on pages 62–3. Where would you place yourself? If you fit into more than one category, consider yourself in one situation in particular; for example, at work. Put your name in the appropriate quadrant above.

2. Think of three other people you know well who you'd place in the other three categories. Be aware that they also may be different in different circumstances. You might want to write their names in the table above to see the next part of this exercise more clearly.

DIRECT AND CONSCIENTIOUS
START WITH THE TASK FIRST

DIRECT:

Outgoing Task-oriented

Needs:
Results, achievement, action, challenges

Fears:
Challenges to their authority
Lack of results from others

Behaviours:
Keen to get things done
Likes to take the lead
Takes action to bring about change
Challenges status quo
Seeks autonomy

When dealing with conflict:

- Be upfront — get to the point.
- State what the problem is and what you want.
- Get back to them if you need more time.
- Don't get emotional or personal.
- Move quickly to solutions, presenting them as options they can choose from.
- They present forcefully, but if your suggestions work they'll take them on.
- Ask directly for their decision.
- Don't hold grudges. Be ready to move on!

CONSCIENTIOUS:

Reserved Task-oriented

Needs:
High standards, structure, logic, quality work, detail, order

Fears:
Criticism of work, imperfection, things not adequately explained

Behaviours:
Reserved
Approaches work systematically
Pays attention to detail
Focuses attention on immediate task
Prefers to stick to established guidelines and practices
Likes to plan and research carefully for change

When dealing with conflict:

- Be punctual, calm, concise, unemotional and not too confrontational.
- Outline issues clearly — come prepared with facts, information and explanations.
- Put forward logical reasons for the way you think.
- Be ready for them to find any errors.
- Praise their detailed work.
- They don't like surprises. Give them time to prepare.
- Don't expect an immediate response.
- Don't pressure them. Give them time to work it out for themselves.

INFLUENCING AND STABILISING
BUILD RELATIONSHIP FIRST

INFLUENCING:
Outgoing People-oriented

Needs:
Change, acknowledgment, new
trends and ideas

Fears:
Disapproval, stagnation, detail

Behaviours:
Leads by enthusing others
Prefers a global approach
Steers away from details
Acts on impulse
Keen to promote change

When dealing with conflict:

- Be friendly. Spend time on the relationship.
- Let them know you value them and why.
- Start with the big picture.
- Talk about the problem and how you feel about it.
- Say what you want in a positive way and ask them to help.
- Make it clear you are including them in the decision-making.
- Ask how they feel about it.
- Keep the situation energised.
- Work together to fix things.

STABILISING:
Reserved People-oriented

Needs:
Security, acceptance, teamwork,
harmony, peace

Fears:
Isolation
Conflict
Standing out as better or worse
Unplanned challenges

Behaviours:
Reserved
Works well in a team
Accommodates others
Maintains status quo
Recovers slowly from hurt
Prefers planned, not sudden,
change

When dealing with conflict:

- Be relaxed and not too quick.
- Ask how they are first.
- Calmly and considerately broach the difficult topic.
- Be aware of their sensitivity to conflict.
- Build up the whole picture — give attention to how others are involved or affected. Then they'll want to help.
- Give them time to digest information.
- Provide them with enough time and encouragement to ask questions, offer input and state their needs.
- They go silent if you put down their contributions and may not offer more.

3. Consider: people you find most difficult are quite likely to be diagonally opposite you in the DISC model. Do you find the person you placed diagonally opposite you is quite often difficult to get on with? How do you think the two people you have placed on the other diagonal get on with each other (or would, if they knew each other)?

4. Consider the lists in the two tables again. Do you notice a need or fear that you might not have recognised as important for that person? For example, the Direct person's need for challenges in their life. Hold them back and they'll lash out. Of course, we all hate criticism, but the Conscientious person who is trying so hard to get everything just right may well react badly when criticised. You might like to write a high-priority need below each person's name in your chart.

Value Clashes

When it is hard for you to understand someone else's motivation it is often because they have high esteem for a value that is low on your own priority list. Someone may value honesty, but use the principle of 'buyer beware' when selling a second-hand car with a faulty gearbox. We may care deeply about intimacy and find ourselves resenting someone who highly values their privacy. Someone may value diligence much more highly than you if you regard yourself as a free spirit.

Often you can find a signpost that says 'this value of mine is being met'. If it is quantifiable, you can negotiate how much of it needs to be present for you or the other person to feel the value is being met. By how much should sales increase to tell you I'm being competitive in the marketplace? Will a phone call a day tell him I care? Does she need a bunch of flowers just on birthdays or every week? How many staff meetings per month will indicate an appropriate emphasis on team? These are questions about quantifying values. The answer may be the key to shift an impasse. Move the focus onto how much of *what* would indicate that the value is being met?

Quantify the value — how much is enough?

Opposing Priorities

There are a number of opposing values that continually seem to cause problems between people. They are described in the diagram below.[5]

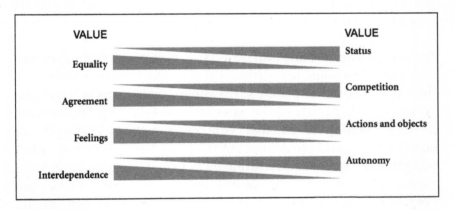

This diagram suggests that people high on one value tend to be low on the value at the opposite end of the spectrum. Integration balances both ends of these four spectrums — valuing both interdependence *and* autonomy, for example. During conflict, a person may well take a stance for one value at the expense of the other. The more extreme they are in demonstrating that value in their everyday behaviour, the more they will attract conflict with other people who prefer the opposite value. For example, the style of a status-oriented person may well arouse deep resentment in someone whose ideal is equality in relationships.

Equality versus Status: People respond to power differently. Some people will always emphasise the *equality* between people and minimise the differences, others demand respect for the *status* power brings. Equalisers will work hard to avoid arousing other people's jealousy; they'll use fairness as their yardstick for evaluating alternatives; they'll come out fighting to support the rights of friends and colleagues. Status Watchers may be striving for self-improvement or self-reliance, building self-respect, creating a clear chain of command, supporting justice and obedience to law and instructions.

Agreement versus competition: Some people use an interacting style that primarily focuses on *agreement*; others enjoy *competition*, even in ordinary conversation. Agreers will keep the peace, emphasise similarities and common ground and are emphatic about concluding disagreements. Competitors value competition because it drives people forward and tests worth. They will accept some aggression as part of the rough and tumble and they thrive on coming out on top after a struggle.

Feelings versus actions and objects: People focus their attention differently. For some their first source of information is *feelings* — their own and other people's. For others their focus is largely on *actions or objects*; that is, the external world. Feeling Focusers are relatively willing to disclose vulnerable feelings and will use emotions as a guide to action. On the other hand, Action Focusers will generally steer a conversation away from feelings. They'll build rapport through the exchange of information about activities and objects. For these people the world of feelings may be difficult and uncharted territory.

Interdependence versus autonomy: For those whose comfort zone is *interdependence*, working in a team or being part of a family are the keys to their life. Others need *autonomy* and may see anyone who doesn't as weak, dependent or interfering. For them, the goal is proving themselves, solving their problems alone and working independently. They might work well with others but they have a clearly defined sense of self and they like sole responsibility in their area.

Listen for hints that one of these values is not being accommodated in complaints like these:

SIGNALS OF A VALUES PROBLEM	
Complaint	Issue
That's not fair!	*Equality*
Show some respect!	*Status*
Why do you always have to make such a fuss?	*Agreement*
If you can't stand the heat, get out.	*Competition*
You don't give a damn about how I feel! You're not listening!	*Feelings*
Stop complaining and get on with it!	*Actions and objects*
We're all in this together!	*Interdependence*
Let me do it myself! Don't tell me what to do.	*Autonomy*

We are very individual on how we'd rank these eight values. Our priorities are influenced by our personalities, life experience, culture and the way we view a particular situation. They may also be influenced by what we grew up believing was a masculine or a feminine style and what we aspired to most. At work, changing management practice is shifting the attention towards equality, agreement, feelings and interdependence and moving away from authoritarian control.

If a person demonstrates one of these values in the extreme, they are likely to draw out its opposite in someone else. If you are highly competitive, someone else is sure to feel that you've got it all wrong. If you put all your attention on feelings, you'll irritate the action-oriented person. Spotting this conflict of values helps clarify the problem and minimises negative judgement. For example, if you become aware that the other person is more oriented towards action, whereas you are more concerned with feelings, then immediately some of the polarising goes out of the situation. It's easier to find a way to accommodate their values as well as your own rather than try to *change* them. You can encourage them to *include* values of a lower priority, which may be key values for you, in their decision-making. If you can achieve this you're well on the way to cooperative problem-solving.

Cognitive Dissonance

In dealing with a clash of values, where the other person's value is not particularly honourable or suitable to the situation, it is sometimes wiser not to encourage them to state the value they hold. Let's consider here a psychological theory developed by Leon Festinger — *cognitive dissonance*, the term he used for the inner tension that causes us to alter values or behaviours.[6] When our values and behaviour don't line up with each other, we change one or the other so that they will both be the same. If there is a discrepancy between what is publicly declared and what is privately believed, this is usually resolved by the person shifting the privately held value to align with the publicly stated one. So be careful: people cement in place values they declare publicly. If someone can be encouraged to state in public a *positive* value, this is more likely to motivate future action. If someone seems to be unfairly competitive in the workplace but can be encouraged to talk about the importance of team agreement they are more likely to start thinking that way.[7] If a manager with a blind spot for sexual harassment is required to acknowledge their responsibility to enforce the law against it, they will gradually become less accepting of this behaviour.

What is the Good Intention?

We often see other people's motivations only from our own perspective. They might be seeing it quite differently. For example, someone speaks harshly, demanding that you leave the room straight after a meeting. If you think they are just being rude and bossy, you'll probably feel very alienated. If you know that they're trying to clear the room quickly for the next meeting to take place, you will probably brush the incident off. Look for the other person's good intention whenever you feel alienated. There almost always is one and it helps to know it or even surmise it. They'll often be supporting a value with which you fundamentally agree. Even if you cannot identify a good intention, presume it exists. It opens the door to the possibility of empathy. You can ask: 'Tell me why that is so important to you?' Even when you don't agree with the underlying value or motivation, understanding it helps you open up meaningful discussion.

Dialoguing

Dialoguing is another method used to shift people's resistance to a set of values very different from their own. Its primary purpose is to build empathy between individuals and groups independently of the problems between them. It is particularly helpful where there are deep differences in culture or ethics. It relies on people telling their personal stories rather than debating the issues. Stories can be very useful whereas debating the issues may only inflame the situation further.

In dialoguing, each person relates parts of their personal history that show where or how they formed their values. They might include the influences on their lives and the difficulties they face. The aim is for people to explore the meanings and experiences behind the values that are clashing.

As people tell their personal stories, the complexities and ambiguities start to surface. People might talk about why the issue is important to them, how they got to this place, their pain and their unanswered questions. This shifts the focus from the conflicting values to the richness of the people themselves. Once they start hearing the stories, people view the conflict in a different way. They see that what the other person is saying is true *for them*, is *their* reality. Diversity can be a rich resource that you can explore by encouraging someone to tell you how they formed a value that is alien to you.

KATHERINE AND JOHN

Katherine and John had been out together several times and their relationship was starting to move into a deeper level. Katherine was discovering for the first time what it was like to trust someone else, be honest about her feelings and reveal her secrets. She felt very close to John. Yet something was getting in the way.

John had children from a previous marriage and she found herself being judgemental about the many gifts he bought for them. Her only attempt, so far, to indicate her feelings on the matter had been the somewhat snide remark, 'You sure give your kids a lot'. She felt guilty that she was so uncharitable about John's generosity towards his children, but she couldn't stop her resentment. This became a problem because she wasn't dealing with it, and it began to interfere with the relationship.

She went to a friend for advice. Her friend said, 'Just imagine for a moment that you are a third person looking down at yourself.

There you are — Katherine and John having a romantic dinner. John's telling Katherine about the latest special toy he has bought for one of his sons. Katherine's getting hot under the collar, wishing John would stop all that. She is debating whether she should suggest that he not buy so many gifts or should she think about giving up on the whole relationship? What would you recommend she do: Leave the relationship? Just sit and say nothing? Tell him to stop buying expensive gifts? Tell him not to tell her about the gifts?'

Katherine found the bird's-eye view of the problem helpful. She looked at her friend and said, 'Why doesn't she find out why he does it?'

The next time John mentioned a gift he'd bought, Katherine held back the acid remark about to slide off her tongue and instead said, 'I've noticed you buy a lot of expensive gifts for your children. I've often wondered why you do that. Why do you?' She carefully kept her tone of voice neutral.

He thought about it for a while and then replied, 'It helps me feel okay about myself as a father. My own father was incredibly stingy with me, with his time and his money. I vowed I'd be different with my own children. You know what my test is for a good toy? I always choose toys I can use to relate to the children with. They're things we assemble together or we all have to go off to a park to use. I think, in part, I'm making up for all those lost opportunities with my own dad.' They talked further about all this. Katherine talked about her childhood and the attitude to toys she grew up with. Toys only came her way at birthdays and Christmas. Her parents didn't regard toys as important. Katherine and John didn't trying changing each other's opinions, simply hearing them was enough.

Finally, John said, 'It's good to feel free to talk about myself so openly.' She was glad she'd opened up the conversation and found out more. It would have been so easy to have shut down instead. Katherine now felt closer to him than ever.

Through reflective dialogue you'll see the person, as well as the problem, and the conflict starts to matter a little less. Positions become less polarised; a more empathic climate evolves. This process has been used with religious and ethnic groups and factions holding opposing values.[8] It is also sometimes used in victim-offender reconciliations. It may seem as though nothing really has happened — there was no resolution — and yet something has changed.

You might encourage a conversation where people tell their stories. It's not usually very difficult to get people to talk in this way, but it's often helpful to have a third person steering the process. Some useful questions are:

- 💡 'How did you come to think/feel this way?'

- 💡 'What important experience in your life led you to believe in this?'

- 💡 'Can you tell us about something that has really affected you personally that relates to … (the topic at hand)?'

- 💡 'When you do … how does it satisfy you?'

- 💡 'When you do … how does that make you feel?'

- 💡 'What doubts have you had?'

- 💡 'If this dialogue is successful what differences will you notice?'

Even with the best of intentions we will never fully understand the other person's views, and so our empathy cannot be perfect; however, if we can manage to put judgements to one side and encourage heart-to-heart communication, empathy will build.

SUMMARY

We have looked at a number of techniques for entering another person's frame of reference.

The DISC model explains differing behavioural styles using the spectrums of reserved and outgoing, and people-oriented and task-oriented. In difficult conversations consider this to accommodate the other person's style.

Spot a clash of values. Common clashes include Equality versus Status; Agreement versus Competition; Feeling versus Actions and Objects; Interdependence versus Autonomy. Can you agree on signposts that say to the person 'this value is being met'? Perhaps with a phone call, a team meeting or a sales or production target? Can you quantify how much of that is enough?

Look for the good intention underlying unwelcome behaviour.

Dialoguing is a method which encourages the person to impart their personal history that supports the values you or another person are finding unacceptable.

These methods can help the flow of empathy beyond and around differences. They help clear negative judgements out of the way and foster respect for other people's values.

Notes

PART I

1 Dianne Collins QuantumThink — Living Wisdom From a New World View (article available on www.quantumthink.com)

2 For more on active listening see: Gerard Egan, *The Skilled Helper: A Problem-Management and Opportunity-Development Approach to Helping* (USA: Brooks/Cole, 2001); and Eugene Gendlin, *Focusing* (USA, Bantam Books, 1982)

3 Kris Cole, *Crystal Clear Communication* (Australia: Prentice-Hall, 2000) See also Genie Z. Laborde PhD, *Influencing with Integrity: Management Skills for Communication and Negotiation* (UK: Crown House Publishing, 2003)

4 Douglas Stone, Bruce Patton and Sheila Heen, *Difficult Conversations* (UK: Penguin Books, 2000)

PART II

1 Carl Gustav Jung, *Man and his Symbols* (UK: Aldus books, 1964) pp 59–60 Another widely used, more complex categorisation of individual difference is the Myers-Briggs model which further explores distinctions made by Jung. See Isabel Briggs Myers with Peter B Myers, *Gifts Differing* (USA: Consulting Psychologists Press, 1980)

2 Alan Parker in *Beyond Yes* makes a similar distinction based on high versus low assertiveness

3 Jung identified this distinction as feeling versus thought. Thought-focused people rely on logical deduction and reasoning and are task- and achievement-oriented. Feeling-focused people are paying the most attention to people and relationships and base their decision making on these factors. He is careful to point out that feeling versus thought and introversion versus extraversion are just two of many possible distinctions one could draw

4 This model was originally developed by William Moulton Marston PHD (1893–1947) and expanded upon by Dr John Geier for Performax Systems International. For information on questionnaires and courses, the Australian distributor is Integro Learning Company P/L, PO Box 6120, Frenchs Forest DC NSW 2086, www.integrolearning.com Tel: 1800 222 902

5 These values are discussed in detail in Helena Cornelius, *The Gentle Revolution* (Australia: Simon & Schuster Australia, 1998). The book focuses on masculine versus feminine relationship styles, though it would be simplistic to regard these value differences as gender-specific. The book and a summary are available through the Conflict Resolution Network's website: www.crnhq.org

6 Leon Festinger, *A Theory of Cognitive Dissonance* (USA: Tavistock Publications, 1959 See also Hugh Mackay, *Why Don't People Listen?* (Australia: William Morrow, 1994)

7 See *The Gentle Revolution* op. cit.

8 Many people are doing wonderful work in this area. Visit the website www.publicconversations.org for information, articles and resources

CHAPTER 4
Appropriate Assertiveness

How can I express myself so that I'm more likely
to be heard?

You need to believe that you have the right to have your needs met and that it is reasonable to turn to others as partners in meeting these. Of course, they won't always do that, but it's just fine to put your needs forward. Assertiveness is about being skilled in when and how to express your needs, feelings and viewpoints — in a way that is proactive, not reactive.

You'll know you've been appropriately assertive when you have expressed a desire in a manner that is respectful to the other person. It will be clear when you haven't been assertive because you'll be saying to yourself, 'If only I had said … or 'I wish I hadn't said …'

Sometimes there will be issues that are safer or wiser to leave alone, which in itself can be a form of assertiveness; however, if you're always saying: 'It's not wise' or 'It's not safe', you're probably avoiding being assertive. Perhaps you're scared of making things worse or anxious about damaging the relationship. You need to develop your skills of appropriate assertiveness.

What's your personal history on assertiveness?

- As a child, did you learn that it wasn't acceptable to have needs, express them and have them met? How was that message delivered to you? 'I'm not hungry.' 'Eat your dinner anyway!'

- Were you told not to feel what you felt? 'There's no reason to be so angry' or 'Don't be upset.'

- Were you criticised or ridiculed for saying what you thought?

- Were you told it was better not to speak up?

- Did you learn that by shouting louder or longer you got your way?

What happens for you now?

- Are there circumstances in your life where you aren't assertive and probably should be?

- Are there issues in a personal relationship that ought to be discussed, so that you are clean and up-to-date with each other, but you avoid them because you don't know how express yourself well?

- Do you find yourself very uncomfortable setting limits on other people? For example, with their use of your time.

- Where are your needs not being met? For instance, do you do too much yourself rather than delegate?

- Do you feel you don't speak up for what you want or feel you deserve?

- With whom do you get into fight, flight or freeze situations?

In Chapter 1, Responding to Conflict, we discussed the amygdala hijack: when we feel threatened, it can launch us into fight, flight or freeze reactions. From those states we attack, defend or withdraw in order to stay safe. We are in a *reactive* playing field. To get to flow, the *responsive* playing field, we need to shift our state. We'll do better if we centre ourselves, respect our emotions and shift our thinking from reaction to what we can do. Assertiveness is not an unconscious reaction — it often takes careful planning. The aim of assertiveness is to be responsive (to ourselves and to others) and elicit a response, rather than a reaction, from the other person. We're taking charge of getting our needs met, or our views heard, in order to make the situation better, not worse.

Take responsibility for your needs

How can you steer your assertive conversation so that you stand your best chance of success?

Premises behind Assertiveness

1. Respect yourself.

2. Respect the rights and needs of others.

3. Respond to early clues that something needs addressing.

4. State how it is for you, not how it is for the other person.

5. There's no guarantee you'll get what you want.

6. Your aim is to create a constructive conversation.

Guidelines for Assertive Communication

- Intent is important. Are you coming from your heart? Are you centred? Is your communication without blame? Are you using a collaborative approach?

- Being assertive with another person requires good two-way communication. Having told them how things stand for you, you'll want to know what they think. Always be alert for the opportunity to switch from talking to listening. This is a necessary part of a collaborative approach. Inquire about their needs. By doing this you are implying: 'I want to be satisfied and I want you to be satisfied too.'

- Avoid telling others what they should or shouldn't do. We want to be able to ask for what we want in a way that makes it okay for the other person to say 'no' without damaging the relationship.

- You may need to examine closely what it is you really want and then be open to a number of ways you might achieve that. If your partner hates action movies and you love them, perhaps you could go to the cinema with a friend instead.

- If you are feeling that you have too many demands on you, you may need to clarify your limits, boundaries or expectations rather than get resentful or over-stressed.

- You might have to be clear about what you are *not* saying. 'I'm *not* saying you're a bad mum!', 'I'm *not* saying you don't have the right. I'm just hoping that in this situation …'

- If another person's behaviour is causing you problems, you need to be truthful. You're the one having the problem and it is you who would like it to be different. They may not be seeing their behaviour as a problem at all.

- If the other person's behaviour is unacceptable, you may have to stand your ground, and set your limits.

- There will be times when you will have to escalate your assertiveness. Often the best way is to indicate the consequences if the person does not change. You may need to say 'No', *politely* but very firmly.

- If you find you're wrong, it need not affect your integrity or self-worth. You simply need to acknowledge the error and apologise if appropriate.

DENNIS

My wife, Sonia, and I have just had our second baby, Ruby, who is only three weeks old. She is gorgeous but life is a real handful now trying to care for two children eighteen months apart.

I had just got home after a stressful day at work and was confronted with my wife, handing me our screaming baby: 'Here take Ruby, I have to feed Max.' I discovered her nappy was very dirty. Being frazzled already, I snapped at Sonia, 'What kind of mother are you? This nappy's filthy.' Of course, she reacted angrily, 'Can't you see I've got my hands full ...' We started yelling at each other and quickly my day went from bad to worse.

I took a beer from the fridge and went to sit on the deck. I felt terrible about what I had said. I just needed a little breathing space when I came home before taking care of the family. I felt guilty and didn't know if it was fair to ask for what I wanted. After thinking about it for a while, I was ready to talk. 'Sonia, I feel so bad about how I shouted at you when I got home. You are a great mother and the issue was really about me, not you. When I get home from work I need some time to unwind before I can be on duty with the family. How would you feel if I took twenty minutes to myself before helping you out?'

Sonia was still upset but at least what I had said seemed to make her less defensive. She responded: 'When you criticise how I take care of the kids I feel really unappreciated. I'm doing the best I can. Take some time to unwind, but then I'd like a break too. I don't want you to dread coming home and I don't want us to stop appreciating each other either.'

We made a plan to have a picnic on the weekend, our way of trying to care for our relationship through all the huge changes in our lives.

Reactive or Proactive?

People who are experienced in assertiveness repeatedly use proactive rather than reactive language. They are careful about *how* they address the issues they are raising and they are constantly reframing their own reactive thinking and language. That's why they sound respectful. That's why it's hard to challenge what they say. Their conversations head towards positive outcomes. It's how assertive people get the leading edge!

The following examples show how proactive ways of saying things can create different conversations.

✗ REACTIVE ➡ ✓ PROACTIVE	
Blame: 'They didn't get the information to me on time.' 'You've misinterpreted what I said.'	**Take responsibility:** 'I need to find a way to ensure I get the information on time.' 'I need to explain this more clearly.' **Say how it is for you, not the other person.**
Generalise: 'You're always late.' 'When you constantly change the TV channels while we're watching ...'	**Be specific:** 'I saw you come in after the start of the last three team meetings.' 'When you change channels three times during the same show ...' **Avoid always, never, keep.**
Emotive: 'You humiliated me ...' or 'You ignored me.'	**Objective:** 'When you left the room while I was still talking to you ...' **Describe the specific behaviour. Don't assume you know their attitudes or motives.**
Judge: 'This report is unprofessional.'	**Describe:** 'This report has no charts or statistics.'
Criticise: 'Your spelling is terrible!' 'Your telephone manner is hopeless!'	**Offer suggestions:** 'Would you consider turning on the spell checker in your computer?' 'Would you feel okay asking each caller how you can help them?' **Focus on what the person can change.**

✗ REACTIVE ➡ ✓ PROACTIVE	
Demand: 'You'll have to …' 'You should!' 'Stop being a pest!'	**Invite:** 'How would it be if you were to … ?' 'Could you …?' 'Would you be able to … (eg find something else to do until I'm finished?)' **Invite behaviour you do want. Don't dwell on what you don't want. Ask for their response to what you have said.**
Negative: 'I don't want to go.' 'I can't see you until 3 pm.'	**Positive:** 'I do want to put in a phone call.' 'I can see you at 3 pm.' **Say what you can do, rather than what you can't.**
Opposition: 'I like that idea, but it is expensive.' 'You can't do that. John would be offended.'	**Inclusion:** 'I like that idea and I'm concerned that it is expensive.' 'We must consider, in any solution we come up with, that John must not be offended.' **Include the opposite point of view as part of the total scene you're working on.**
Problems: 'This filing is a terrible problem.'	**Issues, challenges, opportunities:** 'The filing is an issue. Let's design a better filing system.' **Reframing a problem as an opportunity or a challenge makes it into something you can work on.**
Past: 'I've told you a thousand times …'	**Future:** 'From now on …' **Look where you can make changes, rather than dwell on what was wrong in the past.**

If you catch yourself using reactive language, think about how to reframe your statement. After a while it comes naturally.

Discomforts

A situation is making you uncomfortable. Let that discomfort or disquiet be your guide. Trust your intuition. How and where will you begin to address the issue? You need to set the scene for a good conversation. For example:

'I'm feeling a bit uncomfortable. Is there anything we need to clear up between us?'

'Is there anything we need to discuss before the meeting so that it will all flow smoothly?'

'I've agreed to the plan, and now it doesn't sit well with me. I think we need to renegotiate.'

Such statements sound simple, but they take a bit of thought. On the surface they hardly seem assertive, but a proactive response to discomfort is a key element of assertiveness.

Stating Your Views

You need to add a different perspective to the discussion. Each of us has a unique perspective built on our personal experience, our feelings and our theories of the topic at hand. Assertive people make it safe for everyone, including themselves, to add to the pool of shared meaning.[1] By virtue of your uniqueness you have a contribution to make. You need to be able to speak up even when others are vehemently pushing their point. It is best not to thrust your own insights into the limelight so forcefully that other perspectives are obliterated. Each perspective needs to be respected for the contribution it makes.

STATING YOUR VIEWS ASSERTIVELY	
Make sure you have truly understood their point	'Do I understand you correctly?' 'Are you saying that …?'
Stating your point	'Here's what I think and how I got there.' 'I came to this conclusion because …' 'As I see it …' 'My experience is that …' 'I'm uncomfortable. I need some time to think about this.' Avoid using 'Everyone thinks …', 'Most people know …'

Expressing doubts	'I am concerned by ...' 'I see a difficulty in that ...' 'Will that lead to ... ?' 'I am finding it hard to see ... because of ...'
Stating disagreement	'I see it differently in that ...' 'I respect/appreciate your view that ... and the way I see it is ...'
Getting feedback	'What do you think about what I just said?' 'Do you see any gaps in what I said?' 'What can you add?' 'How do you see the situation?'

Raising Difficulties with Others

'I' Statements

An 'I' statement is an excellent way to raise difficulties. An 'I' statement tells the other person how you see the situation, without blaming and without demanding that the other person change. It might include naming the behaviour, the resulting problem, your feelings and the future. It helps you to hold your ground without treating the other person as an opponent.

An 'I' statement is about taking responsibility for your own feelings. When you're making an 'I' statement you give yourself the right to feel as you do. Don't talk yourself out of your feelings: 'I know I shouldn't react like that'; 'I'm silly to feel like that'. This type of self-talk is non-productive. If you blame others for how you feel, they usually get very defensive and reject the accusation with statements like: 'If you got angry, that's your problem!'; 'It's not my fault if every little thing makes you upset'. When you take responsibility for your feelings, communication about a problem has a better chance of staying on target.

✗ 'She hurt my feelings.'   ✓ *'I am feeling hurt.'*

✗ 'He drives me mad.'   ✓ *'I get mad when ...'*

✗ 'It makes me angry.'   ✓ *'I get angry.'*

NAN

My son Eddie lives two hours' drive out of town. I was upset when I heard he had visited town and not bothered to call or see me. We seemed to be growing further apart, and I had been brooding over this. I did not want to appear to nag him, nor say anything that would make things worse, but I did want to see him when he came to town.

When we next spoke, instead of putting on my pretending-not-to-be-hurt voice, I prepared myself for the conversation with an 'I' statement. I had worked on it for quite a while before I got it both 'clear' and 'clean'. I had a clear intention the conversation would be different from all those times when I had only hinted at the problem.

'When I miss out on seeing you I feel hurt and I'd like to see you when you are in town.'

I said it. Eddie immediately reacted with, 'You're always going on at me with the same old thing.'

But this time I had a clear intention. 'No,' I said, 'this time I said something different. I was simply telling you how I felt.'

For the first time on this issue, he really heard me. There was a moment's silence. Instead of getting defensive, his normal pattern, he said, 'Well, actually I've tried to phone a few times. You weren't home.' I acknowledged that that was so. I felt much better and we then had the best conversation in ages.

When Do You Use an 'I' Statement?

In simple situations ...

✗ 'You're not listening.' ✓ *'I need you to listen to me.'*

✗ 'You're off track.' ✓ *I'm confused as to how that is relevant, could you please explain it to me.'*

✗ 'You're doing that badly.' ✓ *'I need us to find a better way to do this.'*

✗ 'Put your jacket on.' ✓ *'I'm concerned that you may be cold.'*

✗ 'You've overcharged me.' ✓ *'It seems to me that this charge is greater than we agreed.'*

✗ 'Is something wrong with you?' ✓ *'I'm feeling concerned/uncomfortable. Are you okay?'*

In difficult situations ...

An 'I' statement can be particularly effective when you are angry, irritated, upset, just not getting what you want or when the other person's behaviour is causing you problems and it is appropriate to give them feedback. You might want to work out carefully what you are going to say before you see the person. While you're first learning to be assertive having a formula helps. Once you have become familiar with the principles, you can fly free and trust yourself to get the principles right, whichever way you put your case.

As you work on your formula, what you need and how to say it will become clearer. Your 'I' statement is not about being so soft or nice that you don't convey your message, nor is it about pushing your point or being rude. It is about having a constructive conversation.

Constructing an 'I' statement is like combining cooking ingredients: using a recipe to start with is more likely to ensure you put them together in a palatable way.

For the 'I' statement recipe there are five ingredients:

1. The action.

2. Your response.

3. Your preferred outcome.

4. A constructive consequence.

5. An invitation to respond.

You won't always use all parts of the 'I' statement; sometimes just one or two will suffice and you may change the order in which you put them together.

1. The Action

The recipe calls for a specific and objective description of the action or situation that's causing you the problem. Specific and objective here mean that the description is free of subjective or emotive words and generalisations (see Reactive–Proactive table pages 77–8) The aim is to give a factual description of what happened, rather than your interpretation. They may want to argue against an emotive or judgemental description; an objective description of the event can actually serve the other person. They may not have been aware of what they were doing, or how it affected you; for example, you tell them they are shouting at you when they simply meant to emphasise something. To avoid the other person becoming defensive, rephrase less objective ways of stating your point.

✗ 'When you leave me out of things ...'   ✓ *'When I'm not included in planning ...'*

✗ 'When you accuse me ...'   ✓ *'When you say I did ... (a particular thing)'*

When we are angry with someone it's quite a challenge to describe their behaviour objectively. Often it's easier to focus on exactly what the problem is for you.

✗ 'When you leave your junk all over my desk ...'   ✓ *'When my papers get mixed up with yours ...'*

✗ 'When you keep interrupting me ...'   ✓ *'When I don't finish what I am doing ...'*

If you can't think of an objective way to describe a behaviour start with *'When it seems to me ...'.*

✗ 'When you rant and rave at me ...'   ✓ *'When it seems to me that you are talking loudly ...'*

2. Your Response

People don't always know how you are affected unless you tell them. They can underestimate how hurt or angry or put out you are. It's no good assuming that they know what has offended you or what you are feeling. Most people prefer to keep onside with someone else and not to offend, hurt or annoy, so if you explain how it has affected you, that usually prompts them to reconsider their behaviour, as long as you have not attacked them in the process.

Your response might be:

an emotion   *'I feel hurt/angry/helpless/resentful or guilty.'*

an action   *'I withdraw'; 'I lose my train of thought'; 'I scream at you.'*

what you feel like doing   *'I feel like ignoring you'; 'I want to walk out'; 'I wish I could give up'.*

With your spouse or partner it is important to share how you feel. In a work situation you may not want to tell your manager or colleagues about your feelings. In some situations talking about feelings is culturally inappropriate. Describing your actions or impulses can sometimes be more appropriate.

When you are talking about *your own response* you know you're on safe ground. You're discussing your truth. People are less likely to argue the point if you say 'I feel frustrated' or 'I feel ignored'. Beware of statements like 'I feel *that you're* not listening'. This is your interpretation.

Reasons

You may want to add more explanation to your response to explain why there is a problem. Many independent and strong-willed children are more likely to cooperate when they understand the reasons for a particular rule[2] — it works for adults too. Explanations can make it easier for them to appreciate how it has affected you — and often that is sufficient. Use this only when you think an explanation is necessary or helpful.

3. Your Preferred Outcome

Your preferred outcome is not the solution, it's an invitation. Invite what *you* would like to be able to do or have. For example: 'I'd prefer it *if I could finish what I am saying*' rather than 'I'd prefer *you to listen better*'; 'I'd like it *if I could have more help* with the cleaning up' rather than 'I'd like *you to help me* with the cleaning up'.

When you tell other people what they should do, they often resist. They should feel free to choose. A well-formed 'I' statement indicates that you respect their autonomy.

When you discuss your preferred outcome, keep as many options open as possible. If you are clear about what *you want to be able to do or have*, the other person can see who can contribute and how. It can open up options. In the cleaning up example, there are several ways you can get more help: one family member may help per night, you may get a housekeeper, eat out more often, make a roster, or the person you are talking to may volunteer themselves. When you involve the other person in coming up with solutions, it becomes collaborative.

> Demanding invites resisting

4. Constructive Consequence

What is the benefit of the outcome you have suggested? Explaining this often makes it look more attractive:

✓ 'That way I won't be feeling so tired and cranky at night.'

✓ 'That way ... we'll all be able to sleep better.'

5. Invitation to Respond

Add something that encourages the other person to respond, so it is a two-way conversation. For example:

✓ 'How would that be for you?'

✓ 'Is that okay with you?'

SAMANTHA

Having her husband, Nathan, do something special for her on Valentine's Day was very important to Samantha. She had told him so many times and each year he did nothing. It wasn't his thing and he didn't believe in these 'commercial' events. He didn't like to buy Christmas presents either.

Each year Samantha got upset. She spent a lot of time complaining to her work colleagues, checking out how many people did get cards and getting a lot of agreement that he should do something because it mattered so much to her. She knew from her past experience that if she did tell him he should do something about it, it either ended up in an argument or he just ignored it, and if she didn't say anything, she couldn't really hide her disappointment and resentment.

A colleague who was familiar with the 'I' statement method helped Samantha think through an appropriate statement. It took Samantha a while to stop saying, 'He should do something about Valentine's Day' and get down to her underlying need — to be appreciated and to keep the relationship special by doing special things. She was then able to let go of feeling that it had to happen on Valentine's Day and to talk with Nathan about ways they could both agree on, to keep acknowledging and celebrating their relationship. Here's Samantha's opening 'I' statement:

'When you don't want to do anything for Valentine's Day, I feel hurt and unappreciated, because for me it is important to do things to celebrate our relationship. What I'd like is to talk about ways we can celebrate our relationship, so that we can keep it exciting.'

Key Points

'I' statements are openers not resolvers. The best 'I' statement is free of expectations. It's an opener that delivers a clean, clear statement of your side of things and how you'd like it to be. Listen to what they've got to say next; perhaps ask them a question: 'What's happening for you at those times?' Combine your 'I' statements with active listening. Then perhaps another 'I' statement, or part of one, will be needed. You are giving and getting the information you both need to develop options together. You've created a starting place for honest communication, inviting possibilities and improving the relationship.

MARIA

Mike had recently married Maria. They were both in their forties. It was the second marriage for both of them. Maria, whose children were now living away from home, had devoted much of her time over recent years to looking after her ageing widowed mother. Now, after the honeymoon, Mike and Maria were putting a lot of energy into renovating their home and enjoying their relatively new relationship. Maria was spending less time with her mother.

Then Maria's mother broke her arm and became very demanding just when Maria was most reluctant to have her own life pressured. This put her in conflict with her Italian upbringing and its strong family values. Though her relationship with her mother had so far been good, this time she felt resentful.

She turned to Mike for advice. 'What can I do? Vince and his family live too far away, Franco is in America, Angela has got three young children and lots of problems, and Liliana has just got a job because she needs the money — and you know how lazy her husband is. So it's pointless asking any of them.'

Mike thought for a while. Should she drop everything for her mother and leave the renovations aside for a time? Pay someone to look after her mother (which they could hardly afford)? Ask her mother to contribute? Put some pressure on the other family members?

He finally said, 'Could you just discuss the situation with each of them without asking anything of them? Simply listen to them and acknowledge what problems and stresses they have too. Leave them to think what we could all do to help while your mum's arm gets better.'

Maria contacted all her brothers and sisters. She started the conversations with an 'I' statement: 'I'm worried that I won't be able to give Mum all the support she needs'. She went on to explain the situation and listened to them tell her about their stresses and pressures. She said to John, 'Oh well, at least I tried', having listened to their stories and feeling very 'dumped on'.

Within the next few days each member of Maria's family offered to do something. Angela offered to mind their mother overnight, Liliana offered to take some prepared meals over there and her 'lazy' husband agreed to transport mum to hospital for her treatments (he was a taxi driver, after all), and Franco sent some money for a housekeeping service.

Maria wasn't sure what had made the change until afterwards, when Angela said to her, 'I felt like doing something this time because you seemed to care about me and didn't judge my lifestyle, unlike everyone else in the family. I felt needed, not cast out'.

Maria's 'I' statement had been an opener. She didn't know what would happen, but the response was more positive and more far-reaching than she could have envisaged.

Adapt your style. Would it help them to hear you better if you adapted your style to fit their style? Will your assertive statement best serve the situation if it is more direct and fast paced or if it is approached more slowly and tentatively? Does it need to be more task-focused or more feelings-focused, with a softener at the beginning. How can you be most effective?[3]

Check your intent. If your assertive communication is not well received, check your intent. You can't afford to sound insincere. Your underlying motivation and judgements show through. Any attempt to humiliate will go down like a lead balloon and is almost never helpful. Even though your verbal message appears to be blame-free, your non-verbal language and tone of voice may convey a different message. If you think you will sound stilted, adapt your 'I' statement to fit the way you like to say things. Just keep the principles in mind. Be clear that you are not forcing them to fix things. You are not imposing your values or opinions. You are letting them know how it seems on your side and what you need. You can't predict how the other person will take your communication. It is better to just focus on your intent.

Sometimes the most important person you are framing an 'I' statement for is yourself! In the process of developing your 'I' statement examine what the problem behaviour really is — beyond all labels and judgements. Sometimes you'll see

> For things to change, first I must change

that it isn't really their behaviour that's the problem — it's your reaction. If that's so, you may not choose to deliver your 'I' statement at all. There may be something quite different that you want to say. It may lead you from being annoyed with another person, and expecting them to fix it, to understanding your own needs and what you can do about them.

Don't expect to solve the problem straightaway. Don't expect the other person to respond immediately. Sometimes you can't push things home to the conclusion you'd like, but at least you have shared your point of view. Sometimes the most powerful thing you can do for the long term is to stop pushing your point and go back to the relationship. It may need something like this: 'I've said my piece. We both want the relationship to work so perhaps we just have to agree to differ on this one.'

Sometimes the other person may not be able to do anything. Having the conversation may be enough. Undelivered communications can build up to an increasing coldness between you both. Sometimes there is no answer, and the communication allows you to stay close to the other person.

JELENA AND MARCO

Jelena and Marco had been colleagues for a while. They usually talked a lot about work issues and occasionally had a drink and debrief at the end of the day. It had been a while since they had talked and Jelena was hurt and wondered why Marco appeared to be avoiding her. She raised it with him using an 'I' statement. Marco explained that he had been totally preoccupied because his mother was ill and his wife pregnant. He also said that it was going to be like that for a while and he wouldn't be able to spend time with Jelena as they used to and that he was sorry.

Jelena felt better having had the conversation even though the situation wasn't going to change.

It takes practice. If you couldn't quite get your 'I' statement out of your mouth, make another opportunity. The key to good 'I' statements is to make them so often that they become second nature.

Sample Conversations Based on 'I' Statements

When someone's on the computer while you're talking to them:

'*When I am trying to talk to you and you continue to work on the computer, I find it difficult to know if you are listening and I'd like to find a way to get your attention when I need it. Could we work something out?*'

To someone who's let you down at the last minute:

'*When you let me know at the last minute that you can't meet the deadline, I feel annoyed because it puts me in an awkward position with the customer. I'd prefer it if you could let me know at least a week ahead if there are to be delays so that I can make plans accordingly. How would that work for you?*'

To a manager not giving feedback:

'*When I don't get information on how I am proceeding on the project, I feel unsure about how it's going. I'd like some feedback so that I could know if it is proceeding well or if there are adjustments to be made.*'

Dealing with children who are slow to get ready in the mornings:

'*When I have to leave for work at 8.30 am and you're not ready, I feel upset and irritated. I'd prefer to work out a way to be more organised, that way we'll be able to start our day better and I won't get cranky.*'

A small irritation that needs an important conversation:

'*When I've told you I'll be running late and you then say, "Why are you late?" I feel distressed. My work situation is difficult for both of us. If you are upset, I'd prefer you tell me in a less confronting way. Can we discuss how we could make the situation a bit easier?*'

ARE YOUR 'I' STATEMENTS CLEAN, CLEAR AND CONCISE? Combine some or all of the following five elements:	
The action:	Say what happened. *No emotive words.*
Your response:	How you feel or how it affected you. *No blame.* *You may want to explain why you feel that way.*

Preferred outcome:	What you'd like to be able to do or have, or simply: 'I'd like to work something out together'. *No demands.* *Make it an invitation.*
Constructive consequence:	Perhaps describe the benefit of the outcome you are suggesting.
Invitation to respond:	Encourage a conversation.

EXERCISE: using 'I' statements

Want to start practising?

Here are some scenarios. Work out an 'I' statement for each. Only after you have done so, consider the sample 'I' statements at the end of the chapter on page 96. There are no rights or wrongs.

Situation 1: Someone talks too loudly on the phone in a shared office.

When ... _____

I ... _____

What I'd like is ... _____

That way ... _____

Invite a response: _____

Situation 2: Someone you live with has been distant and preoccupied lately and it is making you uncomfortable.

When ... _____

I ... _____

What I'd like is ... _____

That way ... _____

Invite a response: _____

Situation 3: Your manager is not consulting you on decisions about which you consider you have an important input.

When ... _____

I ... _____

What I'd prefer is ... _____

That way ... _____

Invite a response: _____

Consequence Confrontations

The Hardline Situations

There will be times when your carefully worded invitational 'I' statements appear to fall on deaf ears. If you're the manager, you may have to decide whether you should now issue a warning. If it's your child's behaviour that must change, you'll have to work out an appropriate consequence if they continue to misbehave. Even if you are not in a direct power relationship, you have the power to initiate some consequences if the unwelcome behaviour warrants it: you can decide to leave the room; you can end a relationship; you can put in an official complaint. When you are contemplating such major consequences, it's usually fair to warn first. You'll have to confront the person and let them know what will happen if they do not change. It's still up to them whether they change or not. Your intention is to inform not demand.

When ...	Objective statement of the behaviour.
The results ...	Why it's a problem.
The change needed ...	The person should be capable of making this change; don't ask for the impossible.
Consequence ...	What will happen if the change doesn't occur. You are not making a threat. You are explaining a result — your solution if the other person is not willing to contribute.

Switch to active listening ...

When you switch to active listening you may hear an apology, you may hear justification, the person may be upset or angry. Without putting them out of your heart or being vindictive, you may need to tell them yet again the consequence they're facing.

To a recalcitrant teenage son:

'When you came home from the party and it was past your deadline, I was worried sick and wondered if I should call the police. From now on I really need you to come home on time or phone in. If this problem happens again I will collect you from all future parties at 11 pm until I think you've matured enough to take the responsibility for respecting my concern.'

To an unpunctual employee:

'When you are often late for meetings we have to go over information twice to help you catch up. People are making sarcastic comments and I don't want my team talking that way. I also don't want them considering that lateness is acceptable. I need you to be on time to all future meetings, unless there is a major crisis. If you can't commit to that, I need you to resign from that work group so you don't have to come to those meetings at all.'

Switch to active listening: 'How are you feeling about that?'

Consequence confrontations are 'big' moments in a relationship. You make them to avoid a bigger crisis.

Positive Consequences from Change

You may find that there are less confronting ways of achieving your purpose. Offering the person a positive consequence if they are willing to do what you suggest creates a warmer climate for the relationship.

'If you come home on time after the next three parties, then we can extend your deadline by an hour.'

'If you prove to me that you will get your reports in on time, I'll consider making you team leader.'

'If you tell me when something I've done is upsetting you, I promise I will talk it through with you, without shouting or storming off.'

Refusing Requests

Even though it can be difficult to turn someone down, it's much better to do so than say 'yes' and then be resentful or not actually do it. People-pleasers who don't follow through are not well respected. If you need to turn someone down there are some assertive skills that can help it go well.

Acknowledge the requester. It is nearly always best *to give the reason* for refusing. When you need to turn down a social engagement, honouring your needs can be a valid reason. Most people respond better to a 'no' followed by an honest *reason*, than a 'no' reinforced with an *excuse*. There is *no need to overdo the apologies* — it starts to sound insincere. Here's an assertive refusal to a dinner invitation from a friend:

'I'd love to have dinner with you and tonight I need some quiet time to myself. Could we make it another night?'

When you have too many demands placed on you, it doesn't serve anyone if you take them all on. Here's an assertive refusal:

'Thanks for asking — I'd like to be able to do it, and at the moment I have too many things on my plate so I won't be able to do it now.'

If appropriate offer an alternative.

Saying 'No'

At times people might ask you to do things that just don't sit well with you ethically, or on which you are not negotiable, not willing or not interested. These are times when you'll have to say 'no' clearly, precisely and firmly.

If 'no' is not sufficient, give the reason once. | **Be firm, not furious** |
Avoid rambling justifications.

'No, I don't want to move my office. I need to be near accounts.'

If the person persists, repeat your refusal — like a scratched CD.

'No, I don't want to do that.'
'No, I'm not able to …'
'No, I intend to stay where I am.'

Saying No without Saying No

'I would like to be able to do that and under the circumstances it is not possible' (give a reason if appropriate). You could add, *'What I can do or am willing to do is …'*

To an overhopeful twelve-year-old: *'Yes, I know you would like to stay out until midnight, and what I'm going to do is let you stay out until 11 pm.'*

Handling Aggression

If a person is shouting, swearing, or using verbal abuse, being aggressive back is unlikely to lessen the other person's aggression.

'Don't you dare swear at me!' or 'Don't call me an idiot — you're the one who is an idiot!' might seem satisfying in the moment, but could incite an extreme reaction.

'When you use those words with me, I will not continue the conversation. I am willing to continue if those words are no longer part of it.'

'I'm not willing to continue in this way.'

'If we are to continue this conversation, we need to do it differently.'

If your job requires that you frequently deal with angry people, these may be helpful:

'If you want me to keep helping you, then what I need is to discuss this more calmly.'

'If you want me to help you I need you to allow me to finish what I am explaining to you.'

Handling Put-Downs

Perhaps there's an underlying aggression in the other person's communication. They may be questioning your judgement, nagging, inferring you are lying or using emotive language to describe your actions. To get a sense of the way you could handle these, review the table below, *Handling Put-downs*.[4]

HANDLING PUT-DOWNS		
Type of Put-down	Example	Your Assertive Response
Questioning your judgement	'You can't really believe that!'	'Yes, I do believe that.' **Sidestep the insinuation You're entitled to your beliefs.**
Inferring you are lying	'Oh come on, you know that's not how it happened!'	'That's how it appeared to me. Is there something I missed in the way I saw it? How do you see it?' **Affirm your personal perspectives while being open to hear theirs.**

Type of Put-down	Example	Your Assertive Response
Nagging	'How much longer are you going to be before you finish that job?'	'Why are you asking?' or 'About another two hours. How will that be for you?' **Find out the legitimate need behind the insinuation.**
Using emotive language to describe your actions	'You were completely irresponsible not to let me know!'	'I accept that it was a mistake not to let you know.' **Acknowledge.** Take responsibility without grovelling.
	'You're incompetent!'	'What specifically has led you to conclude I'm not competent?' **What specifically?** Find out what their judgement is based on.
	'You were so rude with me on the phone.'	'Yes, I was rushed. You wouldn't have been aware that you caught me taking my daughter to hospital with a broken leg.' **Educate.** Where they're missing information fill them in. You're giving them the context, not making an excuse.
	'That was a stupid decision!'	'I learnt that it didn't work. I'll do it differently next time.' **Redirect.** Focus on learning for the future. Explore options.

SUMMARY

Assertiveness is about respecting yourself: being clear about who you are and what you want, need and feel, and how you believe you deserve to be treated. Ways to be assertive include:

- Being centred and responding from your heart.

- Using proactive rather than reactive language.

- Addressing discomforts and issues before they become big problems.

- Speaking up when you have different views.

- Responding, not reacting, when you have difficulty with other people's behaviours.
- Saying how it is for you, not the other person.
- Using 'I' statements as conversation openers to address difficulties and give feedback.
- Inviting others to respond, not react.
- Adapting your communication to the other person's behavioural style.
- Using consequence confrontations in hardline situations.
- Being able to refuse requests and say no when necessary.
- Handling aggression and put-downs.

Sample 'I' statements for Exercise on page 90

Situation 1: *'When you are talking to someone on the phone in a way that seems to me to be loud, I get distracted and find it hard to concentrate. What I'd like is to find a way that would work for both of us so that I can let you know when it is happening.'*

Situation 2: *'When it seems to me that you are quieter than usual, I feel as though I've done something to upset you and what I'd prefer is for us to talk when something is bothering you. Can we do that?'* Or *'When it seems to me that you are quieter than usual, I get concerned and what I'd like is to find out what is going on for you.'*

Situation 3: *'When decisions are made on things I am working on without my input, I lose my motivation, and what I'd prefer is to be consulted on these before a decision is made. That way I could make a contribution. Would that work?'*

Notes

1 Kerry Patterson, et al., op. cit., p 21
  Useful reference on advocacy and inquiry questions: Peter M Senge, Art Kleiner, Charlotte Roberts, et al., *The Fifth Discipline Field Book* (USA: Doubleday, 1994)

2 Thomas Gordon, *Parent Effectiveness Training* (USA: Three Rivers Press, 2000)
  Robert Bolton, *People Skills* (Australia: Simon and Schuster Australia, 1986)

3 See DISC model, Chapter 3, Empathy Part II, p 58

4 Adapted from Ken and Kate Back, *Assertiveness at Work* (USA: McGraw-Hill, 1982)
  There is more on handling aggressive people in Chapter 6, Managing Emotions, pp 136–40

CHAPTER 5
Cooperative Power

What will steer us to use power 'with' rather than 'over' each other?

In this chapter we look at power relationships. The relative power of each participant is a factor in most conflicts, though usually it stays under the surface, never to be addressed directly. Nonetheless, sometimes it is of primary importance and has a major influence on the outcome.

There's a lot we can do to shift the power balance in the direction we want it. Our purpose is to move away from *power over* and *power under* others towards *power with* them. This is what we mean by *cooperative power* — the power of pulling together. It requires each person in the relationship or group to be empowered, so it is important that we consider personal power — how we can diminish it and how we can empower ourselves.

Take a moment now to orientate yourself to the topic. Ask yourself these questions, and perhaps write down some thoughts:

• What does power mean to you?

• What role does power play in your life?

• Who has power over you?

• Whom do you have power over?

• Around whom do you feel powerful?

• What makes you feel powerful?

• Around whom do you feel powerless?

• How do you diminish your power?

In personal relationships your power is reflected in your ability to have what you want. Anthony Robbins defines ultimate power as:

> ... *the ability to produce the results you desire most and create value for others in the process ... Power is the ability to change*

your life, to shape your perceptions, to make things work for you and not against you ... Real power is shared, not imposed.

It's the ability to define human needs and to fulfil them — both your needs and the needs of the people you care about ... It's the ability to direct your own personal kingdom — your own thought processes, your own behaviour — so you produce the precise results you desire.[1]

Power Bases

What are the sources of our power? What things give us leverage in a conversation so that our point of view is accepted by others? To find out how the different power bases operate, think of people in your life you often comply with, even when you don't really want to — people who tend to influence you to do things their way. Often there will be more than one reason why they influence you. What is the basis of that influence? Here are seven significant power bases to consider. It's by no means an exclusive list.

Valued Relationship

Do you care about the relationship staying on good terms? How would it suffer if you did not comply? Are you concerned about what they think of you?

Expertise

Do you trust their advice because they know more about the matter? What is their special area of competence, information or expertise?

Reward and Punishment

Do they hold the power to reward you — openly or covertly — if you agree? Which rewards, if any, influence you? Can they refuse to deliver something you want? Sex and money are two big ones here. Can they punish or censure you in any way? If so, how? Where conflict could turn violent, larger physical size or possession of a weapon will have a huge impact on the ability to punish you.

Position

Do you respect their authority? How would you describe your respective places in the hierarchy or pecking order?

Power of Law

Does society demand you respect them because their position is backed up by the power of law? A policeman, judge or government officer may fall into this category.

Collective Power

Do you respect their point of view because they represent the combined opinions of many? For example, a trade union representative, the spokesperson for a lobby group, a church representative, a group of allies — a political, social or family 'gang'.

Persuasiveness

Do you respect and trust them as individuals? If so, which of their personal qualities do you particularly admire or respect? Is it, for example, their commonsense, their ability to sell an idea well, their charisma, or their integrity? Other qualities that will add to someone's persuasiveness include: positive energy, clear sense of direction, ability to get things done, good leadership skills, enthusiasm, balanced approach, kindness to others, cooperative spirit, ability to manage rather than suppress emotions, perceptiveness and wisdom.

These sources of power influence people's behaviour so that they get what they want. So long as they are not relying excessively on one power base it remains a hidden agenda. If, however, one — or sometimes more — of these bases is directing the outcome, it's worth being very alert to what is going on.

Manipulation or Influence

Some people regard any influence as a threat, while others are so cautious about influencing those around them that they end up with very little of what they want in life. Yet, cooperation and achieving consensus depend on one side influencing the other. Influence is a necessary process in communication. Nevertheless, if the result is that we feel tricked, used or stood over, then something has gone awry in the influencing process. We've been manipulated rather than influenced. What's the difference?

MANIPULATION OR INFLUENCE

Manipulation	Influence
• The manipulator uses the clout of a power base to pressure for a particular outcome.	• The influencer only uses their power base to be sure their points are fully considered.
• The other person is not left free to choose for themselves.	• The other person is left free to choose.
• The other person feels tricked or pressured.	• The other person feels persuaded.
• Input from the other person is discouraged.	• Input from the other person is encouraged and valued.
• Biased information is supplied.	• More balanced information is supplied.
• Needs and concerns of the other person are not seriously considered.	• Needs and concerns of the other person are considered.
• Outcomes favour the manipulator, often at the expense of the other person.	• Outcomes favour the other person as well as the influencer.
• Generates less commitment from the other person to make the solution work.	• Generates greater commitment from the other person to make the solution work.
• Tends to stunt relationships.	• Tends to build relationships.

The difference between influence and manipulation is not black and white. We've all done a little manipulating from time to time. Whether or not it was acceptable depends in part on how positive the outcome was, and also on motive and process.

- ♀ Did everyone benefit in the process and was that the intention?

- ♀ Were the other people involved free to refuse?

- ♀ Did they know what they were being asked?

- ♀ Were they left free to decide for themselves?

Stepping Stones

What can you do when you notice that you are being manipulated? The purpose of these stepping stones is to create power *with* rather than power *over* the other person.

- Stand up to the manipulator. You need to **state your own ideas clearly and firmly**.

- If the manipulator is stuck in worst-case scenarios, shift away from the negatives by moving towards a vision of possibilities. **Move from problems towards solutions.**

- If the manipulator is overoptimistic, **discuss the possible consequences** of the proposed decision. Encourage the flow of information. Point out people's needs that are not being considered. If you can, organise the affected people to speak for themselves.

Power Tactics

As well as the power bases, which are *sources* of power, people might use other *methods* for extra leverage in conflict situations. Most of us at some point have suffered from the manipulative power of 'the silent treatment' or emotional withdrawal or from the effects of being stood over for physical advantage.

Take a moment to sense the manipulative power behind the following tactics:

- being overcritical

- behaving righteously

- rebelling

- withholding information

- backstabbing

- refusing to discuss the issue.

People might milk their power base in a valued relationship by:

- behaving stubbornly

- sulking

- crying

- collecting allies or withdrawing
- turning on charm or seductive behaviours.

Some of the ways people use their position, expertise or ability to reward and punish include:

- being threatening
- adopting an adversarial style
- dismissing by logic
- pulling rank
- excluding others from decision-making.

Such behaviours don't always start out as a tactic. For example, crying or withdrawing may begin as a knee-jerk reaction but slip into manipulation if the person has found it successful.

Stepping stones
What can you do about it?

First, noticing the behaviour as a tactic reduces its effect on you.

Sometimes naming it as a tactic can take the wind out of the other person's sails. Consider making a statement to someone who is using their tears to manipulate: 'I can see you are upset. When you've stopped crying let's discuss the options.' To someone who is shouting: 'Do you realise you are shouting? It's not really persuading me.'

> When a tactic you dislike is used on you, redirect the flow towards the positive

Sometimes it will be better to sidestep the tactic — ignore it without being overly hurt, overwhelmed or vindictive. If you can recognise the unmet need driving the tactic, perhaps you can take it in your stride and redirect the conversation towards positive solutions.

Is the person trying to redress a perceived injustice? Are they feeling their status or equality is being threatened? Sometimes you might take a moment to support that value directly. 'I really am listening to what you have to say', could address a perceived lack of equality. 'I hope you're clear that you have my respect', could lessen the impact of your opposition for a person who feels their status is being undermined.

Power Game Triangle

We all operate within a variety of power relationships, such as parent-child, child-teacher, employee-boss, male-female. How we operate in these is largely a matter of learning. We have absorbed these from our culture, past experiences and tradition. Transactional analysis[2] defines three entrapping behaviours people can easily get caught up in: Persecuting, Rescuing and being Victim. They are behaviours that keep us stuck, replaying a learnt pattern of relating. They may seem to get us what we want in the short term, but, in the end, will not serve us well. They keep us stuck in pre-programmed behaviour, so we are not free to discover new responses in new situations.

Persecuting

The person reacting with a Persecuting approach uses aggression to get what they want and to silence the opposition. They may shout or use a forthright tone that allows no argument or their insistence may appear to be very gentle while hiding an iron fist or they may demand obedience, relying heavily on rewards, punishments and their position of authority. Perhaps they behave this way as a form of protection against the discomfort of uncertainty or fear of powerlessness.

Most of us will have Persecuted from time to time. You may not even realise that you have done it. If, for example, you've pushed your point without giving the other person a chance to express theirs, you've succumbed to what we mean here by Persecuting behaviour. It is quite different from being assertive.

Rescuing

People who fall into a Rescuing approach *assume* that the other person needs help. They put aside their own needs to focus on fixing things for others. They start from the desire to help someone who seems to be getting a bad deal, which is a thoroughly worthy sentiment! At their best, Rescuers give a lot of support to a person in trouble. They'll provide a friendly ear and do all sorts of helpful things, such as do their work or make their choices for them, but the Rescuer is caught by an extra motivation: they need to be needed. Therefore they'll rescue, whether the person really needs it or not. It may also be that they are highly sensitive to unresolved conflict. They can become addicted to the role and feed off conflict, running from one party to another — taking on other people's issues and trying to make it better. They disempower the person who could find their own way through their problems.

> Too much Rescuing locks the other person into being a Victim

If you've ever put a lot of time and effort into helping a friend or colleague, only to find that they aren't taking on board your helpfulness or that they continue asking for your help, chances are you've been Rescuing and you're very likely to end up feeling used. Moreover, the helped person may well turn against you as they struggle to claim their own power.

Being Victim

In recognising the Victim behaviours, it is important first to distinguish genuine victims of circumstance from people playing the Victim as a social role based on a sense of inadequacy.

Real victims who suffer from hardship, injustice or accident naturally deserve care and sympathy. They need support until they can manage on their own. Of course, you'll give support to a friend or colleague going through a rough patch — you'll know it is a good thing to do because you'll see results. Sympathy is needed when a friend is sick or suffering a loss — it's normal and healthy to need some help, advice or empathy at such times and you'll notice they won't need it any more when things get better. This is not the same situation as the person with a Victim attitude who gives their power away to others. They see others as being powerful while they are not. They feel helpless, stay stuck in inappropriate situations and blame others for their situation. They focus on how bad and hopeless it all is and what's not working, rather than what is. They regularly accumulate new dramas in their lives and seem to attract accidents, mischance and illness. There is little action on finding their way out of their difficulties, though there may be a lot of talk. The trap and the tragedy lie in their ingrained attitudes of self-defeat.

How the Power Game Starts and Continues

Sometimes you can play out the Victim, Persecuting and Rescuing roles on your own. Sometimes a two- or three-way manipulation is going on. Victims might be walking around with their 'Rescue Me' or 'Pick On Me' badges shining. It is easy to be drawn in if you are not aware, and the Rescuing or Persecuting keeps the Victim stuck. Victim behaviour gets rewarded with lots of care and attention, especially if they can hook in a dedicated Rescuer. They're a perfect match until one of them sees the light. The Rescuer and the Victim ganging up together trap the Persecutor in the role of enemy.

Often we've learned our part within our childhood family, unconsciously choosing the role of the person we identify with most. By demonstration, parents teach their own victim-style to their children. Authoritarian parents demonstrate just how persecution is done — 'Do it because I say so'. You may discover you act in similar Persecuting ways with your own children, your spouse and people you work with — particularly when your authority is threatened. Or perhaps your other parent — the partner of a Persecutor — seemed to be the sane, loving parent. You grow up just like them, but they could not demonstrate how to unhook from the Rescuing roles they may have played.

As adults we can fall into Power Game behaviours when our buttons are pushed by an issue on which we're easily inflamed or hurt. Particular varieties of abuse will bring out the Rescuer in us. When we meet incompetence or a perceived lack of respect, it might be our trigger for a Persecuting reaction. Dictatorial teachers, bosses and systems can scare people into a return of the victim state of their childhood.

People in Victim roles can keep others around them stuck in victimhood also. We see this when habits of blaming and complaining are rife between couples or in work groups. If they

POWER GAME TRIANGLE

PERSECUTOR

Coercive power

Uses aggression to silence opposition.

'You'll do it my way.'

'I'm right, you're wrong.'

'It's got to be your fault.'

'I'll show you who's in charge here.'

Pay-off Short-term: often get what they want; feel powerful, in control.

Cost Long-term: relationships out of balance; alienation; lack of commitment from other people who will undermine.

RESCUER

Manipulative power

'Other people are inadequate.'

Often offers unwelcome or uninvited help.

Puts other people's needs before their own.

'Others can't function without my help.'

'I'll do it for you.'

Pay-off Short-term: feeling needed and a worthwhile person.

Cost Long-term: often ends up rejected or used; burnt out; own needs not met.

VICTIM

Inadequate power

Some covert power to draw in help.

Very dependent.

There's always another drama.

'Other people or circumstances are doing this to me.'

'There's nothing I can do to sort this out.'

Pay-off Short-term: sympathy and attention; doesn't have to take responsibility; less scary to complain than to act.

Cost Long-term: unhappy; low self-esteem; life doesn't move forward; other people get sick of helping.

EMPOWERMENT CIRCLE

CONSULT/LEAD/EMPOWER OTHERS

Show what you consider will work best for everyone — and explain why.

Invite and respect the other person's point of view.

Give up threatening, blaming and sulking.

MEDIATE/FACILITATE/COACH

Encourage people to settle their differences.

Support people in helping themselves.

Look at the wider context and see how much help is (and is not) appropriate.

LEARN/TAKE RESPONSIBILITY/SELF-EMPOWER

Use even the most difficult situation as a learning opportunity.

Avoid negative self-talk and disempowering language.

Start with one thing that will make a positive difference.

Celebrate your growing ability to stand up for yourself.

have never seen anyone modelling differently, it may be their only way of expressing frustration. Such circumstances are only one step away from a destructive Power Game: someone will soon be cast in the role of Persecutor, and someone else might fall into the role of Rescuer. It becomes like an improvised stage play, with only slight variations repeated for each performance: one character is the baddie; the least powerful person — perhaps a child or an adult with low self-esteem — plays the innocent victim and a third person takes on the role of Rescuer, defending the Victim from the Persecutor. When they get bored they might swap roles around for a while or rope in other people. In some families the drama includes physical violence; in others it's more sedate and involves subtle put-downs, innuendos and private hate sessions.

The power game triangle might be played out at organisational levels. For instance, workplace union activities or worker's compensation issues can sometimes develop a power-game flavour. Management might be cast as the Persecutors by those Rescuing the Victims. Victims can get together and white-ant projects and other people with malicious gossip. The destructive effects become more widespread, even devastating, when these power games play out in community groups, aid organisations and in the international arena.

Moving Out of Power Games

There are alternatives for the relationships that have sunk into the Power Game Triangle. Once we recognise we've been caught in these behaviours, we're no longer trapped. With appropriate strategies and skills we can step out of the Triangle and into an Empowerment Circle (see the diagram on the opposite page).

Coming from a commitment to self-empowerment, we choose how we relate to people. If we begin to feel victimised we can choose to place ourselves in learning mode. We'll look for ways we have contributed to being a Victim — not to blame ourselves, but to empower ourselves to do it differently. We'll treat our Persecutor as a teacher — whether or not they intend that and regardless of what they might think they are teaching us. They might *think* they're teaching us some underhanded tactic to dodge the system; however, we regard them as

> **Empowerment:**
> **Persecutor**
> **consults;**
> **Rescuer coaches;**
> **Victim learns**
> **responsibility**

teaching us assertiveness by having to stand up to them. Persecuting behaviours become our challenge to raise our standard. From wherever we stand on the Empowerment Circle we can work towards replacing coercion and manipulation with collaborative interactions. We value the interdependence and empower ourselves and those around us. We learn from each other, we help each other grow and we use differences between us to create a shared vision.

STANLEY

I am a headmaster in a small country town. A new teacher had just been appointed to my school. I encouraged him to come to me with any difficulties. The teacher soon came to me with a big predicament — he had punished a consistent troublemaker in his class, but now he realised that the punishment had been too severe. The child had complained to his parents, who were furious, and soon the word would be all around town. A classic victim–persecutor–rescuer game threatened.

Instead of deciding who was right or wrong, and falling into the persecutor role, I wanted to mediate. I'm always loyal to my staff, and I don't expect them to be perfect. I always try to support them in working through problems. I called together all the parties involved. I supported the teacher's acknowledgment to the child and parents that he regretted what he had done. This allowed him to avoid being seen either as a persecutor of the child or a victim of the headmaster. I encouraged the child to see that his behaviour had provoked his teacher and that though people make mistakes, amends can be made and new relationships formed. This took the child and parents into the learner position. A constructive discussion followed on how the teacher, child and parents could find better ways of relating to each other.

Stepping Out of the Rescuing Role

Helping another person in trouble is part of our humanness. It's a wonderful quality and should be encouraged; however, there are times when being compassionate can be misplaced. Others might take advantage of your caring involvement, and wear you down. You might so identify with the role of carer/fixer that you'll care and fix even where it's inappropriate. Do you have a tendency to repeatedly slip into Rescuing, too often putting your needs aside for others?

EXERCISE: spot inappropriate rescuing

Think of someone in your life you are possibly rescuing. Check it out:

Have they actually asked
for my help?   _____

Whose need is this really?
Mine or theirs?   _____

What needs of mine am
I putting aside?   _____

Is the other person more
focused on the problem
than the solution?   _____

How much time do I want
to give this?   _____

What are my boundaries
around advice/support?   _____

Insofar as possible, analyse your motives. Try not to muddy your support with your own need to be needed. Don't overdo it. Don't disempower the other person. If it's starting to hurt you, it's a sign to pull back. Respect that. Try not to hurt the other person as you do so. Get some support for yourself if you must often be in a caring role. If you can trust yourself to monitor how much support you give others, then you really can let it be a wholehearted expression of your caring and love.

First handle yourself

Certain conversational tags can help you identify someone who is falling into Victim behaviours. Be on your guard if you hear: 'This always happens to me'; 'How come I never …'; 'They made me …'; 'If only …'.

- Recognise your own signs that you are doing too much or that the other person is caught up in being Victim.

- You may need to establish clear parameters with the person, about what you will offer and where your limits are. For example, you won't always be available to listen to them and when you are you may set a time limit at the beginning. You won't help write their assignment or report but you may be willing to edit a finished draft.

- Your very caring listening could open conversations that become far more intimate than you have time for or are appropriate in the situation. You don't really want a sales assistant to tell you her troubles or a team-mate to think that each morning starts with an unpaid counselling session on his marriage. You may need to watch how you reflect back what you're hearing. There will be times when you'll want to express concern without encouraging the person to tell you more. You may have to immediately switch topics to an item on the day's agenda.

Then handle the Victim behaviours

When others are slipping into being Victim, you could:

- **Ask them to list what things can be changed and what things can't**. Then focus with them only on what can be changed.

- **Pick one thing that can be worked on.**

- **Stay in the present** — steer them away from conversations which wallow in the past: 'If only …'; 'They should have …'.

- **Set boundaries around which conversations you are willing to have.** For instance, say you are not willing to focus on the reasons why things are so awful or reasons why they can't do something that could be helpful. Their conversations might start with 'I can't …'; 'Yes, but …' or 'You don't understand how bad it is'. Use 'I' statements to set your limits: *'When you tell me what you can't do or how bad things are, I find it overwhelming. What I am willing to do is to have conversations that focus on what you could do.'*

- **Use redirecting questions:**

When you hear:	*Redirect with:*
'I don't know …'	 'What do you need in order to decide?'
'I can't …'	'What could you do?'
'You don't understand …'	'What is it I need to understand?'

- **Raise their consciousness about their victim behaviours.**
  With some people it might work to get them to count how
  many times a day they put themselves down. So that they
  don't beat themselves up even more once they realise what
  they're doing, you might turn it into a game and provide
  some mock trophy for a really high number of self-put-
  downs.

Stepping Out of the Victim Role

Self-empowerment

Perhaps you find yourself at times slipping into being Victim. Your major task is self-empowerment. How might you achieve that?

- **Be aware of when you using disempowering language.**

REFRAMING DISEMPOWERING LANGUAGE		
	Instead of	Try
Don't focus on what you can't do, focus on what you can.	I can't get my job back.	I need to find a new job.
Don't focus on what you don't know, focus on what you could learn.	I can't cope with computers.	I want to learn word-processing skills.
No self-put-downs!	I'm just a shop assistant.	I'm a shop assistant.
Reframe doubts.	I don't think I could manage that.	I wonder what I would need to try that.
Avoid 'if only' ruminations.	If only I'd held my marriage together.	What am I free to do that I wasn't able to try before?
Don't dwell in the past.	I should have given him a piece of my mind.	What can I do now to move the situation in a better direction?
Don't fantasise about fears of the future.	What if I can't pay the mortgage?	I need a good plan for handling this mortgage, including emergencies.

- **Accept the challenge.** Know the difference between wanting to have a moan and getting some advice about a bad day, and wanting the other person to side with you and fix your problem for you. Set yourself a time limit for venting. Recognise when you've complained quite enough and when it is time to move forward. See yourself as the creator of the patterns in your life, *own* the issues and fully engage yourself in their solutions.

You're empowered when you're aligned with what *is* so for you. It might mean you take responsibility for finding your way through difficult financial circumstances or for clearing your reputation. Your personal power task is to accept the challenge, especially in trying circumstances. This is not a passive acceptance. Your anger might be the very fuel you need to bring about changes.

'Choose' not 'should'

Think of something that you will do anyway but don't want to … now *choose* to do it. Give yourself a reason that works for you. Instead of 'I should go to the party' try 'I choose to go to the party because I know my presence makes all the difference to … (a person you care about)'. Instead of 'I should finish my assignment', try 'I choose to finish my assignment this weekend because that is the best way to structure my time'. Still feeling that external pressures are making you do what you don't want to do? Say 'I choose to …' a few times. You might be able to feel the energy shift. If you're not quite there yet, offer yourself some sweeteners: 'I'll play my favourite music in the background' or 'I'll wear my new outfit'. You can resist or flow with whatever circumstances life presents. Develop the habit on small tasks. When the big challenges come, you will be glad you have made a commitment to operating your life out of choice. People with plenty of personal power are those who do not dissipate it in submission or rebellion. They are whole and centred; that is, they are totally involved in the here and now. To others they appear very alive and ready for action. They're also powerfully persuasive!

> Personal power blossoms when you want what you have in your life

ZENA

I am the mother of two teenagers, and I've always resented the amount of time I have to spend in the supermarket doing the family shopping. It's always irritated me. I used to stand in those long lines waiting to be served and thinking of all the things I'd rather be doing. One day, standing in a queue and feeling resentful, I found myself looking into someone else's trolley and was appalled at the amount of junk food piled in it. I started thinking about what I was really doing in the supermarket. I wasn't just 'having to do the shopping'

— I was choosing to make a contribution to my family's health. It has always been important to me that everyone eats healthy, balanced food. I realised that I wanted to do the shopping because I'd rather choose the food myself than let someone else do it. With my change in attitude, I was pleasantly surprised at what other positive aspects I could find — how fortunate I was that I could buy what I wanted and I could read magazines while I was waiting in line. I even started to make a game of my venture to the supermarket. I began smiling at other shoppers and counted how many smiles I got back!

Building indestructible self-esteem

It is difficult to participate powerfully in conversations if you feel undeserving and lesser than those you are dealing with. Of course, there will always be people who you feel have more authority, more intelligence, more skills or information than you have. But no one else has *your* perspective — it deserves to feature. You fall into Victim behaviour when your self-esteem is shaky. Indeed, most of us have some work to do in this area. As you build self-esteem your power base of persuasiveness also grows. Ultimately you are heading towards an indestructible self-esteem that won't be damaged by arguments, adverse circumstances or someone else's opinion of you. You may find you have issues to deal with, but they don't affect your core. A Persecutor mismanaging their power won't be looking for you — they'll find a better target. Here are some useful pointers:

- **Generalise from positive experiences** — 'I completed that task without a hitch. I can complete tasks successfully.'

- **Form a loving relationship with yourself** — be kind to yourself. Be your own best friend.

- **Work against your self-destructive tendencies.**

- **Take in praise.**

- **Build your competencies** — take a course, develop a skill.

- **Set yourself big goals and take small steps** — what would you love to achieve? What can you do towards it this week, next week, next month, next year? Make a plan.

EXERCISE: for a 'poor me' situation

Got a situation where you think you have been badly done by? Perhaps you are feeling like a victim of circumstance. Is there something in your life that's just not fair? Perhaps use a pen and paper while you answer the following questions:

1. What do I feel I need some sympathy or understanding for?

2. What do I need some help or support with?

3. What would be the appropriate way to get that? Who do I need that from?

4. If other people have distressed me, how might they be seeing the situation?

5. What did I do to contribute to the situation? If I was looking at it from outside what might I see that I might have done that got me into this situation?

6. What do I need to learn from this?

7. What can I do now to move forward?

As you face life's challenges you shake off being Victim and instead become a learner, a discoverer, an explorer.

> What is one thing I can do to improve this situation?

Stepping Out of the Persecuting Role

You can fall into a Persecuting style if you underestimate the subjectivity of your own viewpoint. Caught inside your own head you presume you can see objective truths. In fact, you can only see glimpses of them coloured by your own perspective. If you fail to take this into account, it is easy to misuse your power, browbeating others because you are so sure you're right. You can also Persecute if you hold a mistaken idea of how best to use the power of the position to which you've been appointed. You're liable to abuse your power if you think you should be controlling other people, rather than taking responsibility for the end results. If you're an ex-Victim, you might overcompensate for lingering insecurities, and then sound like a Persecutor as you find your feet in a new, more assertive style of operating.

EXERCISE: what's my control issue?

There are many times when you move into controlling others to mask issues with which you haven't come to terms. Think of a person you sometimes try to control. What's your control issue?

EMOTIONAL ISSUES OF CONTROL

I exercise control over: _____ (insert the person's name)

Why?   YES or NO

Am I choosing to control because the other person *wants* me to direct their behaviour?   ☐   ☐

Do I think the other person would tell me if they don't like me taking charge?   ☐   ☐

Am I choosing to control because the other person *needs* me to direct their behaviour?   ☐   ☐

Do I think the other person will control or undermine me if I am not the one in control?   ☐   ☐

If I don't tell the other person what to do, do I expect chaos?   ☐   ☐

Do I sometimes use control to mask my anxiety about things being out of control?   ☐   ☐

Do I sometimes use control to mask my feelings of inadequacy?   ☐   ☐

Do I believe that I can see how things should be and that the other person doesn't measure up?   ☐   ☐

Now present yourself with an alternative point of view.
How might you find an antidote for the 'control freak' part of yourself? For example, 'Of course I won't have a disaster if I let her have her say.'

_____

_____

_____

If you find your finger is pointing in someone's face, your tone is becoming demanding and the other person is reduced to resentful silence, you have slipped into controlling mode — you've become the Persecutor. You're in danger of inviting rebellion or stifling creativity. First ask yourself:

- Does the problem really affect me personally?

- Could I live with the problem their method creates?

- Does their method actually work adequately?

What else can you do to support cooperative power here? Consider the following:

- Change tack from demanding to consulting — offer advice and options rather than providing the definitive solution.

- Avoid making statements that sound like you are presenting a universal perspective on anything that is controversial. Make sure you imply you are talking from your perspective only.

- Use 'I' statements when you present your point of view.

- Stop, listen and acknowledge the other person's position.

- Encourage others to offer their point of view. Allow them the freedom to disagree without fear of retribution, ridicule or criticism from you.

- Use the negotiation strategies outlined in Chapter 10, Negotiation.

Power with Rather than Over

As we have seen in the Power Game Triangle it's easy to get caught up in situations where coercive rather than cooperative behaviour is the norm. At such times we will have to pay attention to the power relationships involved in the conflict. Though different situations require different tactics to address the problems, the underlying principle is always this: a collaborative approach that supports the empowerment of all people involved.

Redirect the agenda to a collaborative approach

Confronting Powerful People

Are you in a position to face up to someone and try to redress a bad decision or an injustice? Can you move beyond being intimidated, address the issue *and* keep the person on side? When you don't have authority, it can be very challenging to say what you need to say and respond well to what that person says back. (The section Handling difficult emotions in others in Chapter 6, Managing Emotions, has more on the issue of handling their anger, and will help if this is part of your problem.)

What can you do when a person you perceive to be more powerful than you says 'No!', talks you down, out-votes or overrules you?

- Use your power base of persuasiveness.[3]

- Keep your focus on a collaborative approach.

Respect their authority — indicate respect by your tone of voice. Approach the person according to their DISC style; for example, Task-oriented people value action and results: respect their time and get to the point without getting emotional or personal.

> *Your boss is furious with a client who won't pay their bill because they say there was something wrong with the order. As they haven't returned the goods, your boss has instructed that a very firm letter of demand for payment be sent.*

Reaffirm their needs — particularly if you are trying to find another way or solution with the person in authority; affirm that it is another way that you believe will still meet their needs. You may choose to indicate you understand the good intention behind their original position. This might be more important for People-oriented styles of leadership.

> *I understand how important it is to keep a tight rein on debtors.*

Offer your suggestions — if you need to, first explain your difficulty; for example:

> *The problem is, at this stage, we don't really know why the client is complaining.*

Offer your alternatives as suggestions only. You will have to leave them to decide. If they are a Direct person, one of their core fears will be loss of authority, so don't stand on their toes. You may come up with a statement something like this:

I know you value this customer and I was wondering if we should send John over to check out their complaint. Would that be okay with you?

For more on confronting people in authority, see Appendix II on pages 244–5.

LUKE

My boss is a very intellectual and dogmatic man. I find it hard to stand my ground with him. He doesn't listen to my views and continually argues his point until others back down. I understand he has a lot of responsibility, but often I feel he uses his power to manipulate people.

Not long ago I received a memo from him instructing the staff to carry out some new procedures. These would create a lot more time-consuming work for all of us. The memo was badly written and sounded dictatorial to a number of other staff members as well as me. I had two choices: to obey or rebel. I had reached the end of my patience. Either way, I was going to feel terrible about the disharmony. Was there another way?

It wasn't just an internal shift I had to make. It was necessary to take a stand against that memo. I went to my boss with a carefully worded statement: 'I just want you to know that when I read this I felt like doing the opposite of what you asked — and I don't want to be like that. I want to be supportive and cooperative.' My approach wasn't challenging but factual.

My boss took it far better than I could have expected. He said, 'That's interesting. Which parts made you feel like that?' Then we talked about them. I explained to him that I would have liked to understand why this new way was best for everyone. I acknowledged that he must make the final decision and suggested that perhaps next time the staff could offer their ideas before a decision is made. My boss explained his reasoning and I got a different slant on the situation in this face-to-face, friendly discussion. I left feeling I could now freely choose to follow the new procedures. I think my boss also gained some helpful insights about how to approach the rest of the staff to implement his new plan.

Equal Power Relationships

To show up for a difficult conversation with a relatively equal power balance in play, we need to use our skills of assertiveness —

Stake your play on 'power with' rather than 'power over'

in particular 'I' statements: 'The way I see it ...'; 'I'm concerned about ...'; 'I feel ...'. If we face an attack we need to remember that dropping into active listening for a while will calm the situation down and move it away from domination back towards equality (see chapters 3, Empathy, and 4, Appropriate Assertiveness).

Equal-power relationships are very precious. These are cooperative partnering relationships in which two people can stand together looking for solutions to their mutual problems. Each side keeps their personal power intact and respects the other's space and integrity. Each will consult the other and outside experts if necessary. Each is willing to explain, coach or educate the other person as needed. They are free to agree or disagree with each other. They accept the consequences of their decisions and take on the responsibility of those choices. Which of your relationships are like that now?

SUMMARY

- 'Ultimate power is the ability to produce the results you desire most and create value for others in the process.' Anthony Robbins

- Power may stem from the emotional tie to a valued friendship, the use of expertise, position, the law, the promise of reward, the threat of punishment, the collective power of a group and a person's ability to persuade.

- If your intention is to serve yourself at the expense of another person, you may be using power to *manipulate*. If your intention is to create benefits for others as well as yourself and you use a collaborative process, your power may help you *influence* the other person.

- The behaviours in the Power Game Triangle (Persecuting, Rescuing or being Victim) can be transformed to consulting, mediating and learning when you take charge of the way you use power in relation to others.

- Set boundaries with others when they are asking for too much help. Empower them to help themselves.

- Reframe disempowering language.

- *Choose* the challenges you face. Personal power blossoms when you want what you have in your life. This attitude encourages your energy to flow, rather than being caught up in resistance.

- To increase your power in all situations work on your self-esteem.

- Ask what is one thing you can do to improve this situation?

- Work towards 'power with' rather than 'power over' others. Examine your control issues and keep them in check.

- Even when your position gives you power over others there is still much you can do to provide a sense of equality for others.

- Find ways to redirect the agenda to a collaborative approach.

Notes

1. Anthony Robbins, *Unlimited Power* (USA: Simon & Schuster, 1987) pp 20–1

2. For a Transactional Analysis (TA) explanation of the triangle, see Muriel James and Dorothy Jongeward, *Born to Win* (USA: Addison-Wesley, 1996). Other highly recommended books on Transactional Analysis are Thomas A Harris, MD, *I'm OK, You're OK* (USA, HarperCollins, 1969), and Claude M Steiner, *Scripts People Live* (USA, Grove/Atlantic; 1990)

3. See also Roger Fisher and William Ury, *Getting to Yes: Negotiating Agreement without Giving in* (USA: Penguin, 1991) pp 107–11

CHAPTER 6

Managing Emotions

What messages are my emotions delivering to me?

How can I use these messages for positive change?

How will I best manage my own and other people's strong emotions?

Have you ever felt:

- So overwhelmed you couldn't think clearly what you wanted to say?

- So outraged you thought something like, 'I'll show them. They'll never do that to me again'?

- So hurt by someone you felt you could never forgive them?

- So scared you were shaking all over?

Don't indulge or deny emotions — use them to build richer relationships

Raw emotions are the triggers for reactions that can be very destructive to relationships — we don't feel as though we're really in charge. To be able to respond to conflict constructively, we need to catch hold of emotions, stay in charge of the thoughts that arise from them, and channel their energy in a positive direction. We can do this for ourselves and support others doing the same. These are the emotional intelligence competencies of managing ourselves and managing others well.[1] This is what the skill of managing emotions is about: the clearer we are about what we are feeling and what really is the matter, the more precise our strategy will be for sorting out the difficulty.

Bodymind

There is a close connection between body and mind. Bioenergetic therapists have coined the word 'bodymind' to describe this relationship. We equate emotions with sensations in our body. Common language bears testimony to this in expressions such as 'I can feel it in my bones'; 'She makes me sick to my stomach'; 'I've had a gutful'; 'He is so open-hearted'; 'You're a pain in the neck'. The body is like a giant computer, constantly reading your emotional relationships to other people, the environment and ideas, and responding with physical sensations of muscular and energy movements. Each time a significant body/energy event occurs a message pops up on the screen of your awareness. You notice a change in your emotional state. Perhaps you recognise that you're angry, fearful or frustrated. If only you could observe that sensation; that is, allow it — not tense up, not shrink away— just observe it as it passes. Past conditioning may have told you it's not okay to have these feelings. Those feelings may make you so uncomfortable that you want to push them away. Few of us are able to relax into a large emotional wave of sadness, regret or anger and allow the emotion to deliver its primary message.

We can think of ourselves as an energy system of flows and resistances. Feelings, thoughts and actions all affect each other via the body's energy flow. As well as responding to what's happening

Emotions are energy, body and mind events

right now, we are likely to embody a huge accumulation of unresolved issues. Our energy flow is affected by these deep unconscious processes, which are stored as muscular tension and are waiting for discharge. If the current situation holds vague similarities to the past, old emotions will flood our awareness. (We explore this further in Chapter 7, Willingness to Resolve.)

The worst of it is that when we suppress such key feelings as hurt, anger or fear, our experience of pleasure is also restricted. We know pleasure by an expansive flow of energy through the body — this can't happen fully when major muscle groups are held permanently in contraction. We lose our capacity to use our emotions as signals for what is immediately important to us in the current situation. We can't be happy if we won't be sad, and we can't be truly loving if we can't also be angry. We must allow ourselves to experience 'negative' emotions, such as sadness or anger, to complete ourselves.

We'll manage our emotions better by trusting the intimate connection between mind, body, energy, feelings, thoughts and action. These interconnections can be explored through:

• **Emotional release** — using the body to discharge feelings out of range of other people.

- **Focusing** — attending to bodymind energies below the surface of our awareness until they reveal their messages.

- **Communication of feelings** — channelling emotions to push for positive change in relationships.

Emotional Release

Most of us know very little about running our bodyminds. The most common misconception we have is that by suppressing tears we stop grief, or by pushing thoughts out of consciousness we stop anger. We may stop the emotion from exploding out, but it is stored in our body waiting for a more appropriate time to surface.

What's the difference between suppressing and containing?

You might *suppress* your emotions because you are fearful of them or you want to avoid the conflict that comes in their wake. You do this by breathing more shallowly, which keeps the emotions out of consciousness. Because you offer your bodymind no release, your overall levels of stress build. Pent up, suppressed emotions don't disappear — they either implode, causing ill-health and burnout, or explode, often causing inappropriate or embarrassing scenes.

> Suppression pushes emotions out of consciousness, containment allows them into awareness

If, however, you *contain* the emotion, you are choosing not to make it public just then, though you still acknowledge it to yourself. A lot of the tension is therefore released. Your breathing rapidly returns to normal and you deal with the conflict in the best way you can in the particular circumstances. Long-term, you'll be less stressed, more empowered and likely to be in better health.

Do I need to release pent-up feelings?

You haven't yet finished with the emotion. However, its energy is accessible and can discharge during your daily activity. Travelling to and from work, exercising and doing housework are excellent opportunities for digesting your experiences — there's more to walking the dog than meets the eye! You also discharge some of your pent-up feelings nightly in your dreams. Meditation, too, can be a useful tool. Exercising, writing a journal, talking out the events of the day with someone you are close to are all useful ongoing strategies for dealing with emotional tension.

Modern somatic psychologists, such as Dr Julie Henderson, suggest you acknowledge emotions such as anger, frustration and disappointment in a playful, childlike way.[3] If you can manage to poke a bit of fun at yourself as you flounder around in a bad mood, you usually

return to a state of well-being quite quickly. Many therapists have now found that too much venting of emotions fosters, rather than completes, your anger. Releasing unexpressed feelings should be relieving rather than exhausting. So, when things are really annoying and hard to handle, find some privacy and stomp around like an angry kid, dramatise groans, pretend to puke, make a noise. Finish it off by blowing raspberries at the situation. Do one right now just for fun. Put your tongue between your lips and blow. Think of something you're angry about while you do it. If you start laughing as you do it, this is already a help. Well, that's managed that emotion!

Counsellors who include body work and somatics in their approach can sometimes help when you could do with support to release suppressed emotion productively. They might include exercise and gentle pressure to release contracted muscles.

Focusing

By far the best thing you can do with a difficult emotion is feel it, explore it and get to the bottom of it. If you do this it yields up its information and has its own way of releasing. Feelings are often at the heart of the problem, but it may be difficult to pinpoint them exactly. Here's where focusing can be very helpful.

Focusing is the art of concentrating on the way your body senses an unresolved problem. You can use this focusing method for business and personal problems, and to increase creativity. Because it deepens your understanding of how things are from your perspective, focusing changes the way you deal with conflict. To focus well, you need to grasp two basic concepts. Eugene Gendlin, in his valuable book *Focusing,* calls these the 'felt sense and the body shift'.[4]

Felt sense

Your bodymind registers everything that is going on in very subtle muscular responses and energy flows. Different issues deliver different felt senses. You may believe you think with your head, but in truth a lot of information is gathered from the energy flowing through and surrounding the whole body.

Try these exercises. You'll find the contrasts help you pinpoint each felt sense.

1. Notice particularly what's going on in your muscles. Imagine you are playing a game of tennis and you are about to serve the ball. When that is clear, switch to imagining yourself playing football and about to kick the ball. The thousands of pieces of information about how to hold your body for each game are contained in an instant of through-the-body awareness.

2. Think for a moment about your mother. Don't go into details about her eyes, the last time you saw her or whether she's alive or dead: just tune in to yourself and into the general body sense of 'all about my mother'.

   When you have some sensation you're tuning in to, switch to thinking 'all about my father'. Can you feel a difference somewhere in your body or energy? Switch between both of them several times if that helps you locate a different felt sense for each of them.

3. Now focus for a moment on some difficulty, big or small, you are having. This is a more challenging exercise than the previous two because the felt sense may not be quite so clear. The more troubling the problem or the conflict, the *easier* it is to get in contact with its felt sense. It's troubling you precisely because you *are* aware of its felt sense.

Body shift

To understand how focusing helps you manage your emotions so effectively, you also need to become conscious of body shifts. These are releases of energy in the body that occur when you remember or first label accurately something that until that moment has been beyond your awareness.

Say you leave the house in a hurry. You know you've forgotten something but you can't think what. Suddenly the thought just appears; it might be, 'I was going to take in the photos of my last holiday to show Rebecca' or 'I forgot to lock the back door'. When you remember, there's a noticeable release of tension. Possibly you'll move in the seat (if you are sitting) or tap your head. That relief is a *body shift*.

A similar relief and release of energy occurs any time you tune in to the felt sense of something that is troubling you and up pops a new set of words describing exactly what is the matter. The accurate labelling of even a small part of the whole problem undoes a knot inside you and you relax. Your label might be: 'The main thing about it is that I feel I can't trust him'. Perhaps you might sigh, relax a tight facial muscle or resettle yourself in the chair. You might suddenly feel very hot or have goosebumps if the insight is particularly significant because trapped energy is discharging.

This unknotting does not occur when you just think about the problem in the same old way. Body shifts, which are real changes, come from a through-the-body approach, not a mind approach. They come with *a new* insight or understanding.

> **Unravelling an emotion releases energy**

The focusing process

The task is to focus on the felt sense without going inside the problem. Stand back from it a little and ask yourself questions such as: 'What's the main thing in this?'; 'What's the crux of this?'; 'What's most important here?'; or 'What's really the matter?' and then, without answering yourself, stop, listen and wait.

After a few moments some labels for the essence of the problem will pop into your mind. Now you're really listening to the part of yourself that senses the whole problem but has not yet made it conscious. As you get your labels right it's a bit like untangling knotted fishing line — as each piece is freed by accurate labelling, you are able to gradually unravel the next bit.

> **Use focusing to find the core of the problem**

If the problem is hard to think about, you might find you have trouble focusing. Don't push across such barriers — use them. If you feel empty or overwhelmed, focus on what it feels like to be empty or overwhelmed by this difficulty. Up might come the label: 'sad' or 'too much'. Check back with the sensation again to confirm you've named it well. Some problems are so complex they can take months or years to untangle completely. You don't need to find all the answers today: live with the question; be open to any helpful insights or information. It might come in the shower or while taking a walk. For people in touch with their kinaesthetic senses, focusing can be a wonderful tool for understanding their unfolding processes around difficult circumstances, but some people don't find focusing easy. If that's you, just let it go. There are plenty of other tools you can use.

If you do have some successes with the process, there may be times when you can support another person in focusing. Have you ever felt irritated by someone who is worrying about what seemed to you a minor issue? If you can help them focus, they'll stop going round and round in circles. Ask them to focus on the core of the issue and then use active listening. Focusing won't in itself solve the issue — it is concerned with clearly *identifying* it — but you might be surprised how well they can find their way forward from the new place they've arrived at.

STEPS TO FOCUSING

Step 1: Relax.

Step 2: Feel for the problem.

Step 3: Attend to the core of the uncomfortable feeling.

Step 4: Find the right label for the feeling.

Step 5: Allow a little time to experience any body shift

Step 6: Another round starting from Step 3.

RACHEL

I am an Australian married to a Greek man, Dimitri. We are living in Greece and are preparing to move to Australia. My husband is used to being surrounded by family and friends. There is very little time for privacy between us as a couple. I have been accustomed to living with more personal space and private time with a partner. This issue often causes conflict between us.

Easter is coming and Dimitri suggested we go away for a few days. He had been really busy organising our move to Australia and I was excited by the thought of having some quality time together. However, his plan was that we go with his brother to visit his uncle in a nearby town. My heart sank, I could just see myself spending the entire time tagging after three macho men. Not my idea of a romantic holiday!

I asked, 'Can't *we* do something, just the two of us?' Dimitri replied gruffly, 'I don't want to leave my brother; you know his wife is away right now.' I agreed rather reluctantly and Dimitri didn't respond well. 'Don't worry. It is better if we just stay here.'

We left the issue but I felt angry and hurt. Later, when I was alone, I decided to try the focusing exercise. I tuned in to this conflict and asked my inner sensation what the real issue was for me. I waited until the words started to flow. Well, it was like a tidal wave: 'I feel so disappointed in him ... I feel like I am giving more to this relationship than he is ... He is not interested in making time for us ... I am tired of working so hard on this ... I miss my family and friends in Australia ... I feel hurt because he would prefer to spend time with his family and friends than with me ... I feel let down.'

That must have been the crux of the problem because a wave of tears came then — and passed. And I went back to focusing. I tried to redefine how I felt about my problem now. I went back and forth into the sensations, feelings and thoughts. My main issue became: 'I feel unappreciated when Dimitri doesn't make time to nurture our relationship'.

Some perspective on his issues came in the wake of this naming of my problem. I could see how much responsibility he feels for taking care of his family. I sensed he might be feeling very torn in leaving his friends and family to move to Australia. Was this why he wanted to spend all his time with them before we left?

Focusing had helped me settle my emotions. I was more aware of my needs in the relationship. I still felt neglected and hurt, but I also had more clarity, which was a relief. I knew we would need to talk about this issue again.

The final surprise came when Dimitri arrived home. Normally he would be resentful and give me the silent treatment after an unresolved argument. This time he was warm and loving. Perhaps he was responding to the internal shift I had made through my focusing exercise. We were able to discuss the issue with less emotion the following day.

Communication of Feelings

The most obvious way to release emotions is by expressing them to the people directly involved. However, you may first need to release some excessive feeling in private before you start. Emotions are a part of what it is to be a human being. Each is delivering you a message. You need to work out what the message is and whether or not it is appropriate to bring it into your relationship.

What's the message?

Anger: Anger is your fire for change. When appropriately expressed, you can use it to let others know their behaviour is unacceptable to you. If there is hurt underneath your anger, acknowledge it. You may find some people respond better when you talk about your hurt as well as your anger.
Messages: 'I need change; I need to communicate this.'

Resentment: Resentment is immobilised anger. You blame others for how you feel and for the situation you are in. It is a way of holding yourself apart from others to maintain a position of being right. Are you waiting for the other person to fix things? Is there something you can do to shift this stand-off? Is there something you need to forgive them for? Is there something you need to speak up about?
Messages: 'I need to take charge of my feeling; I need to take responsibility for changing the situation.'

Hurt: Hurt tells you that your needs are not being met, or that your self-esteem has been wounded. It can be empowering to acknowledge it, especially when the alternative is withdrawal, anger or revenge. Often it deepens your relationship if you can communicate your hurt without resentment.
Messages: 'I need to restore empathy; I need to be healed.'

Fear: Fear warns you that you feel out of control in a situation, that you need to proceed with caution, to seek help, to get more information and to separate fantasy from reality.
Messages: 'I need to take care; I need support; I need more facts; I need to slow down.'

Guilt: Guilt comes about when you act or feel something less than what you expected from yourself. It can be very self-destructive if you let it gnaw away at you. But it is productive when you feel it, take on board its message and move on. Its purpose is to teach you a better way to behave.

Messages: 'I need to make amends; I will do things differently next time.'

Regret: Regret is a huge feeling that can encompass pain and sorrow. It may lurk underneath anger, resentment and guilt. It is the acknowledgment of the unfulfilled potential of a situation. It is often the last emotion before you let go of thoughts such as 'if only it were different' and reach a place of acceptance.

Messages: 'I need to acknowledge my pain and accept it without denial or contraction; I am almost complete with this situation.'

Anger, hostility, resentment and frustration can easily become destructive forces. But these emotions, often presumed negative, are in essence, the impetus for positive change. An extreme emotion can be best brought into a relationship by communicating the appropriate message; for example, your anger about a communication breakdown may be best channelled into establishing a better system for messages.

Use anger as a fire for change

EXERCISE: exploring your emotional responses to conflict

Think of a conflict which has brought up anger, hurt or fear. Delve into your own feelings and responses and answer the following questions.

Five questions to ask when angry/hurt/frightened:

1. **Why am I feeling this?**
   Ask yourself: 'What unmet need triggered my response?'; 'What did someone do? Have they touched on a sensitive issue for me?'

2. **What do I want to change?**
   Your emotions tell you what you do and don't want, so use them to create change. Unfortunately, emotions are often misused to prove the other person wrong and hold grudges.
   Ask yourself: 'What change do I want?'

3. **What do I need in order to let go of this feeling?**
   Once people get hold of an emotion they sometimes have
   trouble finishing with it. If someone makes you angry, you can
   stay angry, and if a difficult confrontation has hurt your
   feelings, you might stay hurt. Emotions should do their work
   and then pass through.

   Ask yourself: 'What will help me let go?'; 'Do I need to explain
   myself?'; 'Do I need an apology?'; 'Do I need to see someone
   making an effort?'

4. **Whose problem is this, really? How much is mine? How much
   is theirs?**
   You may be angry that your teenage son's room is untidy. If you
   have to find something in there, then it's your problem.
   However, as it is your son's room, it's largely his problem. If your
   spouse spends all evening on the phone chatting to friends, it's
   your problem if you are missing the companionship. It's their
   problem if they're not getting done the other tasks they have set
   themselves. It's not uncommon for one person to take an
   inappropriate level of responsibility for the way the other
   person is living their life. That's nagging! You will handle your
   communication more effectively if you are assertive about your
   part of the problem, but do no more than offer a very occasional
   suggestion about theirs.

   Ask yourself: 'What part of the problem is mine'; 'What part
   is theirs?'

5. **What is the unspoken message I gather from the situation?**
   Is it 'They don't like me'; 'They don't respect me'; 'They don't
   appreciate me?' The conclusions we draw about someone else's
   behaviour are often the triggers for our excessive emotional
   reactions. If someone is abrupt with you, you might assume
   that they don't think you're worthy of their attention. If
   someone doesn't return your call you may assume they are not
   interested. If someone walks out and slams the door you might
   presume that they don't love you any more. If your boss won't
   let you print up your own business card, is it because she
   doesn't respect what you do and doesn't acknowledge your
   status? Knowing how you interpret the unspoken message
   gives you a chance to evaluate that response and decide how
   realistic it is.

   Ask yourself: 'What am I telling myself this situation means?'

Five Goals for Communicating Emotions

You will sometimes decide that it's not wise to express your emotions; however, if you do choose to speak out, here are five goals that will help your communication be clean, clear and helpful.

1. **Aim to avoid the desire to punish or blame.**
   Take responsibility for how you feel. If you plan action, check that it is not vindictive. Are you blaming someone for your feelings? People do what they do, we respond how we do. There's an important difference between 'You make me mad' and 'When you do that, I get mad'.

2. **Aim to improve the situation.**
   High emotions indicate where change is wanted. Be sure you are going to make the situation better.

3. **Aim to communicate your feelings appropriately.**
   If something hurts you or angers you, you have a right to say so. Bottling it up jeopardises the relationship, but watch that you express yourself in a way that won't make them defensive. Consider if you would get defensive if it were said that way to you. A well-chosen 'I' statement is invaluable for expressing anger and hurt. For example, 'When you leave suddenly without talking about our problems, I feel hurt. What I'd like is for us to discuss our problems more openly.' (See Chapter 4, Appropriate Assertiveness, for more on 'I' statements.)

4. **Aim to improve the relationship and increase communication.**
   When talking about your good and bad feelings you are offering something immensely precious to the other person — the opportunity to know you. When someone tells you about their feelings they offer you the same gift. Treat them with care.

5. **Aim to avoid repeating the same situation.**
   If someone doesn't telephone when they say they will, you may well feel worried, hurt or annoyed. Managing your emotions also involves making sure that the situation won't recur. Explain your situation; say what you find difficult; ask to be treated in a particular way; fix the problem. This way you're looking after yourself and, in so doing, preserving the relationship.

> 'Anyone can become angry — that is easy. But to be angry at the right person, to the right degree, at the right time, for the right purpose, and in the right way — that is not easy.' Aristotle (384–322 BCE)

EXERCISE: communicating your emotions

Think of a situation in which it may or may not be helpful to express your emotions. Answer the following questions:

What is it that I would like to communicate to the other person?

_____

_____

_____

_____

If communicating my emotions is not appropriate, what other action can I take?

_____

_____

_____

_____

Handling Difficult Emotions in Others

Responding to another person's strong emotions

Even if you love and respect someone deeply and would never wish to hurt them, sooner or later you probably will. Their 'hot' buttons are pressed (those areas in which they're supersensitive) and there's a wave of angry and hurt emotions breaking over you. Their amygdala hijack has been set off (see Chapter 1). They are now in reaction mode. If you know them well, you will recognise the body, thought and emotional clues that indicate they are reacting. What will you do? Ask yourself:

💡 Am I reacting or responding?

To react would be to fight back the wave, deny its validity, angrily defend yourself, or try to suppress it. Have you ever tried holding back a wave? Our objective can be to treat other people's emotions as we treat our own — neither suppressing nor denying them, and listening to the messages they bring. The strange thing is, if we can surf well on a wave of high emotion from the other person, in the long term the relationship can deepen. Here are some suggestions to help you stay upright (like a skilled surfer) as the wave comes crashing in.

Don't be reactive!

Don't try toning them down. Reassuring the person without really acknowledging how they feel is actually a version of disrespect and many people will react badly to attempts to pacify them. They are likely to get more emotional even though they can't speak about the emotion directly. You'll read it in their intensity and tone of voice. That's often the way you pick up on frustration, hurt or anger. You may need to acknowledge these unspoken feelings if the conflict is to move towards problem-solving.

Be tolerant when others discharge emotions. It's a sign of maturity when you can allow some leeway for others to discharge their pent-up emotions without taking offence or being caught up in them.

Try not to defend or explain yourself, attack back, withdraw or change or close down the conversation. Don't blow up! Don't leave the room in a huff! Don't immediately start defending yourself — however much you'd like to!

Try not to block their flow by offering advice or criticism at an inappropriate moment.

With the best of intentions, Jim had interfered in his daughter's relationship with her boyfriend. She was furious with him. He had started giving her advice on how she should handle her boyfriend and criticised what she'd done in the past. At that moment it wasn't helpful and Jim wondered why his daughter never discussed her boyfriend with him again.

Be responsive

This is not the time to get caught up in the content. Move your thoughts away from what they are saying and what you think. Focus instead on how to connect to the person and what's going on for them. Your attention is also on how to turn this into a safe and constructive conversation.

Centre. As soon as you can, tune in to yourself and centre (see Chapter 1, Responding to Conflict, for more on this). Monitor your own reactions. Try to stay calm. You might need to check that you are breathing deeply.

Use active listening. Pay careful attention to what you are picking up from the communication. Separate feelings from content. Support those aspects that seem justified and, if you possibly can, let some irate remarks pass you by without reacting.

Repeat back to the person what you understand of their feelings and the content of their communication:

- 💡 'It sounds like that matters a lot to you.'

- 💡 'Let me check with you ... Is what you are saying ... ?'

Shift to discovery mode. Ensure that you really do understand both their feelings and what they are saying.

Stay focused only on acknowledging what they are feeling and saying until they have calmed down. Do not make any comments or add anything to the conversation.

Try a redirecting question. After they have expressed how they feel and you have indicated that you have heard, ask questions to move the focus on to exploring the issues. It's useless and unhelpful to do it too soon. At an appropriate moment, however, it can support the other person to shift out of their swamp of feelings and into a thinking state. Switching from feelings to thought will tone down an amygdala hijack (see Chapter 1, Responding to Conflict).

Clarify their needs and concerns. What might be their unmet needs — including unexpressed needs that might underlie the angry outburst? Acknowledge the validity of their needs.

Repeat the cycle as necessary, returning to active-listening mode several times if their high emotions are not yet dissipated. See that the issues that need to be dealt with are on the table.

Consider the next step.

- 💡 Do you need to acknowledge your contribution to their problem?

- 💡 Have you ignored a need of theirs or done something that appears disrespectful?

- 💡 Now might be a good time to take responsibility for that.

- 💡 How might you fix other issues together?

🔅 Is it a suitable time to develop options, for you to make an 'I' statement about your needs and concerns, or to take time out?

Addressing emotional blackmail

The above suggestions are helpful when the other person is delivering you an urgent and highly charged message of negative feelings. There are other situations where offering that

Emotional blackmail — return to sender

much attention to a negative emotion may not be the best thing to do; for instance, if you have to deal with power struggles, attention-seeking, desire for revenge or helplessness. In many cases you are being manipulated though they may be unaware of that. In some people these blackmailing behaviours and their underlying negative emotions come along with a dreadful frequency. Every knee-jerk reaction of yours only feeds the problem. How can you respond?

Disengage from the behaviour and the emotions driving them wherever possible, suggests behaviourist Rudolf Dreikurs.[5] Pay attention instead to their deeper motivations — their underlying need for self-esteem, a sense of significance, justice, identity or belonging.

While you might deliver an 'I' statement about what is unacceptable behaviour or offer valuable information on what won't motivate you to help them, you might also consider more long-term strategies.

Support the real needs under the emotions and behaviour you're finding difficult. Remember that behind this mess are *unmet needs*. You might try a mapping exercise as described in Chapter 8, Mapping the Conflict.

Disengage from power struggles. People often use power to build their own self-esteem. It can make you furious if their ability doesn't match their position, or if they test you with confrontations such as, 'You can't make me'. Disengage from this kind of power struggle as soon as you recognise it. Walk away or don't react. Fighting and giving in both reward negative behaviour. Give them other support for their self-worth. Praise something they do well.

Reward the behaviour you do want. It's easy to react negatively to someone seeking attention. Perhaps they're always jumping into the spotlight — boasting, showing off, making repeated requests or talking excessively. How do you react? Do you remind them they've asked that already, rebuke them for showing off or just raise your eyebrows? Unfortunately, any of these could reward their attention-seeking and, behaviourally, whatever you reward you get more of. So reward the behaviour you *do* want. Support their involvement and contributions as soon as they are constructive and ignore their negative bids for attention, where possible.

Don't retaliate. One of the most difficult emotions to handle is another person's desire for revenge, especially when you are the target. Sometimes it springs from deep hurt, which may have very little to do with you. Try not to feel hurt or to retaliate. Consider instead: what can you do to build trust; how might you convince them you respect their needs; can you explain how you believe you are being just and fair with them? Your best efforts may not work, of course. You might just have to back away.

Avoid nagging and criticism. You may be driven mad by someone who acts helpless for no good reason. The child who plays dumb to avoid helping cook dinner; the coworker who pretends to be stupid so he won't get an extra task; the woman who plays stupid under the mistaken belief that it's feminine and appealing; the depressed friend who maintains no one could ever love or employ them; the relation who pleads illness so the family will be at their beck and call; the parent who whines that their adult children never do enough for them. You might have tried and already given up on pity and endless support. It's so tempting then to switch to nagging or criticising to bring them into line, but this rarely helps. You are more likely to cut through the discouragement or the manipulation by supporting any positive attempts, however small, they make to help themselves and get on with managing their lives.

Nourish Core Needs — Become a Source of Positive Emotions

There are some people — perhaps in the top one per cent of the population for emotional intelligence — who can harness cooperation, creativity and trustworthiness in the most difficult of people. The competency they rely on is to become a source of positive emotions for those around them. They do it all the time with everyone. Fisher and Shapiro in *Beyond Reason* recommend we make it our priority in relationships to nourish five core underlying needs that are common to most people, and when fulfilled stimulate helpful emotions in others.[6]

We are wise to:

1. Express **appreciation** of the merits and difficulties in how the other person thinks, feels and acts.

2. Help them build a sense of **affiliation** or connection with us.

3. Indicate our respect for their **autonomy** (their need and ability to make decisions for themselves).

4. Respect their **status** and not demean them in any way.

5. Help shape fulfilling and meaningful **roles** for them whenever appropriate and especially when designing solutions.

What can you do if someone's negative emotions seem to be getting in the way of the relationship or a successful conclusion to a conflict? Look first to see if you have ignored or disrespected one of these core concerns. Make sure the other person knows that you appreciate them, regard them as 'one of the team', respect their decision-making, acknowledge their skills, expertise and the important parts of their identity position where appropriate, and offer or support their meaningful activity. As you become a source of positive feelings, of course they will be more willing to become partners, rather than opponents. This is a preventative approach to difficult emotions. You forestall negative feelings with positive ones. Ideally, you do it all the time and before there is any problem.

EXERCISE: become a source of good feelings

Look around you. Your mission, should you choose to accept it, is to find:

- At least one opportunity to show your appreciation of someone.

- One opportunity to increase your connection (perhaps e-mail, call or include the person in a social occasion).

- An appropriate situation to show your respect for a person's decision-making.

- What genuine expertise of theirs you can show your respect for.

- An opportunity to communicate your admiration for expertise you notice in another person.

- Where you can contribute to another person finding more fulfilment and meaning in their activities.

If you do this exercise every day until it becomes second nature, you'll become a constant source of good emotions for those around you.

SUMMARY

- Don't indulge or deny emotions — build richer relationships with them.

- Emotions are energy, body and mind events.

- Release pent-up feelings away from other people.

- Try focusing to find the crux of the problem.

- Each emotion delivers a message: you must decide what is appropriate to communicate to others. In particular, you can ask yourself what you want to change.

- Respect other people's communication of strong feelings.

- Support the real needs under emotions and behaviours you find difficult.

- Nourish core needs — become a source of positive emotions for others.

Notes

1 See Daniel Goleman *Emotional Intelligence* op. cit.

2 Richard Carlson, *Don't Sweat the Small Stuff ... And it's All Small Stuff* (USA: Hyperion, 1997)

3 Dr Julie Henderson, *The Lover Within* (USA: Barrytown, 1999)
   Dr Julie Henderson, *How to Feel as Good as You Can in Spite of Everything* (USA: 1995)

4 Eugene Gendlin, *Focusing: How to Open up your Deeper Feelings and Intuition* (USA: Rider & Co, 2003). See also www.focusing.org

5 Rudolf Dreikurs and Vicki Soltz, *Children: The Challenge* (USA: Plume, paperback ed, 1991)

6 Roger Fisher and Daniel Shapiro, *Beyond Reason: Using Emotions as You Negotiate* (UK: Random House, 2005) pp 203–4

CHAPTER 7
Willingness to Resolve

Am I ready to move beyond personal issues towards forgiveness?
What feelings or issues do I need to release?

Can you remember a time when you were so hurt, angry or resentful that you didn't want to fix the problem? Perhaps there's someone in your life right now who angers you so much you'd rather have nothing to do with them. What might stop you from wanting to resolve such a conflict? Are any of these relevant to your situation:

- How unfair the other person has been.

- How bad their behaviour has been.

- Your need for self-respect — or is it pride?

- Are you proving that you were right and they were wrong?

- Do you need an apology first?

- Are you playing on a desire for revenge?

- Have you been too deeply hurt?

- Are you just too angry to even think about forgiving them?

- Your resentment is so old and deep you wouldn't know how to let it go.

- Does hanging onto the problem have any benefits or advantages?

Willingness to resolve is a key factor in conflict resolution — sometimes good will is all you need. However, it's not always easy to come to the point of being willing to resolve. It can be even harder helping another person to get there.

Secondary Gains from the Conflict
What's the Pay-off for Hanging onto the Problem?
You sometimes hold onto a grudge for some secondary gain or pay-off. Willingness to resolve can begin with a quiet moment in which you explore *the pay-off for not resolving the conflict*, and

assess the temptation to leave the problem as it is. For instance, by keeping your distance you can avoid confronting or dealing with a difficult issue or hearing something you may not wish to hear.

What's the Pay-off for Solving the Problem?

What are the benefits of being willing to resolve? Think of times when you have resolved a conflict even though it was quite difficult. Did you gain relief, deeper understanding, feel better about yourself, or become closer to the other person? Perhaps you got some new perspectives. You might avoid another person for years, but if you haven't handled your willingness to resolve, you're still connected. Dealing with your unwillingness to resolve can bring proper completion to a finished relationship.

For things to change, first I must change

Deciding to resolve a problem can require a major internal shift. Hurt and anger are like two sides of the one coin. Many people resist examining the underside. To come to a place of peace, the angry person may need to experience their pain; the hurting person may need to find their anger. Anger can hide in the form of cold spite or resentment — and this icy condition can be preserved for ages. You may know of situations where the people involved refused to speak to each other for twenty years!

There's a grim satisfaction in being very cold to people with whose values we deeply disagree, but pigeonholing people as baddies and goodies is an over-simplification. If you acknowledge the other person's full range of qualities, it's not nearly as easy to dismiss their viewpoint and you might also be faced with acknowledging some bad points of your own.

Sometimes it's difficult to admit that you, too, have a part in the conflict, and have contributed in some way. Maybe you handled a situation badly, treated someone with a lack of respect, or hurt a person you love. Can you accept your own faults as well as theirs? Be willing to express your sadness in causing another person pain. Be willing to listen to how another is hurt and move towards asking for forgiveness. Sometimes you will need to forgive yourself.

Would I rather be right or happy?

How important is being right compared with resolving the problem? Sometimes you feel so strongly about something you keep hammering the point or defending yourself for fear of losing what's so important to you. Sometimes you can't see the cost of hanging on so hard; it can be better just to let go of the issue. It's not giving in — you are just not trying to prove the point any more.

Perhaps you'll develop some strategies to deal differently with problem areas, or you may choose to limit or end the relationship. Whichever way it goes, you're finished with debates about the rights and wrongs of the whole situation.

People caught up in resentment are often defending against a blow to their self-esteem. They'll justify their position excessively to convince themselves they're right. They'll sound self-righteous, while underneath they feel rejected or betrayed. They block off these feelings with an impenetrable resentment. If they are ever able to bring their vulnerable emotions into awareness or re-examine the roots of their low self-esteem, their viciousness will fall away. If you can penetrate their façade and work out what's really going on for them, you may begin to see them as just 'mistaken', rather than 'malicious'. It's easier to forgive them for being mistaken than for being vindictive.

Forgiveness

Two people locked in resentment are tied to each other emotionally and energetically. As long as you say, 'I can't let go until they do', you're still locked in, whether the other person is physically present or not. Forgiveness is really up to you alone. Your forgiveness may free the other person to change, but, more importantly, your forgiveness frees you. Not to forgive means you are locked in the past. The case for letting go of hurt and anger is overwhelming!

My forgiveness frees me

Forgiveness doesn't mean forgetting. If someone has hurt, offended or abused you, you're unlikely to forget it. What you could do is try to understand what motivated them, accept their inadequacies and forgive them for not knowing or being able to do better. That way you free yourself from continuing to suffer. Until you do, you remain in pain, trapped by the other person's offensive behaviour.

Certainly, you may never want to put yourself in the same situation again. You could develop strategies to deal with it differently. You may want to put limits on the relationship or break all contact. Once you have forgiven them, you can choose what's wisest in the situation. Ending a relationship because it's not healthy or supportive for you is quite different from ending it out of anger and resentment.

When someone has deeply offended you, broken your trust or hurt you, it is not easy to forgive.

> *Sasha was well into her thirties and desperately wanting to marry and have children before it was too late. When her boyfriend ended their two-year relationship, she was deeply hurt and angry. She had invested two years and all her emotional energy in the relationship when he announced he was unable to commit to a future with her. She would wake in the night, rehearsing in her mind all the things she wanted to scream at him. One day in tears she cried, 'I wish I could forgive him and move on, but I'm so angry I can't seem to let go.'*

Sasha was, in fact, taking a first step towards forgiving him. She could see that she was *willing to become willing* to forgive him. Primarily she wasn't taking this first step for him, but for herself.

The alternative — staying locked into the pain and anger — was excruciating.

Stephanie Dowrick in her book *Forgiveness and Other Acts of Love* writes:

> *Let's suppose those first stages (of forgiveness) go something like this: forgetting about the matter some of the time; not actively wishing the other person harm; feeling that you are able to be patient with yourself ... Wanting forgiveness to come and waiting for it may be all that one can do[1] ... The process of assimilating our scars may take months, years, decades. The original events will not have changed, but you will.[2]*

Forgiving the other person hasn't got a lot to do with the words you might say. In fact, you might not say anything at all. Forgiving is a shift in attitude that arises from yourself, an inner shift that comes from the heart. Of course, you will not come to this acceptance right away. You will need time to withdraw, incubate, get angry and allow yourself to experience your pain. That's how you heal your wounds.

Although you may not be able to condone the other person's actions, you might be able to accept that we all have imperfections and faults, sometimes major ones, that come with being human. It can help to try to understand what motivated them to behave as they did.

EXERCISE: understanding their motivation

Think of someone with whom you are or have been in an unresolved conflict.

- Write down what the person did that has caused you anger or hurt.

- Look at why that made you angry. Consider how you may have made judgements or assumptions about those behaviours.

- Put yourself in their shoes and contemplate all the possible reasons for them doing what they did. What did they need to protect or defend?

- Are you still holding onto some resentment?

- What do you need to forgive them for?

- What do you feel you could ask their forgiveness for?

- What do you need to forgive yourself for in relation to them?

Use this as an exercise of self-awareness. You may or may not talk about it to the person in question.

At some point, take what you have written and discard it, turn it into a ceremony or celebration of your freedom. You may want to burn the paper, or tear it up and throw away the pieces. Things change when you change.

LUENG

I moved to Australia mainly, I'm afraid, to escape from an impossible relationship with my mother. Over the years we had shared fierce scenes and bitter feelings. For twelve months we had not even spoken to each other. I was the second son in the family and had not been nearly as clever at school as my older brother had. I felt my mother always compared me with my brother and that I, the second son, was second-best in her book. One day, in a personal development workshop, I unlocked some of my resentment about my mother. It was a very significant release for me. I arrived home late that night. Within minutes my mother phoned from Singapore. She had been trying to reach me for some hours. She was ready to talk again and my recent insights helped me to accept the love she was trying to offer. Why did she ring just then? Had she intuitively responded to the shift I'd just made? I had let go of my anger. Things certainly changed when I changed.

While forgiveness is fundamentally an inner process, you nevertheless may want to involve the other person directly. Consider the actions you are willing to take, no matter how small, to open up or change the situation. You may need to tell the other person how you have been affected by their behaviour. Use some elements of the 'I' statement format and be very careful to adopt neutral language. You may want to offer a small gift or a helpful deed. Do you want to apologise for your part in the problem? Do you want to ask them for an apology or for some form of recompense? Be sure you are not attached to the outcome as the other person may not be ready to move on or to acknowledge their part. We explore how you might handle the other person's unwillingness to resolve conflict towards the end of this chapter.

Informed or Inflamed?

Have you ever noticed that a particular person or characteristic really irritates you, but doesn't really irritate others? Have you watched someone get really irritated by something that doesn't particularly distress you at all? Negative views and strong reactions are usually filtered through pain or anger deep inside us. Our view is coloured by rights and wrongs, likes and dislikes, past experiences and upbringing. We can see the distortion when others' reactions are more extreme than the situation calls for; however, when you're the one who's furious, it all seems perfectly justified.

There may be someone in the office who talks a great deal about themselves. Others in the office, not influenced by unconscious prejudices, may simply think: 'There she goes, showing off again. I wonder why she needs to do that'. They disapprove and may even express their dislike, but they are not emotionally hooked. But a person who grew up under the shadow of a more attractive and outgoing sister may find the situation throws up unresolved jealousies. They can't stand how the office chatterbox behaves. The situation inflames them rather than informs them.

When a situation inflames or angers you, this tells you as much about yourself as about them. When your response is relatively free of undue negative feelings, the situation has merely informed you of a problem. If that's the case, you have only the difficulty to deal with. Whenever you are inflamed, the point is always why do you respond that way? The more someone irritates you, the more you know you have something to learn about yourself in this situation.

Am I informed or inflamed?

Unexamined anger blocks our willingness to resolve. You will find it easier to let go once you understand the fundamentals of *unconscious projection*.

Projection

Projection occurs when your own unconscious thoughts and feelings appear to be in the minds and behaviour of others. You push something out of your awareness and see it, instead, coming towards you from others. Many conflict situations present an opportunity to examine your own projections.[3]

Some psychologists find it useful to work with the idea that your personality is a complete package of human characteristics with positives and negatives, good and bad points — the full spectrum of human potential. Your upbringing allows you to be conscious of only a part of who you really are. The famous psychiatrist Dr Carl Jung used the word 'persona' to describe these conscious aspects of personality.[4] Whether these aspects are good or bad, the significant point about the persona is that it is known to the person. It is made up of things that you accept are true about yourself. The persona is your self-image.

Jung used the term 'shadow' to describe the unconscious part of ourselves — our unconscious desires, feelings, intentions or beliefs. It is the potential that has not unfolded: aspects of ourselves that we are not ready to know about; our emotional responses that

Hello

are too painful to fully experience. It also includes the opposites of all our conscious wants or dislikes, as well as abilities or talents we are not ready to accept or express.

Few of us acknowledge all the bad things about ourselves, or have enough self-esteem to acknowledge all the good. Positive or negative when unacceptable, they become the shadow side of our personality. Indirect anger can work like this: you 'accidentally' spill tea over the person you are angry with; or you inadvertently comment on how you hate red on a day that they are wearing that colour. Your aggression may be passive — and be expressed as ignoring, excluding and avoiding. Others are often much more aware of your repressed feelings than you are. You often have a very misleading self-image. You think you are kindly while unconsciously you can be very cruel. There's an aggressive element in all of us. It's much less dangerous when you can allow it into consciousness and then hold it in check with your other caring, ethical and law-abiding qualities.

When you are inflamed rather than informed — look within. You are probably caught in a projection from your shadow. Consider the hook, the symptom and the projection.

- **The hook:** the behaviour in the other person that is inflaming you, in itself a neutral event. A mannerism, a style of relating, a repeated behaviour, draws your anger and hooks you in like a fish on the end of a line.

- **The symptom:** high emotions (usually variations on anger and hurt).

- **The projection:** the unconscious material (your shadow) that is causing your strong reaction.

It can help you break free of the projection if you focus on the part of their behaviour that particularly inflames you, the hook, and describe it in a neutral way. The hook may be just a particular look in the other person's eye, the way they laugh, an innocent gesture or unconsidered action.

Next, consider why that might arouse such anger or resentment in you. Find reasons that have to do with you rather than them. The following examples are three possible processes that can feed such projections.

Can you get to the future if the past is present?

Unresolved personal history

An event may trigger your emotional baggage — unresolved stress or anger from a similar situation in your past. Here are some examples:

(a) Your job requires you to deal professionally with someone who is abusing a child. Anyone would demand justice and protection for the child, but you are so distressed you miss some important facts of the case because the situation triggers memories of abuse in your own childhood.

(b) Your boss criticises everyone's work. Nobody likes it, but you become particularly anxious and depressed. Did you face destructive criticism some time in your past? Does this remind you of a teacher who really had it in for you?

(c) An intimate relationship breaks up and your distress and depression seem bottomless. Grief in this situation is natural, but you have an extreme reaction. What are you reminded of? Abandonment by a parent through divorce or death are good candidates for the primary cause. If you didn't deal completely with the distress then, it is highly likely to resurface now.

Suppressed needs

You can become excessively inflamed in a situation where you haven't recognised a need you have and it's not being met. You'll then become unreasonably angry with the other person who has let you down. Perhaps you are inflamed because someone else takes the credit for work you have done. Are you underestimating your own need to be recognised? You may be deeply hurt when a friend cancels an activity you planned to do together. Suddenly you notice how much the outing meant to you. Is your need for companionship undernourished? When we are unaware of needs that underlie our behaviour, we are unreasonably inflamed when they are not supported.

Unacceptable qualities or characteristics

Do you see in another person a quality that you would not allow in yourself? You may be projecting your own unacceptable qualities onto others. If you have not come to terms with your own anger, hatred, jealousy or destructiveness, wherever you go you'll meet those exact qualities in the people you deal with — and it will probably make you wild.

Some examples:

- You feel alienated from someone who frequently explodes in anger. You would never be so volatile. Is it worth asking yourself how you deny or push away your own anger?

- You are critical of someone who flaunts their sexuality. Are you jealous? If so, what is that jealousy based on? Do you suppress your own sexuality?

- Someone speaks to you disrespectfully. You react with a curt remark. You don't think you are being unreasonable, but others say it is out of proportion. It's time to look within. Teenagers can be very aggressive if they sense any lack of respect. If the adult is also projecting onto the situation, they can become very alienated from each other at a crucial time. This means the adult has less scope to influence the developing teenager to adopt important values. Parents may need to become aware of and set aside their personal issues when handling such matters as teenage rebelliousness.

> **Acknowledge projections:**
> **1. Unresolved personal history.**
> **2. Suppressed needs.**
> **3. Unacceptable qualities.**

- Your unwillingness to accept your own good qualities can make you project ideal virtues onto another. You put them on a pedestal. This can form the basis of romantic love where the loved person is seen as perfect — until the day that the scales of projection fall from your eyes.

EXERCISE: self-discovery

The aim is to explore your own projections and why you over-react to certain people. Choose people that you imagine might irritate or upset you if you were with them for a long time. The facts of how they behave are less important for this exercise than what you project onto the other person from your own subconscious. Fill in the Self-Discovery Worksheet on the next pages.

SELF-DISCOVERY WORKSHEET

Choose three people with whom you sometimes have difficulty relating	Focus on their qualities or ways of behaving that irritate or upset you	Focus on your reaction. How do you feel about these irritations? Write several words until you have just the right one
Someone you work with: _____		
A person you live with or a close friend: _____		
A parent or child of yours: _____		
HERE IS AN EXAMPLE: The person I work with: Daniel _____	_He's always so organised. He is very rigid, always has a plan and is a stickler for being on time._	_I feel controlled, tense. Not free to do my own thing. Resentful at having to follow his lead._

Why do you feel this way? Give reasons that concern you rather than them. Focus on unresolved personal history, suppressed needs or unacceptable qualities	Summarise the three columns by constructing a statement of self-awareness. You would not normally communicate this statement to another person
	When he/she _____ I feel _____ Because I hook into my _____ _____ _____
	When he/she _____ I feel _____ Because I hook into my _____ _____ _____
	When he/she _____ I feel _____ Because I hook into my _____ _____ _____
I find it difficult to be on time, follow the rules. I can't block off my emotions to fall in with him. I was controlled by my father and I can't stand it when anyone else tries to put boundaries on me. I have the desire to run. I must feel free.	When he *tries to organise me into his plans* I feel *resentful and suffocated* Because I hook into my *history* *with my controlling father. Old* *anger at Dad gets directed at* *Daniel.*

If you have completed the Self-Discovery exercise and have constructed your statements of self-awareness you could ask yourself whether you've gained some new insights. Do you sense a change in your attitude to these people?

I've sought out the enemy and I've discovered it's me

What can you acknowledge about each person that makes you glad they are in your life?

Circumstances: Personal Design or Fate?

Our unconscious state colours how we see other people, and it does more than this. It constantly affects and changes what is actually going on. Carl Jung says that when an inner situation is not made conscious, it happens outside us as fate. At more obvious levels, here are some examples of this mechanism at work:

- Others become disturbed by our disconnection from our own feelings, so they become more emotional than usual when they're around us.

- A person who can't show their own anger and displays it as unconscious resentment can often make others very angry.

- A person who is unaware that they act in a very superior way provokes other people into pulling them down a peg or two.

> I do not like thee, Dr Fell
> The reason why I cannot tell
> But this I know and know full well
> I do not like thee, Dr Fell.

This old rhyme points out a fundamental truth: we respond constantly to people's shadow side. Our unconscious behaviour can provide a hook on which others hang their own projections. The task is to become conscious of this and free each other from the enmeshed qualities of the relationship.

Apparently random coincidences can shape our lives. Someone who was battered in childhood often grows up and marries a physically violent partner. The boy who was browbeaten by his mother can end up working for a very difficult female boss. It's most useful to presume we are attracting these patterns. This seems borne out by times when we see the same

My thoughts draw the events of my life to me

pattern repeating itself until we resolve it — when we address the present situation using the greater power, wisdom and skill we have developed since the original situation.

The circumstances you most resist are often the very ones that you attract, such as a financial disaster or a marriage breakdown. It's as if your excessive fear or dislike draws the event to you. The cure can lie in coming to terms with the circumstances and growing beyond limiting beliefs, such as 'I'm a success only because I make a lot of money' or 'I'd never manage on my own'.

What you resist, persists

Look for unacknowledged projection wherever there are undesirable circumstances or patterns troubling your life. The situation you see is telling you something about yourself. Although it is true that you can be caught up in a grander sweep of events than your personal dilemmas, generally it is useful to presume you are a magnet attracting whatever you need for your development.

It's worth weeding the garden of your own mind, quite apart from considering what the other person may or may not have done wrong. Seeing each conflict as something you have attracted for your growth helps you take charge of your response. Blame, resentment and regret will hold you back from taking this ultimate responsibility. Your learning may be as straightforward as recognising where you have contributed to a problem, or you might begin to see a place where you don't love yourself enough. You can use your life to reveal your hidden self and move beyond its limitations.

Presume you are a magnet attracting whatever you need for your own development

We might choose to take on responsibility for the bigger picture or for the issue itself. Whenever we can do so, we may find an unexpected leap in personal power available for our response.

ALICIA

Recently I started an exciting new relationship. Ahmed was courting me in a way I loved — ringing me often and telling me how much he wanted to see me. We started to get very close. Then, suddenly things changed. First, he rang far less frequently. Then, instead of him asking me out I had to say I wanted to see him. The conversations shifted. I no longer looked forward to his calls. I sometimes found myself being quite short and sarcastic.

I confided in a friend, 'You can't trust men. They're all the same. They say things they don't mean.' When I looked back, I saw how my relationships had often made this sudden turn. That made me really angry. I decided I'd really rather not bother with men at all.

I stayed with that for a whole week, but it didn't sit well with me. I wanted to understand myself better than that. Why was I so mad? What was I really feeling? Then I saw I was scared of being hurt and left alone. I remembered that I felt like this when I was a kid. I would get close to my father. I'd want to be with him more, but then he'd go away and I'd feel it was not safe to love him. Now I could see that there was a pattern to my relationships with men: at the point when we'd become close, it appeared to me that the man suddenly withdrew. My unacknowledged fear was that if I became close, I would be hurt or left. That fear was drawing the reality of hurt and rejection into my life. It was an eye-opener!

Then I started to wonder why Ahmed had decided to withdraw. Perhaps he wasn't doing it to me at all. Maybe he wasn't trying to hurt me. What if he, too, was scared for his own reasons and 'shadows' he had? Maybe he was afraid I didn't want to hear from him?

I softened towards him and decided I was ready to try a different approach. Next time I felt myself wanting to withdraw I decided to tell him the truth and say, 'It seems to me that you've been calling me less often. I find myself feeling hurt and scared that you don't really want to see me.' I was ready to tackle a hurdle I'd always baulked at before.

Managing Others' Unwillingness to Resolve Conflict

For smooth resolution of conflict both parties need to be willing to resolve. In this chapter we have discussed ways in which you can bring yourself to that state of mind. Frequently your greatest challenge will be to guide the other person to that point too.

To get a better response provide a better stimulus

Although you might understand that they have their own suppressed needs, unacknowledged personal history or unacceptable qualities, it will rarely be appropriate for you to point this out.

Therefore consider these alternatives:

Correct Your Part of the Problem

When someone else is projecting onto you, you are rarely entirely innocent. How are you *hooking* their projection? Are you irritating the other person? To clean up your own act, it's always worth looking at what is behind someone's complaint about you. The important thing is to adjust what needs correcting while maintaining a sense of proportion. There is no value in punishing yourself with guilt because you have upset them. The largest part of their inflammation is their problem — you're just correcting your piece of it.

Is there Something You'd Like to Apologise for?

There should be no need to grovel, but you may want to check if there's something you'd be happy not to do again if you know it distresses them. Obviously it's not the whole of the problem, but the apology may help them move on.

Look at How You Come across. Ask yourself:

- How am I using my power? Do I disempower or empower them? Am I playing victim, persecutor or rescuer roles? Did I offer clean choices, or did I make threats?
(See Chapter 5, Cooperative Power.)

- Did I manage my own feelings first? Is my own shadow in the way of resolution?
(See Chapter 6, Managing Emotions.)

- Did I really listen to them? Did I use empathy blockers?
(See Chapter 3, Empathy, Part l.)

- Did I use 'charged' language or did I use 'clean' messages?
(See Chapter 4, Appropriate Assertiveness.)

Look at Where Misinterpretation Seems to have Occurred

- Did we misinterpret each other's position, motives, requirements, values, feelings?

- How can I clarify the issues?

- Do I need a mediator to help with this?

Put Yourself in Their Shoes

- How might they be feeling?

- What might be their needs and concerns around the issue?

- Do they need to save face?

- ·💡· What could make it worthwhile for them to want to resolve the situation?

- ·💡· What needs of theirs might be met if the conflict were resolved?

Try a Positive Statement

Use it as a defuser during conflict, or a reopener when the dust has settled and the atmosphere is calmer; for example: 'I'd really like to clear this up, how about you?'

Discuss the Mutual Advantages of Resolving the Problem

What would make it worthwhile for them to want to resolve? Paint a picture of how it could be if you were both able to cooperate or get along well again. If they cannot hear you, you will have to consider if perhaps they gain more from the problem than from its solution. If this seems the case, you may need to distance yourself. Disengage and understand that you are not responsible for them. Work towards your own resolution. Your changes may free the other person to change, but, most importantly, your forgiveness frees you.

SUMMARY

- What is the pay-off for hanging onto the problem?

- Would you rather be right or happy? Commit yourself to the resolution of the problem rather than to self-righteousness.

- Your forgiveness is up to you alone. How will you make an internal shift and let go?

- Are you informed or inflamed? What colours your view?

- Uncover your own unresolved personal history, suppressed needs and unacceptable qualities that you may project during conflict.

- Your thoughts attract events to you. What you resist, persists. Use troublesome circumstances to weed the garden of your own mind.

- Be aware that the other person is also hooked in and ask yourself what you can do to help them. Consider:
  - Correcting your part of the problem.
  - The benefit of an apology.
  - How you come across.
  - Whether misinterpretation has occurred.
  - What would make it worthwhile for them to want to resolve?
  - Discussing with the other person the advantages of resolution.

Notes

1 Stephanie Dowrick, *Forgiveness and Other Acts of Love* (Australia: Viking, 1997) p 299

2 Op. cit., p 334

3 For a more detailed explanation of projection, see: Ken Wilbur, *The Spectrum of Consciousness* (USA: Quest, 1993)

4 Carl Gustav Jung (1875–1961) was a Swiss psychiatrist and founder of analytical psychology.

Additional reading

Peter O'Connor, *Understanding Jung, Understanding Yourself* (Australia: Methuen, 1985)

Joseph Campbell (ed.), *The Portable Jung* (USA: Penguin, 1971)

Claire Dunne, *Carl Jung: Wounded Healer of the Soul* (USA: Parabola, 2002)

Have you ever had a problem and felt like this?

- I'm confused. I can't work out what's really going on.

- I'm stuck. There seems no way out of the problem.

- There are too many factors involved. Where do I start?

- Something else is going on, but I don't know what it is.

- The situation is hopeless — it's a personality clash.

It's moments like these we need … *maps*. Maps give a clear picture, show how different elements relate to each other and help us to discover what we may not otherwise see. Before moving into action to resolve a conflict, create a map. You can do it alone, with a friend or partner, with others involved in the conflict, especially in problem-solving meetings.

We (Helena and Shoshana) invented this mapping process in 1986 and we've been using it regularly ever since. Mapping puts the spotlight of awareness on the motivational factors in the conflict and combines that with a method for creating a common vision. As people unify their vision by creating a map, somewhere during the process in sneaks the magic transition. While looking at your map together, considering all the issues that must be incorporated into the solution, you turn from being opponents into problem-solving partners.

We have now, between us, done thousands of maps — of our own issues and those that have arisen when working with others in conflict counselling, coaching sessions, team-building, mediations, as part of organisational change processes and facilitating public meetings. Our colleagues who were part of Conflict Resolution Network also use it regularly as a management tool. Judging from the requests for

Step back from conflict about solutions and get down to needs and fears

copyright clearance to include creating a map in training manuals for schools and workplaces, it has gained in popularity around the world. Pondering this, we conclude that it's so successful because it's such commonsense, so easy to do and so powerful in its result.

Remember the story about the orange in Chapter 2 and the importance of going back to needs to find win/win solutions? This is what maps help you to do. Their great value is in their orderly, systematic approach and how they help you see things more clearly.

Creating a Map

A MAP DISPLAYS:
▶ the issue
▶ who it affects
▶ their needs
▶ their fears

Step 1. What's the Issue?

Label the issue in broad terms using neutral and unemotional language. There is no need yet to focus on or analyse the nature of the problem. Where the issue is someone in the workplace who is not doing their fair share, the label you might write down is 'workload distribution' (not 'Bob is not doing his fair share'). Where there are personality clashes and communication has deteriorated, the label could be 'communication'. At home, where the problem is who does the washing-up or the kids are not keeping their rooms tidy, perhaps label the issue 'washing-up' or 'household chores'. Don't get anxious about whether or not the wording is exactly right, simply write down the nature of the area or topic to be mapped. Don't define the problem in terms proposing a yes/no, either/or choice. Keep the problem definition open-ended.

Step 2. Who is Involved?

Decide who the major parties are — you might list each individual (each member of a family or team) or whole teams, groups or organisations (for example, salespeople, receptionists, directors, clients, public, government). As long as the people involved share needs on the issue, they can be grouped together. A mixture of individual and group categories is fine too. If you are mapping a

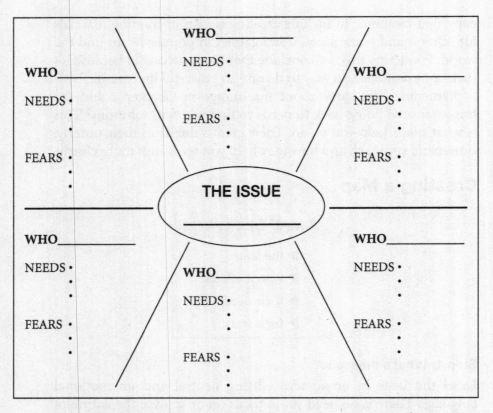

WHO_____
NEEDS ·
        ·
        ·
FEARS ·
        ·

WHO_____
NEEDS ·
        ·
FEARS ·
        ·

_____

WHO_____
NEEDS ·
        ·
FEARS ·
        ·

THE ISSUE
_____

WHO_____
NEEDS ·
        ·
FEARS ·
        ·

WHO_____
NEEDS ·
        ·
        ·
FEARS ·
        ·
        ·

WHO_____
NEEDS ·
        ·
FEARS ·
        ·

_____

WHO_____
NEEDS ·
        ·
        ·
FEARS ·
        ·
        ·

new university policy on teacher-student ratios, the parties involved might be teachers, students, the dean, the board of directors and perhaps the media. An internal problem might involve only the first three.

If you are mapping two people having a clash in an office, you might list the two people separately, but put the rest of the team together in one segment if their needs around this issue are substantially the same. You could probably include the manager and whoever the team provides services for. Although they may not be part of the immediate situation, they may have needs and fears that need to be taken into account.

Step 3. What Do They Need? What Do They Fear?

For each major party, you then list the significant needs and fears that are relevant to the issue. You clarify the motivations behind the issue. People are motivated to move towards what they want and to move away from what they don't want. By mapping needs and fears, we map the dynamics. We broaden the picture and the number of possible options to consider when the map is complete.

Needs

Use this term lightly — it could mean wants, values, interests or the things you care about. Simply ask the question: 'Around the issue of ... what are the major needs that are currently not being met?' You may be asking it *of* yourself, *of* another person, or *about* another person or party. Needs might include: satisfying and secure work; a tidy desk/house; being allowed to make a mess; having everything legal and aboveboard, being able to work in a quiet place. Sometimes the same need applies to several or all groups. It can be worthwhile to repeat the need under each heading to reveal how much the people have in common. Sometimes it's difficult for people to shift their focus from solutions and think about their needs. You can lead them with questions like:

💡 'Your answer to the problem is to do ... What needs of yours will this meet?'

Their reply to this is likely to reveal their underlying needs. Occasionally mapping goes off on a tangent when another person starts talking about their problem in the midst of charting one person's needs and fears. You might complete their digression skilfully by extracting one of their needs or fears from what they are saying. This can then be charted on their place on the map. Continue by asking them whether it would be okay to return to where you originally were in the mapping process.

When asked what they need, many people reply with solutions that they think are needs, such as 'I need him to ring me when he's going to be late'. The underlying needs are, in fact: planning accordingly and knowing he is safe. There are a variety of solutions which meet that need. Ringing when late is only one of these. During the process of mapping the fencing issue (see Map 1 on pages 165–6), the facilitator asked, 'What do you need?' and the woman answered, 'A lower fence!' This was, in fact, a solution rather than a need. In recognising this, the facilitator was then able to draw out the woman's real needs — such as open space and so on. By identifying these needs, progress was made towards uncovering a number of possible solutions.

If you come up with very general words such as 'respect', 'acknowledgment' and 'understanding', probe deeper. The needs you list should be quite specific if they are going to be really helpful. So, for example, if the word 'recognition' comes up ask: 'From whom?' and 'Of what?' Include in the map answers such as: 'Recognition from my manager for the extra work I do'. If the words 'acknowledgment' or 'understanding' come up, you might ask: 'How will you know when you have that?' Write into the map answers such as: 'I'd like to be included in decision-making'. This could later be built into the solutions you come up with after you have created the map.

You may find some of the following questions useful when you are preparing a map:

- 'What needs does this meet?'
- 'What benefits do you see if you ...?'
- 'Tell me more about why that is important to you?'

If a need is intangible, ask:

- 'How would you know if this need were met?'
- 'What would you need in order to get this?'

Fears

These can be concerns, anxieties or worries. You do not have to debate whether or not the fear is realistic before it is listed. For example, you may have a fear about something your rational mind knows is very unlikely to happen, yet the fear still lurks unbidden, wanting to be recognised. These are important to have on the map. One of the real benefits of mapping is the opportunity to air irrational fears and have them acknowledged.

Fears are acknowledged by mapping

Sometimes you can dig deeper. For example, someone says their fear is 'not getting the work done'. Probe beneath this — what is the fear? Is it 'Being seen as inadequate or inefficient', 'Losing the job', 'Loss of their reputation'?

Fears might include:

• failure and loss of face

• doing the wrong thing

• financial insecurity

• being rejected, disliked, unloved

• feeling unsafe in the relationship

• loss of control

• getting stressed

• loneliness

• being judged or criticised

• uninteresting work

• being ordered around

• paying too much.

The fears category draws out motivations that don't surface so easily when considering needs. Fear of failing may be a primary motivator, and if you ask only: 'What do you need?', you won't uncover it. Its opposite, 'To be successful', might not be so vital. It will pop up immediately when you ask: 'What are you concerned about?'.

MAP 1

A woman was unhappy because her neighbour wanted to build a high brick fence between their properties. The plan is about to go to Council for approval. She came to a Conflict Resolution course feeling very angry and helpless. She mapped the situation and left the workshop deciding to invite her neighbour in for a cup of tea to get to know him a little, rather than fighting over the fence. She felt far less angry and helpless. The others in the course, who participated in the mapping, saw the value of mapping the needs, rather than immediately seeking a solution. They had started off siding strongly with the woman about how horrible the neighbour was, and made suggestions about how she could make it difficult for him. After the map, they were also concerned about the neighbour's fears as well as how the woman could help him, and herself too.

```
┌─────────────────────────────────────────────────────────────┐
│ HER                                                           │
│ NEEDS                          FEARS                          │
│ • open space                   • feeling boxed in             │
│ • property left intact         • being walked over            │
│ • to maintain property value   • reprisal if he's knocked back│
│ • good communication and         by Council                  │
│   friendly relationship with   • isolation                    │
│   neighbour                    • paying towards something she │
│                                  didn't want                  │
│                                • having to look at a high brick│
│                                  wall                         │
│                                • losing rosebushes planted    │
│                                  where the fence would go     │
│                                                               │
│                    ╭───────────────────╮                      │
│────────────────────│    THE FENCE      │──────────────────────│
│                    ╰───────────────────╯                      │
│                                                               │
│ HIM                                                           │
│ NEEDS                          FEARS                          │
│ • privacy                      • losing dogs                  │
│ • security                     • dogs being a nuisance to the │
│ • to keep dogs enclosed          neighbours                   │
│ • the neighbour's cooperation  • burglary                     │
│   and communication            • social contact he may not    │
│                                  handle well                  │
└─────────────────────────────────────────────────────────────┘
```

Listing needs and fears

Keep the focus on the needs and fears of all parties until the map is complete. Don't be sidetracked into background stories, explanations, 'But what about …?' or solutions. As quickly as you politely can, get back to the map in question. Stick doggedly to: 'What are the needs? What are the fears?'

Focus only on one person at a time and do both their needs and their fears before you move on to the next person. Of course, if they later think of something they forgot you could add it in.

What would the absent people *say* are their needs and concerns? For example, you may think that person needs 'to communicate more'. They may not see that as their need. Their need may be 'to have more quiet time' or 'to have longer to think things through'. Be conscious that you are only guessing, as you can never really know what another person needs. What would they be most likely to *say* if they were asked? That's what you write down.

Who really has the need? The way we say things can disguise this. 'They need to be more understanding!' is not about their needs, it's about yours. Put it down on your own list. When in doubt ask: 'Whose need is this?' What they may need is more information so that they can understand you better. If you suddenly get an insight into what you need, consider the possibility that they need it too.

DANIELLE

I'd become a stepmother to a ten-year-old boy and was keen to be a good mother to him. I thought he should take a shower each night and he didn't want to. We were clashing over it frequently and it was interfering with our new relationship. So I started to mentally map the problem: 'Showering every evening ... whose need is this?' I asked myself. I realised very quickly it was my need, not his. So I talked to him about it, asking him what his needs were. He said his need was not to be asked to shower every day! I asked him how often he thought he needed to shower. He reckoned he only needed a shower when he was dirty — which was every few days and always after soccer. I asked him when he thought he would need to shower more often and he immediately said — 'Soon as I start to have BO.' So we agreed that when that happened he would shower every day!

When that time came a few years later he willingly started to shower daily ... and not long after that getting him out of the shower became the new challenge!

Handle digressions by going back to needs. While mapping the needs and fears, it is important to not allow participants to start suggesting solutions. Don't allow questions such as 'Why don't you try ... ', 'Have you thought about doing ... ?'

Don't spend time on long background stories. They're not necessary in order to do an effective map. They can often colour the picture unnecessarily. Go to needs as soon as possible.

Avoid 'Why did you ... ?' questions. Don't allow questions that cause people to defend what they did.

Reshape a 'dissatisfied' comment as a need or fear. Find out what's behind a comment about something in the conflict that isn't working or makes them unhappy; for example, you receive a comment like: 'Meetings are a waste of time. They go on and on.' You could ask: 'What do you need?', 'To spend less time in meetings.' You could also ask, 'What do you fear?', 'Not enough time to get my work done.' This converts what might otherwise be a digression on whether meetings go on for too long, or should go on at all, into part of the mapping process.

Clarify the legitimate needs behind a hidden agenda. You may get a sense that there are hidden needs and concerns such as a particular advantage for one party if a problem is solved one way and not another. Commissions, bonuses, getting the credit, recognition and time out are some of the advantages people like to keep hidden. Legitimise these by including them on the map. A common unexposed pay-off is the need to save face. You will read how this was very important to Albert in Map 2 (see pages 170–1). It appears, sanitised and legitimised, on the finished map as 'to have his authority and power recognised'. Express these hidden needs with compassion. It's okay for people to want such things and it's often okay for solutions to support them.

Mapping Difficult People

We have quite frequently been asked to facilitate maps where the issue was a 'difficult person'. By the way, we really dislike that term. Everybody is somebody's 'difficult person'.[1] We label them 'difficult' because *we* are having difficulty with them. 'We have a personality clash' often really means 'I don't know what is making this person tick and my standard methods of dealing with people are not working here'.

> Behind difficult behaviours are unmet needs or hidden fears that the person is defending in clumsy and often unaware ways

Mapping opens you up to discovering why people are doing what they are doing and how your behaviour is affecting that. You'll often find that people will act in difficult ways if psychologically they feel unsafe. By exploring their needs, we may see what we can do to make them feel safer. We might see what they really want: perhaps it's to be more included. By exploring your own needs, you may see that your expectations may be unrealistic and look for other ways to meet your needs.

Focus on discovering needs. You may start receiving a totally different response from them once you have. There may be ways of meeting their needs that you hadn't previously thought of, and your map might lead you to see new solutions. The crankiness of a teenager may mask a fear that they are not loved by the parent. Perhaps a special outing planned just for them might show them you really do care and fix a lot of other problems at the same time. A lot of negativity from a fellow worker may be mapped as a frustrated need for recognition. You might address this with some positive feedback the next time you meet.

Doing a map with the whole team — including a 'difficult' person — can create an amazing shift, but it needs to be handled very diplomatically — or with the help of an external facilitator. Sometimes we realise that we know so little about what the difficult person really needs that we're motivated to get more information.

How to Read Your Map

READING YOUR MAP:

▶ new perspectives

▶ common ground

▶ special concerns

Look for new perspectives and insights. Once you've drawn up your map, consider individuals' needs and fears you had not taken into account before. Mapping helps you see what it's like to be in the other person's shoes. You might come up with new perspectives on the issue and become aware of factors that hadn't been quite so clear before.

Discover the common ground already present. Create a common vision: point out those values and ideas that are upheld by all. Look for similar needs or interests. They may already appear on your map. They may need discussion to bring them out. In Map 3, on pages 174–5, 'a happy and productive team' was listed by the supervisor. The receptionist and the other team members recognised that it was important for them as well. This was a vision they all shared.

Build new areas of common ground. Ideally, the united goal should be broad enough to include the individual values of each party; for example, a parent cares about homework being done, while their child cares about having fun. The common vision should contain both homework *and* fun.

Look for special concerns. Can you see the areas of difficulty that most need attention?

Analyse the above considerations with all the participants, then list the points demanding attention.

MAP 2

Roger, an account executive in an automotive parts manufacturing company, is required to have daily dealings with his company's biggest client — a large car repair organisation of considerable repute. Albert, the contact person Roger must deal with in the car repair organisation, is very difficult — he can fly off the handle at any moment; he is limited in his capacity to answer questions directly; and is painfully slow to provide necessary information from his own organisation.

Roger has been struggling with the issue for years, and has tried a number of strategies. At one stage he was able to bypass Albert and deal directly with Albert's manager, but that had to stop when the manager found he couldn't handle Albert's irate distress about having his role undermined. The manager asked Roger to bear with the problem, explaining that Albert had spinal degeneration which was often painful.

The frustrations of this situation are a daily challenge for Roger. So he jumped at the opportunity to map his problem at a team-building workshop with a group of his colleagues. They helped him clarify the key people's needs and concerns and then brainstormed options with him. The session revealed several new perspectives and strategies. Roger was re-energised and hopeful that some more support in the situation would make a difference for him. He was willing to try some of the suggestions on how he might negotiate better with Albert and build more rapport.

ROGER, the account executive

NEEDS
- ways to resolve things more quickly
- to be able to get information from others
- to vent frustrations
- more understanding of this situation from colleagues
- less stressful relationship with Albert
- more support from management of the client organisation

FEARS
- this one client takes up too much time
- all dealings are more complex than needed
- lost opportunities with other clients
- sales could decline

ALBERT, the contact person

NEEDS
- to maintain profitability
- to control inventory with a just in-time policy
- to have his authority and power recognised
- to keep things as simple as possible
- to look after his own health

FEARS
- stress and its impact on his own well-being
- losing his competitive advantage
- Roger going over his head

LIAISING WITH ALBERT

ROGER'S MANAGER

NEEDS
- Roger to be happy and productive
- quick results
- quicker decisions out of the client organisation

FEARS
- business decline
- Roger may have had enough
- Roger losing his cool with an important client
- the client organisation placing such big orders that it influences direction and decision-making

ALBERT'S MANAGER

NEEDS
- occasionally to vent his frustrations about Albert (because he is being forced to keep him on)
- maintain acceptable working relationship with Albert
- support Albert in his illness
- continue smooth purchasing through Roger's automotive parts supply company without holding large stocks

FEARS
- stock not arriving as he needs it
- loss of reputation and status
- becoming a low priority for supplier because they get too frustrated

Some of the options arising from the brainstorming included:

- The automotive parts supply company and the repair organisation could put together a joint forecast of stock movements.

- Create some standard documents for frequently required explanations.

- Roger invites Albert over to the company to show him over the factory and to take him to lunch.

- Roger introduces Albert to other peers in the industry.

- Simplify processes for Albert.

- Acknowledge Albert's strengths and his value.

- Build more rapport by addressing the needs of Albert's style (which was Conscientious).

- Understand his illness more.

- Ask for Albert's feedback.

- Someone else manages the account for a while.

- Do a map with Roger, Albert and their managers to focus on ways to smooth and enhance how business is done between them.

- Roger's team to show more support for Roger.

When is a Good Time to Make a Map?

You can make a map any time, anywhere and with anyone! It is best to do your map on a large piece of paper, although many a first-class map has been made on a paper napkin in a restaurant! At a meeting, you are best to organise butcher's paper clipped onto a whiteboard. Write with thick pens so everyone can see. Try to use several colours — one colour for the issue and the parties' names, another for needs, another for fears.

Make a map quickly in your head before starting on a new venture: a job or living arrangement, planning a holiday with friends, making deals or agreements. You don't need to be involved in a conflict to create a map — use it to prevent conflict. Maps can be used before drawing up a plan; for example, where a financial cutback is essential, a mapping exercise with all concerned can make a huge difference to implementing the cutbacks and to the attitudes of those involved.

You can create a map by yourself. At times you'll only be guessing how it is for the other parties, but the process broadens your perspective. It will probably highlight some areas you want to know more about, which will give you some good questions about needs to ask others before you head into solutions.

It's great to do a map together with other people. You can initiate a mapping session at work, at home or with any other group activities you are involved in. It's quite simple to say: 'Let's get a clear picture of the situation before we go further. Let's hear everyone's needs and concerns on this issue.' Sometimes creating the map with the help of others who aren't involved, and can see it freshly, can have advantages.

Maps can be productive for:

• personal relationships

• business relationships (see Map 2)

• households

• team-building and team problem-solving (see Map 3)

• preparations for business negotiations

• negotiations that have broken down (see Map 1)

• custody arrangements and property divisions at the end of a marriage or long-term relationship

• where communications are difficult or there is a 'problem' person (see Map 2)

• advertising briefs

• factions not working well together

• planning meetings

- impending change; for example, forming or carrying out new policies and regulations in large organisations

- mediations.

Mapping addresses the future. You make maps so that you can come up with some real options. Use mapping for current situations, not those which are no longer negotiable; for example, mapping an office policy which is already in place is pointless, but some unresolved effects from the policy may be helped by mapping. Stay on track with your map. If you find that you are sidetracking or that other issues keep coming up, a second map may be required. While mapping the issue of liaising with Albert in Map 2, the issue of the whole business relationship between the two companies emerged as significant. It needed to be dealt with and warranted another map.

Reveal conflicting wishes in terms of needs and concerns. We often think that if we have obviously conflicting needs — for example, two people wanting the same promotion — then it is dangerous to make the clash visible. Concealing a difficulty is usually far more risky than exposing it. Revealing the problem often helps new options emerge.

MAP 3

A section supervisor felt very uncomfortable about confronting a receptionist who was taking so much time off that other staff members had to cover the reception area. The receptionist, a single mother, was often called away over difficulties with her three-year-old child. The supervisor, a reserved woman, found it hard to handle the situation, and her hesitancy annoyed other section staff. A mapping exercise made the supervisor more confident about tackling the problem. Some of the options she went off to work with were:

- Hold a staff meeting and map the issue.
- Help the receptionist set her priorities. She herself could decide if it was appropriate for her to hold this job.
- Help the receptionist explore more reliable childcare options.
- Consider the reception work as a job-share position.
- Create a backup roster system with the staff so that relief would not be so random.

SECTION SUPERVISOR

NEEDS

- to have the work done
- to carry out her responsibilities and report to her supervisor
- to care about the receptionist and her personal life
- to nurture the people in her team
- to overcome her difficulty with being assertive
- a happy and productive team

FEARS

- loss of respect and status from above and from her team
- being bossy or hard
- loss of control
- others will gang up and report her
- the other workers' anger and resentment
- upsetting the receptionist

COVERING RECEPTION

RECEPTIONIST

NEEDS

- to look after her child
- to have an income
- support as a single mum
- to cope as a mum and to show that she can
- respect and acceptance from the team
- stability

FEARS

- job loss
- failure as a mother
- being reprimanded by supervisor
- discussing her situation and being seen as not coping
- loss of control
- stigma of being a single mum
- having her child reported as neglected

OTHER TEAM MEMBERS

NEEDS

- to fulfil their own roles without disruption
- to have their status and time respected
- to show support and care for the receptionist but not at the expense of their own workload
- a receptionist they can rely on

FEARS

- the problem won't change or will get worse
- being manipulated
- not being able to refuse to cover reception
- feeling powerless
- being used
- being unsupported
- being seen as inadequate in their own jobs because of not having enough time

The Benefits of Mapping

- **Mapping structures the conversation** and usually keeps it away from excesses of emotion. People can lose their tempers any time but do tend to keep them toned down while mapping — quite unconsciously they redirect their energy away from attack and start pointing at the relevant spot on the map.

- **The tone shifts from confrontation to exploration.** It creates a group process so that the problem can be aired and solved cooperatively.

- **Mapping provides a forum where people can say what they need.**

- **Mapping builds empathy** and acknowledges people who may feel they were not being understood before.

- **It enables you to see your own and other people's points of view more clearly.**

- **It makes common ground obvious and creates the opportunity to structure a common vision.** It organises everyone's views on an issue.

- **It points out new directions.** Analyse your map for new insights, common ground and a common vision. Focus on key issues and design solutions or managing strategies that support as many needs as possible for all the people involved.

Now you are ready for and may have already started on the next stage — developing options (see Chapter 9, Designing Options).

EXERCISE: your own map

The best way to teach yourself to map is to practise. Try one now. Is there an issue you are dealing with that could be helped by a map? If you can't think easily of an issue, consider the division of household chores in your home. Any problems there? It's a common issue in most households! Perhaps it deserves a map.

SUMMARY

Maps can be done alone, with those involved or with others with a fresh view.

Doing a map:

STEP 1: Label the issue in a general statement.

STEP 2: Name the parties involved.

STEP 3: Contemplate and write down the needs and fears of each person or group you have listed.

STEP 4: Read your map. Look for:
- new perspectives
- common ground
- special concerns.

Remember that behind difficult behaviours there are unmet needs.

Note

1 See Andrew Floyer Acland, *Resolving Disputes without Going to Court* (UK: Century, 1995) pp 159–60 on 'difficult people'

CHAPTER 9
Designing Options

Can we explore creative options together?

Mapping has given you the opportunity to survey the terrain. Developing new options for better solutions is the next logical step. Good conflict resolvers excel at designing options, thinking spontaneously, breaking old habits and trying new ways. Explore as many possibilities as you can. This is a creative process that is like diving into a treasure-trove of possibility. What you bring to the surface depends on what you are looking for. When you are looking for solutions where everyone can win and everyone's needs are met, that's what you're more likely to find. Moreover, you'll reduce power struggles and help the relationship in the process. Power politicking takes place when people don't believe that their needs will be considered. When we search for solutions that acknowledge other people's needs as well as our own we are saying: 'I care about you', 'I respect you' and 'You have needs and so do I!'

There are three distinct stages:

• creating options

• choosing the most suitable ones

• acting on the chosen options.

Stage 1: Creating Options

Define the problem in terms of needs (see Chapter 8, Mapping the Conflict). Once you are clear what everyone's needs are, open up the possibilities. You are trying to design an answer that incorporates a win for everyone and turns the protagonists into partners in the search for a solution. When you get the process right, the substance usually follows. The process should demonstrate in practical ways that your heart and intentions are in the right place.

This is the time to be creative; it needs a different head space to the analytical and reflective mode you need for mapping. Do something to stimulate the creative juices. If you've been working on a problem for some time, it might be good to take a short break.

Get up, move around, break the tension. Perhaps find a reason to laugh. Perhaps take a moment to play — toss a ball around if you can! If you consider you've been stuck in one mindset, consider turning around the seating in the room by ninety or 180 degrees. You're trying to engage the other side of your brain. Left-hemisphere thinking is where your logical, analytical and sequential processing of information takes place. The right hemisphere, the part of your brain that will give you substantially new and creative solutions, focuses on holisitic thinking, is less dependent on speech and more dependent on pattern recognition. You want to move out of the old ways of seeing the problem and change perspective. You have to be willing to dislodge old assumptions and manipulate your new data in different ways. You want to transform the situation, perhaps bring into being something that didn't exist before. You want to use the power of synergy to accomplish together what you could not do alone. It's a sign of your emotional intelligence when you can act in synergistic ways. It means you'll accomplish more than can happen with each person acting independently. It gives you a new equation: 1+1=3!

Collect suggestions without evaluating them yet

This phase is about exploration and discovery. Allow possibilities and let them remain as possibilities. Even mutually exclusive possibilities can be allowed to enter and sit alongside each other. At this early stage, don't judge the ideas that are coming up, just keep encouraging their flow.

Brainstorming

- Brainstorm to create a smorgasbord of options. Your aim is to come up with as many ideas as you can before stopping.

- Appoint one person to record all suggestions. If a group is involved, write up suggestions with thick coloured pens on a large sheet of butcher's paper so that everyone can see the ideas.

- Welcome all ideas, no matter how crazy. Allow a little humour and nonsense if at all appropriate — this can release tension and generate some lateral thinking. Be bold — what seems impossible might be the seed of good ideas.

- This is the time to explore, to look for possibilities, not to judge, assess, reject or choose.

- Take in all the ideas without prejudice, commitment or evaluation and write them down. Avoid stifling new possibilities or implying people should stand behind any option they come up with. During a difficult negotiation, you might choose to hold a brainstorm and define it as a process without prejudice or commitment to any solutions developed during the session.

The more options and potential solutions there are on the table, the more likely it is that people will find one or two that will work. Remember that people feel more committed to solutions they have had a hand in developing, so make every effort to involve the other person or people in the process.

Using Questions

Questions open our minds to new possibilities. They are especially helpful if we see one solution to the exclusion of other options. Don't let the solution 'set' too quickly; instead, use questions to prod creativity. Here are some questions you might find useful:

- 'What are all the possible options for creating the outcome you/we want?'
- 'How else could this situation be addressed?'
- 'What would happen if …?'
- 'What can we do that would help?'
- 'What else might work?'
- 'How else could we do it?'
- 'If you had a magic wand what would you do?'

If you can't make a decision, it's usually because you haven't got enough information or can't understand it. What would help?

- Is more information needed? From where? Who should have it?
- Do you need information presented more simply; for example, illustrations, summaries?
- Do you need clarification?
- Look for leads. What is worth following through?

Being Practical

Conflict resolution is not just about people skills — it's also essential to design practical solutions. You don't keep on yelling at the toddler not to touch the vase; you move the vase. You can often structure situations so that the problem doesn't arise. If people keep using a short cut and it is annoying, lock the door. Many issues can be solved by practical design.

Information and its flow

Does the solution you design need to include strategies for information flow on a regular basis? Consider:

- earlier reporting

- regular times to talk

- more commitment to passing on the information.

Structure and procedures

Do structures or procedures need to be updated? Consider:

- new lines of authority and responsibility

- updated report-back systems

- changed instructions

- introducing a formalised set of procedures

- more planning.

Objects and services

Are physical objects or available services part of the solution? Consider:

- purchasing equipment/furniture

- employing someone new

- hiring equipment/furniture

- hiring services; for example, physical help, medical, business, personnel, legal advice, mediation

- reallocating or relocating space, equipment, furniture

- reallocating tasks.

Currencies

Everyone is a potential ally. How can you support each other?

What is cheap for me and valuable for them?

Find out what they need that you could easily offer. Look for something they could easily offer you that is helpful or valuable for you.

These are the 'currencies' in which you can trade. Currencies might include services, timing, recognition and security. Good solution-building works on a broad front. The aim is to develop a package plan that encompasses a wide range of factors. Generate balanced benefits for all parties. What would it take to meet more needs for more people? The aim is to survey everyone's needs and sweeten the pie for yourself and for the other person, starting with low-cost components. You will often be able to trade concessions.

Best Alternatives

In designing options in a difficult situation it is thoroughly worthwhile to design a good alternative in case you can't reach an agreement. Professional negotiators, including Roger Fisher of the Harvard Negotiation Project, use the word BATNA (Best Alternative To a Negotiated Agreement) as shorthand for this key concept.[1] If your best alternative is a good one, you'll have more power in your negotiation. Being too eager can be a disadvantage when you're bargaining. The other person can sense how badly you want something and knows you will agree even if they are inflexible on terms. You can't sit back and wait for a BATNA to just appear, you'll need to create it and that might mean doing some research. If having a BATNA would help, first create a list of possible alternatives, then polish some of the more promising ideas and finally convert one at least into a real possibility. If the problem with the boss doesn't work out, your best alternative might be to look for another job. Is it worth calling a recruitment agency to find out what's on their books? If your negotiation with your preferred dealership doesn't go as well as you'd like, what price can you get that car for from another dealer?

Consequence Confrontation

If you are dealing with someone who refuses to budge or won't listen to you, it may be important to work out what your options are. You may need to outline the consequences if they refuse to change their behaviour. Don't threaten, just inform them of the inevitable consequences if things go on as they are. Save consequence confrontation as a last resort (see pages 91–2).

Consequence confrontation: Would it help or hinder?

Chunking

Sometimes you can't solve the whole problem but you can solve bits of it. When the task is huge, break the problem down into smaller, more manageable chunks. Consider what would at least manage aspects of the problem and deal with some of the issues if the whole thing is too overwhelming or unchangeable. Chunking nibbles around the edges — it doesn't fix it, but it helps.

Break down the problem into manageable chunks

SVEN

Sven has two children by his first marriage. He doesn't have custody but he still keeps regular and devoted contact with his children. His ex-wife Ingrid's new husband has been offered an excellent promotion in another city. It seems that the family will move and Sven is very upset about losing the close contact with his children. He tried breaking down the problem into smaller parts and considered the following questions: what are my needs, values, limits and priorities? What are their needs, values, limits and priorities?

He could manage parts of the problem with the following strategies:

- Plan long school holiday visits.
- Clarify agreements on child support and air fares.
- Take time off work when the children visit.
- Telephone often. Telephone mainly before Ingrid's new husband comes home.
- Children to know what Sven provides them with; for example, he pays for school fees, new shoes, etc.

EXERCISE: chunking

Consider a current problem, one that seems to have no simple answer. List three major needs, values, limits or priorities for you and three for the other person. Put one item from your list with one item from theirs to build a common vision; for example, for a teenager who wants to leave home, what could you do so that she has her independence *and* keeps in contact? Is there anything that would help just that part of the problem? If you can't think of a new option to help the bit of the problem you've chosen, put together two other items from both lists and try again. Don't give up until you come up with at least one new creative idea to handle some piece of the problem.

Stage 2: Choosing the Most Suitable Options

Evaluate each option:
1. Is it feasible?
2. Is it enough?
3. Is it fair?

The creating stage can be bypassed if needs are clearly understood and one solution jumps out as the perfect answer. However, if you have used a brainstorming approach, don't move to choosing options until time is up or a good number of suggestions are on the table. At the end of brainstorming, you might rate each suggestion: 1. very useful; 2. lacking some elements; 3. not practicable. This helps consider all the suggestions.

Suggestions can also be evaluated according to these criteria:

Is it feasible?

💡 How feasible? When can it happen?

💡 What if ...?

💡 How would you feel if ...?

💡 If ... happened would that help with ...?

Is it enough?

💡 Does it solve the problem?

💡 Does it satisfy everyone's needs adequately?

💡 Is that sufficient to satisfy your need for ...?

💡 What will you do if ...?

💡 How will you know when it has happened?

Is it fair?

💡 How do you judge if something's fair?

Fair often means *equal*. If you can, find an objective yardstick: equivalent money, time, benefits or workloads might be considered. 'Fair' might be based on *precedence*. It may be worth researching independent evaluations of market price or recent sales. 'Fair' might be influenced by *savings*. Perhaps you might calculate how many hours or how much money this suggestion would save. 'Fair' might be judged by your *legal rights*. What does the law say? After a divorce with similar circumstances, what property settlement arrangements are common? When loud sound is the problem, how many decibels constitute unreasonable disturbance? 'Fair' may be what is regarded as *ethical*, though this can be hard to measure, and is culture-specific. Finding the right independent yardstick can cut through unrealistic expectations and make a big difference to satisfaction levels when the agreement is reached. Relevant questions include:

💡 'Does that sound fair to you?'

💡 'Do you think you can live with that?'

💡 'How would we be able to tell if that is fair?'

Many other factors will affect the options you choose. Consider the areas of common ground: if you both want better communication, set meeting dates may get a high priority. Consider where your needs dovetail. Consider what must be included in the plan for it to be acceptable to the other person. For instance, must they be seen to have a win? Does the plan need to include something that helps them save face? Is there someone behind the scenes pushing a particular point of view that must be acknowledged? Are there other vital issues, yet to be discussed, that still must be considered? You may use other people's suggestions, if they're reasonable, even though you believe you already have a perfectly good plan. That's because they're likely to be more enthusiastic about their plan than yours, even if it's substantially the same!

Stage 3: Acting on the Chosen Options

Many a great plan fizzles for lack of follow-through. Formally or informally, plan the steps.

• What are the tasks?
• Who will do what?
• By when does each task need to be done?

Discuss what each of you will do and draft a schedule. If the solution works for you both and you have arrived at it in partnership, both sides can be trusted to carry out their part of the plan. Make sure you each understand what you have to do, and plan a specific review time. Put it in your diaries!

SUMMARY

Develop solutions that build in wins for everyone. Wherever possible, do it together.

STAGE 1: Creating Options

1. Define the problem in terms of needs.

2. Develop options together.

3. Brainstorm: • Do not debate • Do not justify • Do not censor

4. Be practical. Consider: • Information and its flow • Structures and procedures • Objects and services

5. Design your currencies, your best alternative to a negotiated agreement (BATNA) and consequence confrontations, if needed.

6. Chunking: break up the problem into smaller and more manageable portions.

STAGE 2: Choosing the most suitable options

Evaluate: • Is it feasible? • Is it enough? • Is it fair?

STAGE 3: Acting on the chosen options

Tasks to be undertaken: • By whom? • By when? • Review when?

Additional reading

1. Edward de Bono, *Serious Creativity* (UK: Harper Collins, 1992)
   Edward de Bono, *Six Thinking Hats* (USA: First Back Bay, 1999)
   Roger Fisher and William Ury, *Getting to Yes: Negotiating Agreement without Giving in* (USA: Penguin, 1991)

CHAPTER 10
Negotiation

How can I be hard on the problem and considerate of others and their needs?
How can we make the best deal possible that is fair for both of us?

Have you ever had to do any of the following:

- Ask your boss for a raise or some time off?
- Deal with too many people asking you to do things all at once?
- Buy new equipment for the company?
- Work out who will do the household chores?
- Plan how you will live with someone else?
- Organise repairs or renovations for your house or office?
- Sort out where to go on a holiday or an outing?

We are constantly negotiating and exchanging commitments and promises. Any time two people need to reach an agreement, they have to negotiate if the terms are not clear. Negotiation is what business is all about — arrangements for buying, selling or exchanging goods and services. It is also what relationships are about — working or living in the same space, planning who does what and who decides what. It goes on between countries, over the exchange of products or in an international crisis.

Take a minute to place negotiation in the context of your life. When do you negotiate? Which aspect of negotiating is hardest for you? When a negotiation is not going well, it's easy to see it as some sort of contest where one person will win and the other will lose. Where one person takes too aggressive a stance, the other can polarise their position and the negotiation can break down. Depending on your natural tendencies and how you see your power in relation to the other person, you may go into fight or flight mode (see Chapter 1, Responding to Conflict). In fight mode the hardest thing might be controlling your temper and not pushing for what you want at the expense of the other person. In flight mode the hardest thing is to stand your ground and not give in too easily.

The objective of negotiation is generally not to come out on top, but to reach a balanced agreement that seems fair to both parties. That's an agreement the parties will stick to. Neither fight nor flight modes are likely to achieve this. What is needed is a flow of purpose, direction, power and flexibility.

Preparation

What practical steps help negotiations to flow?

1. Remember, Conflict is Opportunity

Edgar ran a small importing company and had just received delivery of a well-known brand of sunglasses. He emailed a flyer to his usual customers and one replied saying he would take 100 pairs at $30 a pair. To move 100 pairs with one e-mail would be excellent, but Edgar had asked for $40. He'd done his costings carefully and felt this price gave him a reasonable profit. If conflict is opportunity, his challenge was how to do something creative with this problem.

2. Move into Discovery Mode

Edgar phoned the customer: 'Phil, I really need $40 a pair for these, to make it economical for me. What could we do about that?'

3. Look for Ways to Improve Both Parties' Situation

Phil said he didn't feel his small boutique business could really afford to pay more than $30. It could have looked like an impasse. Phil, staying quite friendly but firm on his limit, said to Edgar: 'Oh well, let's leave it. Next time you're in town come and show me your range. Maybe there's something else I'd be interested in.' Edgar wanted to take him up on that and started assembling what he would show Phil.

4. Free Yourself from Fixed Ideas about Solutions

Edgar was going through his stock and was reminded of some old stock of sunglasses cases that hadn't moved and he'd just written off. He'd be happy to move them at almost any price. He threw a couple into his sample bag. He had a few more written-off items like this with only small numbers of stock left. Freeing himself from any fixed ideas about what deal he could strike, he put more samples of leftover stock into his sample bag. Here was the germ of an idea.

5. Make a map

For most negotiations, the most effective preparation is to make a Needs and Fears map (see Chapter 8, Mapping the Conflict). Fears include anxieties and concerns — those 'I wouldn't like it if ...' or 'I'm worried about ...'. It's particularly valuable where there's a large psychological and personality-based component in the negotiation — and there nearly always is.

Edgar met Phil that Thursday and took him to the little cafe in the arcade where Phil's shop was located. Edgar put his sample bag on the bench seat between them. Edgar sounded like he was chatting, but mentally he was making a map: 'When you buy from me, Phil, what do you need?' 'Well, I need to like the product. It has to be a fair price, of course, so that I can get a reasonable mark-up. Sometimes I can use a really cheap item in an advertising campaign or to draw people into the shop. I like it that I have an account with you and I don't have to pay up front as I have to do with some of the fly-by-nighters who come in flogging their wares.' Edgar offered Phil some of his own needs. 'Phil, I find it helpful that at the end of your thirty days you pay your bill. I can rely on you because I've seen you trade here quite successfully for, what is it, ten years now? I really value that we've done successful business for that many years. You're not afraid to be innovative. You're always interested in the latest stuff. I can test my market on you.' Edgar's major concern was losing Phil as a client, and he hated being seen as too expensive to deal with. The coffee came just then, so he didn't say that. Perhaps it could have weakened his ability to stick to his bottom line.

6. Ask Yourself, 'What Outcome Do I Want?'

If you want a specific outcome, what needs, values and long-term issues are you taking into consideration? Don't forget the intangibles, such as recognition, security, or an improved relationship.

Edgar asked himself what outcome he wanted from this visit with Phil. He did want this deal. Of course, he hoped for $40 per pair for the glasses. He wanted these sunglasses in Phil's shop. It would encourage other retailers to stock them. Equally important was his desire to maintain the good working relationship with Phil.

7. Estimate the Range of Tangible Results that Might Define this Outcome

You'll have more flexibility if you set upper and lower limits.

For Edgar this meant he would like $40 per pair, that is, $4000 for the whole deal. If Phil was going to stick to his $30 limit, Edgar needed another angle.

8. Have the Facts Ready

Do your homework thoroughly, even though you will rarely need to bring into conversation all the facts and possibilities you have considered. It's a bit like an exam — you don't know what area you will be tested on until you're faced with it.

Edgar had gone over his costings before he visited Phil. He'd checked out how much similar models from that manufacturer were costing and he knew Phil was unlikely to get that brand for $30 from anyone.

9. Work on Your Case

Be well prepared on all the substantive issues that might come up. Prepare concise answers to:

(a) What do I want? What's the heart of what I intend to say?

(b) Who am I asking? Am I approaching the right person for decision-making? Does that person have a preferred way of operating that I should take into account?

(c) How will this person benefit? Carefully consider what their needs and interests are — and how to address them. What tactics and strategies will move them?

(d) Consider the best way of building rapport with this person. It is worthwhile identifying the behavioural styles and values of the people you are approaching. Consider where they fit on the DISC model (see Chapter 3, Empathy, Part II). Adapt your style to present a case that is appropriate to the needs of their style.[1] Consider also the five core needs discussed in Chapter 6, Managing Emotions: people's need for *appreciation*, a sense of *affiliation* with you, their own *autonomy*, respect for their *status* and meaningful and fulfilling *roles*. How might you address some of these?

(e) Consider currencies — what we can trade with each other. Your map outlining needs and fears of the people involved is a useful starting place. What can you do to meet the other person's needs? What can they do to meet yours? What is cheap for me to offer and valuable for them to receive? What is cheap for them to offer and valuable for me to receive (see also Currencies, page 184)?

Edgar already knew Phil's operating style pretty well. Phil liked to hold the reins. Edgar saw Phil as Direct in the DISC model style. He knew he'd better get to the point fairly fast. He had only the time for that one cup of coffee to cut the deal. He had several options with small things that Phil might be willing to stock. If he could interest Phil in stocking about 100 of these things at about $8 an item, Edgar would still make a profit on goods that were low-cost to him and high-value to Phil. Phil might go for it, but he would want to feel free to make his own selection.

It's worthwhile thinking outside the square. People need things you can offer that may not be directly related to the negotiation at hand. You might be negotiating a price with a tradesman for some work around your home or office. Apart from the

**Become a better
negotiator:
consider a wider
range of options**

tradesman's needs for fair recompense for his efforts, he might also need a reference to help him capture future business. This could become a currency you trade with him. 'If you give me a really good deal, I'm happy to write you a reference.'

Take another example: in negotiating a salary package, you might consider such currencies as money (of course!), but also flexible work hours, status, job title, office and equipment (the latest computer is often tempting!), special superannuation benefits, help with a housing loan, make of company car, performance-based bonuses, holidays, career path, on-the-job learning, further education and child-care. Choose which issues you'll put into the negotiation arena and be flexible.

Consider tangible benefits such as goods, services, price, orders, volume and future orders. Also consider intangible benefits such as self-worth, friendship, public image, reputation and experience. What you can offer is your bargaining power. Their power comes from what you need from them.

You might plan to use the format '*If* I do this for you, *then* will you do that for me?'[2] If you give a benefit, you may need a benefit in exchange. If you go for this method your aim is to investigate and swap currencies. There are many ways of being creative with currencies; for example, 'I need my plants watered while I am away. Could I offer you my car space for two months in exchange for watering the plants?'

**If you give me
something, then I'll
give you something**

A note of warning: If you overdo trade-offs, the other person can feel bribed or coerced. 'You do the washing-up and I'll give you money for an ice-cream' may not develop the spirit of voluntary cooperation in a child that makes a family work well.

'If ..., then ...' can be a useful format to discuss terms without committing yourself to them immediately. 'Under the right circumstances I would be willing to ... What would you be willing to offer in exchange?' is another format you could consider during preparation. Sometimes you can create a complete package with all that each side offers and receives lumped together. Your strategy might be to introduce the elements slowly rather than all at once. It's very helpful to know in advance what you have up your sleeve if you need to sweeten a deal. Your purpose in the preparation phases is to work out how you will conduct the interaction so that you can build a fair and balanced deal for all parties.

> Remember: fair deals are the ones that stick

'I've included some sale items today, Phil. The price really depends on how many you take. Do any of them interest you?' Phil liked the idea, and enjoyed making his own choices on items and quantities. A couple of times Phil wanted to include something in the package that was this year's stock and Edgar knew he didn't want to let it go at $8. Phil seemed keen to include some $10 lipsticks. He wanted only ten and as a sign of goodwill Edgar threw the lipsticks into the pile of sale-price goodies. If his negotiation came out as he had in mind, the lipstick was a deal he could live with.

10. Work on the Other Person's Case

Try to think as they think. Put yourself in their shoes:

(a) How would they see their case?

(b) What are their options?

(c) What are their immediate difficulties?

(d) What are the implications for them if they say 'yes'? Are they acceptable? Can you spell out positive implications or change the plan to address the negative ones?

(e) What steps will you both take if the other person agrees? Think the steps through for them. Can the plan be built around something that is easy for them to do? Make 'yes' easy to say by helping to lighten their follow-up tasks. Have information ready that they may need — such as a tentative itinerary and costing for a holiday, a list of people available for a job.

Edgar sensed that as Phil had twice stuck to his $30 offer on the original sunglasses, he probably wouldn't budge now. Phil prided himself on smart trading and Edgar suspected Phil's wife in the background often set limits on his purchasing budget. It was looking like Edgar would be able *to get Phil to take some of these last-season items. Edgar phrased his big move in the negotiation carefully. He needed to have a deal that included the 100 pairs at $30 to make it worthwhile. So he said: 'Phil, I could give you a really good deal but the only way I can see it working at my end is this: so long as you take the 100 pairs of sunnies you're interested in at your price of $30, I could let you have 100 of these (waving at Phil's pile of items) at $8 each.' Phil was interested but hesitant.*

Edgar could see he needed to sweeten the pie a little more. 'Phil, would it help you say "yes" if I gave you two months rather than one to pay for the extra items?' A little glint came into Phil's eyes. Had Edgar found a way round the wife's budget? Now they had a deal that suited Phil as well as Edgar. They shook hands and finished their coffees, chatting about the weekend's big soccer match.

With some negotiations there is no time to think first. For example, the phone rings and someone springs a surprise request

Make yes easy to say

on you. It is quite acceptable to explain that you need to collect more information and will get back to them. That way you can take the time you need to prepare.

11. Consider Your Own Personality

Did you decide which was your usual DISC style (see page 58)? Armed with this information, consult the table on the opposite page to see what steps you could take to minimise problems your weaknesses could cause.

DISC: TURN YOUR WEAKNESSES INTO STRENGTHS

Find your style — when negotiating focus on:

DIRECT	CONSCIENTIOUS
• listening attentively	• thinking laterally
• showing empathy	• being flexible
• giving constructive feedback	• listening sensitively
• including others in decision-making	• allowing more time for exploring feelings and concerns

INFLUENCING	STABILISING
• preparing thoroughly	• making 'I' statements
• focusing on the task	• setting limits on others talking
• putting sufficient emphasis on others' concerns	• ensuring that adequate attention is given to the task
• listening carefully to others' comments	• encouraging flexibility and constructive change

Edgar was an influencer. It had been a challenge for him to prepare thoroughly. He would have much preferred, before striking his deal, to have taken half an hour to 'warm' Phil up, talking soccer and family — but he realised that wasn't Phil's style. He'd noted Phil's hesitation when he'd suggested that the extra $8 items would have to be part of the sunglasses order. It was then that he realised he could strike a deal that would work not only for Phil, but also for Phil's wife, the careful money manager in the background.

12. Prepare Your Opening Statement

Your opening statement needs to present your objective. It should be clear and concise. Author and negotiator Milo Frank suggests that ideally it should take thirty seconds or less to deliver.[3] It helps to consider the other person's needs, as well as your own, when planning what to say. The following exercise shows how to create your 'opener'.

EXERCISE: opening statement

Think of a situation you want to negotiate on, or use one of these suggestions:

- Arrange a week's leave from work.

- Plan how you will divide up the household chores.

- Extend your deadline for completing a task.

Write a brief statement to open the negotiation.

1. **Engage interest**

   What would make this person interested? How might they benefit?

2. **State objective**

   What do I want to achieve? Present what you want in terms of what the other person needs.

3. **Invite response**

   Where do we go from here? How will I invite the next step?

For example, 'I know you want the business to run as efficiently as possible. I'm wondering if we can get a courier service to collect the mail from the post office each day, then we can be sure when we'll get it and it won't be forgotten in the rush. Also, it would free up the staff to get on with other things. I've inquired and the cost would be about $ ... a month. Would you be willing to give this a trial?'

Points to consider:

- Is the statement concise and clear?

- Will the other person feel that you have addressed their needs?

- What other information might they need?

- Is there anything in your words or body language that may encourage a 'no' rather than 'yes' response?

Once you have done all the preparation you are able to do, it is time to move into interaction with the other party.

STEPS OF NEGOTIATION

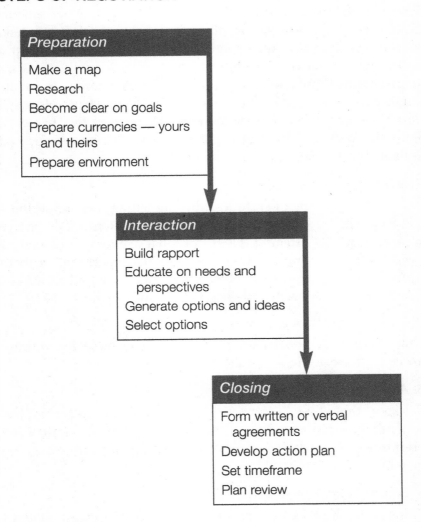

Preparation

Make a map
Research
Become clear on goals
Prepare currencies — yours and theirs
Prepare environment

Interaction

Build rapport
Educate on needs and perspectives
Generate options and ideas
Select options

Closing

Form written or verbal agreements
Develop action plan
Set timeframe
Plan review

Interaction

1. Centre, Flow, Make Contact

Centring is a great way to calm anxiety. Don't forget to breathe deeply into your belly. You may want to deliberately calm and deepen your breathing pattern. Use the image of flow to remind yourself how you want your energy to move throughout the negotiation. Don't contract; make contact. Fill the relationship 'space' with the energy of your attention. You will need to monitor yourself frequently to make sure you stay out of reaction mode (See Chapter 1, Responding to Conflict, for more on these issues).

2. Set up a Climate of Agreement

Focus on the process before the content. Make some agreements on how to do the negotiation, plan when you are both free to talk, how much time is available and where you will meet. Set up a collaborative approach with a statement such as, 'Let's work towards something that will suit both of us'. Remember, in a truly successful negotiation everyone wins. Start to build trust. How will you build rapport? Consider the empathy openers in Chapter 3, Empathy, particularly when negotiating with the people-focused Influencing and Stabilising behavioural styles.

3. Stay in Discovery Mode

Listen to how it is for the other side. Tell them how it is for you

Be open to learning something new or seeing a different approach. Be patient. Use active listening. *Listen* for what's missing, not said or implied. Look out for what makes you or them uncomfortable. *Listen* for feelings behind the words and observe the tone of voice.

4. Use Appropriate Assertiveness

Talk about your needs and the outcome you hope for without arousing defensiveness. Use short 'I' statements.

5. Avoid Win/Lose Outcomes

For sport that's fine — competition is the challenge to accomplish something — but for personal and business relations win/lose is a poor tactic. If one party remains unsatisfied, there may be ongoing hostility.

6. Broaden the Possibilities or Perspectives

Things often look like a win/lose situation. Your previous analysis of currencies (low-cost for you, high-value to them) should help

Can you change the perspectives?

you here. Use extra factors to build your own and the other person's wins.

Sometimes you can introduce a new factor to change the perspective; for example, 'We could see my movie choice or yours this Saturday night' or 'We could see one of the movies this week and the other next week'.

If only one person can be promoted, the other person might broaden their perspective to consider their wins; for example, what did they learn from the experience? What opportunities are they still free to explore?

7. Be Brief and to the Point

Many a good case has been spoilt by someone being longwinded and unclear.

8. Don't be Afraid to Sell Yourself

Have the courage of your convictions: good plans will work for both parties. People are often afraid to ask for what they really want. In truth, if other people knew what you wanted, they might at least meet you part of the way.

> Ask for 100 per cent of what you want, be willing to hear a no, and work towards a compromise

EMMA

I needed to fix up my garden. I discussed with the gardener, Gary, what I wanted to have done. We planned something quite lovely. He got back to me with a quote for the work: 'Hi, Emma, I've done a costing for you and it will be around $1300.'

I was in shock, I needed to understand why it was so much. 'Wow, that seems like a lot. How did you come to that amount?'

'Well there is a lot of weeding to do, so there's about twenty hours' labour in that. Then you want fertiliser and the irrigation system put in. The plants themselves won't cost too much,' said Gary.

I was thinking on my feet. I could see I needed more information. 'Gary, I'm wondering how much you charge per hour?' Gary said it was $38 an hour for each man. Trying to come up with a cheaper alternative, I asked him, 'Is there any way we could cut down on the hours of labour?'

Gary replied, 'I don't think so, but I could buy a few less plants and a cheaper fertiliser.' That sounded like a good option to me.

Gary asked, 'How much were you wanting to spend?' His mobile cut out; this was perfect for me. It gave me some time to consider what the job was worth to me.

When Gary called back I told him, 'I was hoping to spend around $700.' He asked, 'How about I aim to keep the total under $800?' It was a compromise I could live with.

'That sounds okay, Gary. It makes me feel much more comfortable.' We left our negotiation on good terms and I still got a beautiful garden. The total came to $799! Not quite as many plants as I had hoped for, but I could add the finishing touches myself later.

9. Use Questions to Steer the Negotiation

Asking the right question is an art form: it can open up and redirect negotiation. If you feel that the negotiation is not heading in the direction you would prefer, you can change the flow with a well-placed question; for example, 'Is this plan going to get us where we want to go?'

If you are unsure of what you want to do or say, questions can buy you time and give you more information. Rather than trying to work it out yourself, ask: 'What else is important to you in this situation?'

Specific 'how' or 'what' questions can cover the ground more effectively than assumptions can. When the other person expresses themselves very generally — 'I want the best . . .' — clarify with a question: 'What would be best for you?' If they say: 'It's under control …'; 'I will take care of it …'; 'It'll be looked after …', ask: 'Can you tell me how that will happen?'

Don't assume they mean what you think they mean.

When faced with a blanket statement such as 'All my friends are allowed to …', try asking 'All your friends?' Question 'every' and 'never' statements, too. In the face of too expensive, too much or too many, try a question that raises a comparison. For example, if you are told that air-conditioning is too expensive for the office, ask: 'Expensive in what terms? Are we talking only money? Are there other benefits and losses?'

Questions lead the mind

If the terms are dollars, you could question the cost of sick days or low-work output due to poor conditions.

When faced with rigid statements, go for what is possible. Frame your question so that it leads to the consideration of other possibilities.

Ask: 'What would it take to make it possible?' rather than 'Why is it impossible?'

When faced with can't, won't, must, mustn't, should and shouldn't, accept the difficulty and then ask some leading questions.

(a) 'I can't get the report done in time.'

🔆 Question: 'What do you need in order to get it done on time?'

The reply may be, 'Well, if I had more help, or access to more information …'

(b) 'I don't want to make a fuss about it.'

-?- Question: 'What would make it easier for you to approach him?'

(c) 'I won't do what you're asking — your plan is unacceptable.'

-?- Question: 'What would the plan have to address in order for you to accept it?'

(d) 'I can't come to the meeting. I'll feel self-conscious.'

-?- Question: 'What would you need for you to feel more comfortable attending the meeting?'

When faced with unwillingness to negotiate, or defensiveness, ask the other person what would make them more willing, interested, or more sure about the situation. See more good questions to use when negotiating in Chapter 4, Appropriate Assertiveness.

When faced with high emotions from the other person, the temptation is to defend yourself, top them or justify your position. When you feel defensive, don't defend! It's usually better to wait until you have calmed down before you respond. Instead, sidestep the emotion — sometimes it helps to move physically. Change your position to indicate a change in your mental position.

> **When you feel defensive, become an active listener**

Concentrate on active-listening questions in order to learn the needs and priorities at the source of the other person's problem. Then ask a question that redirects the interaction towards a constructive outcome:

-?- 'What do you really want?'

-?- 'How can we put it right?'

-?- 'I didn't handle that as well as I might have. Is there anything we could do now to help the situation?'

> **Be hard on the problem and considerate of the person**

If it is important to state your own case too, use an 'I' statement after you have acknowledged the legitimacy of their unaddressed needs, otherwise people can misinterpret the statement about your needs as a denial of theirs. For example, 'I can see that you are upset about me being late. I had problems with a sick child at home this morning.' If you must argue, stick to the subject under discussion. Don't drag in other issues.

10. Avoid Using Irritants

Avoid phrases like, 'Well, I'm only being fair and reasonable'. This may suggest that you are implying that they are not being fair and reasonable.

11. Separate the People from the Problem[4]

Be hard on the problem and considerate of the people involved. Let the focus be on the issues rather than on personalities. Forget about being an opponent and act as though you are partners, side by side, facing the problem together. Where possible try to reinforce this physically. A whiteboard or piece of paper on which you can both make notes and from which you can read helps place you in a non-confrontational position. People can then attack what has been written down rather than each other.

12. Include Their Point of View

You needn't agree with it, simply acknowledge it; for example, 'I can see your point of view. From my point of view it's like this ...' or try, 'What I like about that idea is this ... and my concern is that ...'. Notice '*and* my concern'.

Consider the ways door close when you say *but*:[5]
    'Come to lunch!'
    'I'd like to, *but* I've got too much work to do.'
    'Oh well, perhaps another time.'

On the other hand, doors can open with *and*:
    'Come to lunch!'
    'I'd love to ... *and* I've got too much to do!'
    'Oh, is there anything I can do to help?'

Treat opposing points of view as contributions, rather than rejecting them. They add a rounder, more realistic perspective to the problem to be solved. One way you can do this is to use *and* not *but*. Another is to include them as a broader picture of the whole: 'Yes, we must include your point about factory safety. How can we work that into the new plan?'

AND not BUT

13. Emphasise Areas of Agreement

Pay particular attention to common ground — places where your interests, priorities and concerns match each other. Talk often about what you agree with. If stuck, go back over common ground. Each time you take a step forward in the agreement, spell it out.

Research has shown that skilled negotiators comment over three times as much on areas of anticipated agreement and common ground than do average negotiators. This technique is particularly helpful during a negotiation between parties who have little in common and who have previously viewed each other as enemies. From time to time, restate that the objective is to reach agreement: 'Let's see how far we've gone with the agreement now' or, 'What we've achieved so far is …'

14. Shift Unrealistic Expectations

Sometimes the other person doesn't know what is reasonable or feasible. You may need to set them right about money, resources, time or conditions. If they think the service they want costs $50, they are going to be shocked if you're asking for around $200.

Sometimes your own expectations will be unrealistic, too. Asking questions, taking time to collect more facts, and staying flexible will help you to adjust your expectations. Part of your task is to close the gap between their expectations and your demands. You may need to use an objective yardstick with which to assess what's fair (see Chapter 9, Designing Options). Talk, educate them; this will save them loss of face, among other things. Before your child tells you that they want 100 children at their party, tell them you were thinking of about twenty.

15. Be Flexible and Know Your Bottom Line

Negotiation is a bargaining process. You are not negotiating if all you can offer is, 'Take it or leave it'. Be clear in your own mind about your range of flexibility — from what you'd like, to what you would settle for. You may set a bottom line, but aim towards something above it. Without a top limit it is easy to get carried away.

Make a reasonable offer, or ask for a reasonable offer to be made, and then be prepared to negotiate further. For example, to a teenager: 'I think 10.30 pm is a reasonable time for you to be home'. Your child won't agree if they were thinking more along the lines of 2 am — after all, it's their first party! You'll probably end up settling on a time somewhere between 11 pm and midnight. Your bottom line might have been midnight — it would be great if you could pick them up early and be asleep by then.

16. Be Culturally Appropriate in the Negotiation

Before a negotiation, you may need to research the cultural differences of the parties involved. In some cultures there is a lot of margin to bargain, and in others there is less room for movement. A customary level of familiarity might need to be observed. Some cultures require far more formality than others. Even body language can be interpreted differently in various countries.

17. Maintain Your Goal, not Your Route

Keep your long-term purpose in sight and be flexible about how you get there. For example, Bill, an advertising account executive, devised an excellent advertising campaign and outlined it to his client. They were not convinced, so Bill tried even harder to sell his plan, but was getting nowhere. Pushing his point was causing the relationship with his client to become very tense.

What was Bill's long-term goal? Much more than selling this particular campaign, he wanted a satisfied client who would maintain a relationship with the agency. He realised that he would never achieve this while the client did not trust Bill's judgement. Bill saw that he needed to change his position on what he thought should happen. If a good campaign had to be sacrificed for the long-term outcome, then so be it. He began to concentrate more on the client's needs. The relationship warmed again and trust was rebuilt. In fact, within a few weeks the client quite enthusiastically accepted the original plan — with a few minor alterations to save face.

Feed off the feedback

Be willing to change tack if a particular approach doesn't appear to be working. There is more than one way to achieve your goal.

18. Use Conflict-resolving Counter-tactics

People don't always negotiate fairly. They might talk for all the available time, be rude, ignore you, throw in red herrings or come up with unreasonable demands. Many negotiation books offer one-upmanship tactics to counter these tactics. We don't, because they take you away from your position of long-term strength — being partners, not opponents. While it's possible to misuse any tactic, we offer this list to help you steer a win/lose negotiation back to a win/win approach:

✓ Ask a question.

✓ Positively reframe their negative comment.

✓ Let some hostile remarks pass.

✓ Use humour.

✓ 'Please tell me what you think I said.'

✓ Breathe deeply, speak calmly.

✓ Call time out.

✓ Name the ploy. A ploy perceived is no longer a ploy.

✓ Change tack.

✓ Can it be dealt with privately?

✓ Agree to discuss it later.

✓ Write down what is being said.

✓ To counter their biased position, say: 'Show me why that's fair.'

19. Take Notes

Many negotiations require a number of meetings. Some negotiations may extend over years, so accurate note-taking becomes crucial. Always take your own notes even if someone else is formally writing up the minutes. There is enormous potential to distort or misinterpret a conversation while minute-taking. Use your notes to check the accuracy of the minutes. Use your notes to reopen negotiations where you left off last time. Use them to prepare for similar negotiations.

20. Know When to Stop

(a) If emotions run too high, call a break.

(b) If the situation reaches an impasse, leave it alone for a day or so.

(c) If someone uses an unfair tactic that throws you off balance, give yourself time out. Go to the bathroom or make a cup of tea. Centre yourself before responding.

(d) Deflect to another topic if an issue becomes too hot.

(e) If you think information is being withheld, take a break and talk to people separately.

(f) Sometimes a negotiation just won't work, even though you have tried everything. Break off in a way that makes it possible to return to the negotiation on some other occasion.

Closing

Assess the Agreement

Tune in for a moment to your emotions. These questions may help you decide if your agreement will work well:

- Is there something you still need to cover? Have both parties really chosen this contract?

- Will the agreement resolve or at least manage the problem?

- Can both parties really fulfil their promises?

- Is the agreement specific enough about how, when, where, who and how much?

- Is it balanced — do both sides share the responsibility for making it work?

- Is a follow-up or review time built into the plan?

Confirm Your Agreement

In informal negotiations, summarise what has been agreed to. It's always worth going over an agreement in case the other person has understood it differently to you. Jot down the terms for future reference.

In business it pays to document the agreement and provide both parties with a copy. Documentation can take the form of a memo, an invoice, an exchange of letters, or a formal contract. In the home, it is surprisingly valuable to post a note on the refrigerator with significant agreements, such as the division of chores. The purpose of a clear contract is to minimise ambiguity so that misunderstandings and reinterpretations, which might lead to future conflict, are unlikely.

Clear contracts minimise future conflicts

When you reach an agreement, stop, acknowledge — and celebrate!

SUMMARY
Preparation

1. What are the needs? What are the fears? What outcome do you want?

2. Collect the facts.

3. Work on the other person's case as well as your own.

4. Make 'yes' easy to say.

5. Prepare a concise opener.

Interaction
Set up a climate of agreement.

1. Listen to how it is for the other side. Tell them how it is for you. The elements of 'I' statements may be useful.

2. Build in wins for everyone.

3. Avoid win/lose outcomes.

4. Ask questions to steer the negotiation.

5. Be hard on the problem and considerate of the people.

6. Include opposing points of view, rather than rejecting them. They add a rounder perspective to the problem to be solved. Use *and* not *but* to incorporate them.

7. Be flexible. Know your bottom line. Maintain your goal, but not necessarily your route. If something's not working, try a different approach.

Closing
Make clear contracts that minimise ambiguity so that misunderstandings and reinterpretations are unlikely.

Notes

1 The DISC profile has been developed by Performax Systems International. For information on questionnaires and courses, the Australian distributor is Integro Learning Company P/L, PO Box 6120, Frenchs Forest DC NSW 2086, www.integrolearning.com Tel: 1800 222 902

2 See also Chapter 4, Appropriate Assertiveness: Positive consequences from change

3 See Milo Frank, *How to Get Your Point Across in 30 Seconds or Less* (UK: Corgi, 1987)

4 Roger Fisher and William Ury, *Getting to Yes: Negotiating Agreement without Giving in* (USA: Penguin, 1991), pp 17 ff

5 See more on using non-adversarial language in Chapter 2, Partners not Opponents

Other useful reading

Roger Fisher and Scott Brown, *Getting Together: Building Relationships as We Negotiate* (USA: Houghton/Mifflin, 1989)

Douglas Stone, Bruce Patten, Sheila Heen and Roger Fisher, *Difficult Conversations: How to Discuss what Matters Most* (USA: Penguin, 1999)

Allan Parker, *The Negotiator's Toolkit: A Practical Guide to Success in the Home, Office, Factory and Boardroom* (Australia, Peak Performance Development)

CHAPTER 11
Introduction to Mediation
Can I make a skilful mediating intervention here?
How could I help the process and stay neutral?

Once you're managing well with your own conflict resolution skills you'll find you become super-sensitive to others around you who aren't doing a very good job of resolving their differences. Sometimes you'll itch to interfere: comments will perch on the tip of your tongue: 'But can't you hear he's not saying that?'; 'It seems to me you two actually want the same things'; 'I haven't heard you explain to her what you do want'. Before you know it the words are out and you have used a *mediating intervention*. The chances are it will move the conflict a step further forwards, but be careful. Being a third and neutral party in a conflict can be tricky. Even if no one's paying for your services, it is worth understanding some ground rules and procedures for good mediation.

You rarely are really neutral in these situations. If you have some stake in the outcome, you may need to put that on a back burner and work around it. Be very clear and open if, at the moment, something is influencing your behaviour. For instance, it's hard to be an effective mediator, even informally, if you are close to one party and not to the other.

Let's define what we mean by *mediation*. Some societies use the word interchangeably with arbitration and conciliation, but as the field becomes more precise it is better to keep the distinctions clear. Mediation means coming between parties in conflict and helping them move towards a resolution. It refers to situations where people in conflict come together to attempt to address their conflicts with the assistance of an uninvolved person whose role is to facilitate good communication and problem-solving skills between them. The role may be formally appointed or informally assumed. A mediator aims for an objective and neutral stance and focuses on helping the parties to find their own solutions. A mediator doesn't try to fix problems or give advice. It's this aspect of a mediator's role that can cause a well-intentioned friend or colleague the most problems. We are so used to offering advice that it can require huge self-discipline not to do so. Asking reframing questions of the type we've mentioned throughout this book can be wonderful mediating interventions.

The mediator helps both parties achieve what they need

A mediator is an independent party to a problem who is generally not directly involved. A mediator makes sure that each party expresses their side and listens to the other side. The mediator then steers both sides towards finding mutually satisfying solutions. At the beginning and throughout the process, they will keep checking that both parties are having a fair say and are listening to each other.

Mediation empowers people to solve their problems themselves as they will be more committed to solutions they have crafted themselves. The mediator does not *impose* a settlement. The only real power the mediator has is the authority to guide the communication and settlement process. If you are mediating completely informally you won't even have been given that much power. Your mediating interventions will be permitted only in the context of what we can say to each other in normal conversation. If you get it very wrong — start siding with one party, start advising, start being too pushy or formal — you will lose your unspoken permission to mediate. One or both parties will close up, change the subject or become angry with you. That's not to say you can't put a foot wrong, but if you do, your very next statement needs to be back on track. So that means staying alert and reading all the signals. In other words, you must be a very good empathic listener. Whether you're mediating formally or informally don't expect a high tolerance for error from people in conflict.

Resist advising

In the right circumstances, you can be very helpful mediating informally when you find yourself around two people fighting. You might step in to help in arguments between children, friends, teenagers and parents, or work colleagues. Skilful mediation interventions can become part of everyday life. An understanding of mediation techniques can help you turn other people's fights into fair play. It is an opportunity to put into practice the conflict resolution skills outlined in this book.

There will be times when it's better to use a professional. Unless you have some formal training or there's just no appropriate professional to call on, keep out of the following: relationship break-ups, custody and property disputes, workplace harassment, and bullying. Our own experience suggests that it's better for the non-professional to take no part in relationship disputes where the parties are highly emotional, seriously entrenched in their positions or the issue has been going for a long time.

JASMINE

I'm a professional mediator, but when two friends were recently going through a very emotional divorce, I found I could not even serve as their counsellor. I started to and then realised they were using me as their go-between. If one knew I'd seen the other, they'd pump me for information about what the other had said on an issue. Keeping professional levels of privacy was excruciating. I had to watch every word. Our social relationships were interfering with my abilities and obligations as a professional.

I realised that I felt strongly about how they should handle their divorce settlement. But it did not look as though it was shaping up to my image. When they asked me to mediate it, I knew they needed to ask someone else. I was much too close and too involved.

I was in danger of losing one or both of them as friends. To save my friendship with both of them, I explained how tense the pull of my divided loyalties was making me feel and we agreed that we'd ban talk of the divorce from our conversations. Over the following months I was often busting to know how their settlement was shaping up, but I knew I must not satisfy that curiosity. I think you've got to be tough on yourself when something is none of your business.

When they finally reached a settlement some twelve months and two expensive lawyers later, each told me it was over and I breathed a sigh of relief. We had finished with the no-go zone in our friendship.

Are there conflicts around you in need of outside assistance? A wide variety of conflict resolution procedures are available when disputants need help. Mediation is the method we emphasise in this chapter, but it's important to know that alternatives exist that offer both more and less control over the process and outcome. The range starts from an outside ruling by a court judge and progresses to complete self-direction.

WITH THIRD PARTY

CONTROL

WITH PARTICIPANTS

- *Court system and arbitration*: Third party hears the case and makes a ruling — a binding decision.

- *Conciliation*: Third party gathers facts and arguments. Makes a recommendation with substantial weight. Non-binding, invites compromise.

- *Shuttle diplomacy:* Go-between. Third party sees each participant separately. Carries options and offers backwards and forwards between them. Sometimes makes suggestions. Has great power to selectively inform.

- *Mediation*: Third party has tight control over process but not content. Doesn't have power to decide or recommend. Assists parties to isolate issues and options, and to reach a settlement by consensus that jointly satisfies their needs.

- *Facilitation:* Facilitators provide processes that enable groups and meetings to reach a desired outcome.

- *Expert appraisal*: One participant consults an expert in the particular field, eg, a property adviser or a stockbroker. Adviser provides data on effective practices.

- *Conflict counselling*: One participant consults an expert in conflict resolution and mediation to receive assistance in presenting their own case well.

- *Negotiation*: Parties work directly with each other towards exchanging promises and commitments in order to resolve their difficulties.

Conflict Counselling

Conflict counselling is a little easier than mediating: you are working directly with only one party at a time. You are not trying to manage the dynamics of a difficult relationship. Here advice is more acceptable and a little bias towards the person you are with may feel like welcome support to someone in the thick of conflict. Just don't jump into a Rescuing role (see Chapter 5, Cooperative Power) and make the absent person into the Persecutor. Don't become caught up in agreeing how awful the situation is and how right they are. Don't make their enemies your enemies. Even if you do think they are right, your overt agreement gives them *permission* to stay stuck. Generally you are of more help being as neutral as possible and working with them to try to understand the other side and to see how they can change the situation. Use all your active-listening and reframing skills. You might work with them to develop an 'I' statement, which objectively states what is upsetting them and how they would prefer it to be. Discuss how they might be able to communicate that to the other person. Leave them free to do something quite different to your suggestions if they wish.

Informal Mediation

When are you likely to intervene as an informal mediator? First, it will appear that the people in conflict are not coping well alone and need outside help. Then you need to be motivated and able to assist at the time they need you. It's best if you don't have a vested interest other than the desire to reach a successful outcome for both parties.

In informal mediation you will want the conflict to be resolved speedily if it presents you with problems in your close working or living relationships. As an informal mediator you may sometimes be invited by both parties to participate; sometimes you might make the offer; and sometimes the situation may be so informal that you are mediating without either party even noticing!

Setting it Up

You don't have to wait to be invited to mediate. Here are some points you might use to introduce the possibility of an informal mediation: 'If you'd like to, I'm happy to mediate while you two work through the problem you've got … Perhaps you can find some answers that work for both of you … I'd make sure you're really hearing each other … I'd support both of you and not take sides … I won't come up with answers … I'll do my best to remain objective … I'd just be steering the process.' It is quite common for only one party to actively seek mediation. A similar speech might persuade the other party to try it. When you have that agreement, decide upon a time and place.

Holding the Space

When you hold the space, you put yourself in charge, like a host or hostess making sure your guests are comfortable and have whatever they need. How do we make truly helpful interventions? Psychiatrist and somatics educator Dr Tony Richardson often says in his workshops: 'The greatest intervention you make is what you embody'. We discussed some key embodying skills in Chapter 1, Responding to Conflict — getting centred, flowing with the energy in the situation, redirecting thoughts towards the positive, and making caring contact. This is part of holding the space. It's about your presence. You bring your presence to the situation by concentrating on the two people, what they are saying and how the issues unfold.

You'll know you're being successful at creating a helpful atmosphere when each person starts speaking less defensively. Your intention is to make it safe enough for each of them to open up, become more willing to shift, give, share, examine, reconsider and resolve the problem jointly.

You need to come to a mediating situation with an attitude of discovery, discarding your biases and judgemental thoughts. A degree of self-awareness is needed because sometimes a judgement will slip in without you realising it. It's very important to put it aside as soon as you notice it and get back quickly to the job of working towards a positive outcome to the situation.

If you feel so strongly about an issue that you can't remain objective, don't mediate. If, for example, you can't get past seeing one person as a despicable bully, or you have a fixed opinion on what conclusions the people should reach, you're not really in a position to do a good job!

There will be times when nothing at all is set up — you just slip into mediation. No one has really given you consent to do so, and if you want the conversation to continue with you mediating, you have to play your cards carefully. Of course, you'll use many of the conflict resolution skills outlined in this book. Here are some particularly useful strategies to bear in mind when you find yourself mediating on the quiet.

Mediating on the Quiet

- 'Hold the space' for your participants: that means be aware of both parties, wishing them both well, wanting them to reach solutions that take them forward.

- Steer their conversation away from blame.

- Try to 'traffic cop' their interactions so that each person gets to speak without being interrupted.

- If you suspect a person has not taken in what was said, you might ask them to repeat what they think they heard. The first person can then correct any misunderstanding.

- If one person switches off or seems too irritated to continue, you might want to gently ask that person what's going on for them.

- Make sure that a conversation centred around each person's needs, not just their positions, is included.

- At times you might need to say what's going on for you. For example: 'I'm uncomfortable. It seems to me you're not considering ... Is that important?'; 'I don't know about you, but I'm finding this pretty intense. Do we want a tea break?'

- Use good listening skills and questions that turn conversations around.

- Ask option-developing questions: 'What might it look like if you had an arrangement that was really working?' You might want to pop the *miracle* question: 'Imagine a miracle has happened — you wake up tomorrow morning and the whole problem is solved. What would be the first thing you'd notice? What would you notice about the relationship (or other relevant topics)?'

ATTITUDES FOR MEDIATORS

Be objective — validate both sides, even if privately you prefer one point of view and even when only one party is present.

Be supportive — use caring language. Provide a non-threatening learning environment where people will feel safe to open up.

Be non-judgemental — actively discourage discussion about who is right and who is wrong.

SKILLS FOR MEDIATORS

Use astute questioning — don't ask, 'Why did you?' Ask, 'How do you see what happened?' and 'How did that affect you?'

Don't advise — encourage suggestions from participants. If necessary, offer options not directives.

Use a collaborative approach — work towards benefits and wins for both sides. Turn opponents into problem-solving partners.

Steps in Mediation

Let's presume you have been asked to mediate. The situation is far from being resolved, or obviously you wouldn't have been asked to get involved, but emotions are not so high that only a professional would dare touch the case. You need to know about the stages a mediator steers the process through, and how to conduct yourself in each of those.[1]

Preparation

Prepare the participants. Before the mediation formally begins, there may be groundwork to be done in preparing the parties to participate effectively. You might spend some time with them before the mediation. This can be wise if you don't know each other. It's hard for people to focus on sensitive issues when they are in the presence of a complete stranger and they don't know whether they trust you or not. If you spend time with one person you should spend a similar amount of preparation time with the other.

During this time you could address their concerns about the process, and help them frame how they will present their issues in a neutral and constructive way. Help them consider their purpose and develop an agenda for the session — how they will name the issues they want to raise and what they want to achieve. Don't enter into debate with them about their views or opinions. You may need to strengthen their commitment to participate in the mediation process. You might get them to recognise the costs of not resolving the conflict.

Prepare the space. Attention to seating is important. It is better not to have opponents sitting opposite each other. A round table is ideal, with you seated between the participants, and the three of you positioned so that you can see a big board or a sheet of paper. Have pens at hand for listing issues and recording agreements.

Open: Introductions and Agreements

• Explain your role, establish ground rules or the operating principles for the session.

• Decide together upon timing. How long will the meeting last? Seek a commitment for everyone to stay to the end of this time.

- Ask them to take responsibility for themselves — to mention if they're not happy about something, if they need a break or if they feel unheard.

- Clarify the role of the mediator. Emphasise that you will not be judging the situation. Your task is to steer the process, the participants are in charge of content.

- You might wish to explain that you will help them focus on building agreements that are fair for both or all parties involved, rather than a victory for any one party.

- To facilitate openness you may offer to respect confidentiality. Professional mediators would normally do so. The participants may or may not want to make a similar agreement.

- Make sure procedures and agreements are clear from the outset and that everyone agrees to them. Check if anyone wants to add something more. Agreements can be added to or renegotiated at any time, particularly if one party is not happy.

- Make an agreement with all parties that you will help them use 'I' statements. Explain this as simply as you can. Perhaps ask them to begin statements with 'In my experience ...'; 'As I see it ...'; or 'It's my opinion that ...' so that all statements are seen in a personal context and are not presented as indisputable facts or generalisations. Explain that participants should avoid blaming or putting interpretations onto the behaviour of the other party.

- Make an agreement that they will each allow the other to finish what they are saying.

Establish: Overview and Details

What are the issues? It is very helpful if you can have a single purpose for the mediation that is clearly stated — for example, restore working relations; handle social situations; sharing resources. You may have worked this out before you start the mediation, or defining the purpose might be the starting place for the meeting. Encourage each person to express their view, the issues and their feelings. Make sure that the parties participate equally. It's not important who goes first, as long as it's clear that each participant will have a chance to express their point of view.

Summarising key points is useful for everyone. Restate core messages using a format that opens options; for example, 'You're both not happy with things as they are and you would like to find some ways to improve the situation'. To stop a monologue, summarise the point, confirm you understand it correctly and ask a question that may direct the conversation forward.

You might use their opening remarks to develop an *Agenda of Issues* to be discussed. Choose agenda items that are relevant and helpful to the stated purpose. For example:

💡 'What do we need to discuss to achieve our purpose of restoring working relations?'

Ask them to add to the agenda or you create it from your summary of their key points. Then check that they agree with what you select.

Use the conflict mapping process — invite participants to talk about their needs and concerns. Participants can then see each other's needs and concerns about the issue, develop new understanding, identify common ground, and find ways to open up possibilities.

Mirroring — when emotions run high, it may be helpful, when one person has spoken, to encourage the other(s) to repeat what they have just heard before they respond. This technique is particularly useful when one person is reacting to an inaccurate reading of what the other person has said, or when one person significantly changes their attitude or makes a concession and it's important to ensure that the other has recognised this. People frequently do not absorb information that requires them to change their perception of the other person or the situation.

Define the common ground where both parties agree or have similar needs. Be careful how you phrase it. Focus on common ground that will move them forward. Try: 'You both want what's best for the children' or 'You are both concerned about the way in which communication occurs between you'; not 'You each feel the other person has been uncaring/rude/uncommunicative'.

Move: Identify Areas of Agreement and Negotiate

Key tasks are:

- Move the conversation forward.
- Recognise areas of agreement.
- Reinforce common ground.
- Highlight movements made.
- Seek out flexibility and movements from both parties.
- Develop options.
- Help design agreements.
- Help define measurable criteria for change.
- Clarify commitment.

Close: Completion

Agreements You will need to bring the session to an end with at least some agreements made by the parties. Summarise and, where possible, write down the agreements that they have made together. People find these documents very important as it gives them something concrete to take away and serves as a future reference.

Review Ask them to make a specific time to review how they are progressing, what is working and what needs some adjustment. Ask them to describe how they will correct a problem if things don't work as expected. You may decide to meet again. You may set them or remind them of tasks that they are prepared to go away and try.

Acknowledge After the mediation is over, acknowledge the participation and contribution of each party.

Conclude Will participants exchange a handshake, share a meal or a hug? Perhaps it's time to celebrate!

MARTIN

Recently I watched helplessly as two of my closest friends ended their relationship. They mixed in the same social and business circles and, unfortunately, when they attended the same functions they became angry with one another very easily. It was very uncomfortable for those around them as well as for themselves. In the end, it became such a problem that one of them would not attend a function if they knew that the other had been invited. Finally, I couldn't stand it any more, so I offered to mediate for them. They said they'd give it a try.

A week later we met on neutral territory (a park), made agreements about how we would operate together, and set a time limit. The purpose of the mediation was to reach an agreement for handling social situations.

I then gave each of them time to speak, and checked that the other person was listening without becoming defensive. After a while, they both softened a little towards each other as they acknowledged the good times they had had, along with the present difficulties.

Because each had recently annoyed the other by not greeting them at all at functions, they agreed that when they met socially they would immediately acknowledge each other with a special greeting in recognition of their past closeness. They also agreed that after greeting each other they would keep at a friendly distance for a while. There was still a lot of hurt and anger between them and time was needed for that to heal before a more comfortable friendship could develop. It wasn't part of my brief that day to sort out the difficulties that had led them to part. We had come together to look at what they would do now. The focus was on the future. It was enough that each now felt comfortable to be at the same function — neither would have to miss out because the other was planning to attend.

Troubleshooting

At the Beginning

Problem: Mud-slinging, accusing, bringing up the past.
Tip: Emphasise that mediation is about looking at how to make things work better in the future. You might need to remind participants of this to stop them if they're revisiting old resentments. You may need to allow talk about the past in order to clear misunderstandings or to work out what needs changing in the future, but do not focus on who is to blame.

Problem: People can't see past their difficulties.
Tip: Ask each party to create their vision of the future with the outcome they want. Ask:

-💡- 'How would you like it to be?'

-💡- 'What would it look like if it was all working well?'

Action-oriented questions might make the parties more likely to want to take action. Questions can include:

- ⚡ 'What can you do to make the outcome as you want it?'

- ⚡ 'Where do we go from here?'

Problem: Someone is harping on about all the things they don't want.
Tip: Ask them to tell you what they *do* want.

In the Middle

Problem: One person in the mediation has much more power than the other and is using it to unfair advantage.
Tip: Ideally you will have spotted this in the planning stage, but if it only becomes obvious as the mediation progresses, you may prefer to adjourn until power can be rebalanced. This might be achieved by the disempowered person getting support — from their union, a lawyer, a friend or a relative — as the situation suggests. If this isn't an option, you might be able to provide extra information about what's usual to expect in terms of a final agreement. You may need to enforce processes which reveal information that the disempowered person needs to know. Don't be enticed into the role of Rescuer, but be alert to situations when the person is, in fact, a genuine victim and needs the help you could offer as a mediator to protect them from danger, exploitation and injustice. Unfortunately it is often true that lions get the lion's share and lambs get the lamb's share and you can't always alter this. Training helps you steer around these dangers. Sometimes it can help to ask a question like:

- ⚡ 'Is that fair for both of you?'

Problem: Participants don't seem to be considering options that would be very helpful.
Tip: You may have no choice but to offer them a suggestion if they are not able to come up with one in reasonable time. Make it sound like an option and not a direction. For example, 'I heard of a situation in which a couple solved a similar problem about finances by having a joint account, to which they contributed equally, as well as separate accounts. Would that be relevant here?' Be careful that you don't usurp the participants' role as the problem-solvers.

A MODERN FABLE

A desert sheik died bequeathing his nineteen camels to his three sons, leaving

> his first son half his camels,
> his second son a quarter of his camels
> and his third son a fifth of his camels.

As it isn't economical to carve up camels, the three sons invited a mediator who arrived on *his* camel. The mediator assessed the situation and lent his camel to the estate. There were now twenty camels.

> The first son received his half (ten camels),
> the second son his quarter (five camels)
> and the third son his fifth (four camels).

This added up to the nineteen camels left in the estate, leaving the mediator with the camel he came with. He mounted it and rode away. Had you been the mediator would you have felt that justice was done? Or would you have asked awkward questions like: 'What about the sheik's daughters ...?'

Problem: Someone is assuming they know their opponent's motivation or is making sweeping generalisations.
Tip: Monitor assumptions. Ask:

💡 'Tell me what you mean by *not caring* or *unfair.*'

If you're hearing many generalisations, such as '... always forgets'; '... never has time', ask:

💡 'Can you give an example of when it really mattered to you?'

Problem: No one's talking.
Tip: Allow some silences, even quite lengthy ones. They give everyone time to think and integrate ideas, but if they cannot speak in front of each other, offer to meet separately.

Problem: Your participants seem to stir each other up every few sentences.
Tip: You may have to intervene frequently in such circumstances, taking firm charge of the process. Sometimes participants use words that inflame the conflict. Point out the impact of their remarks on the process; for example, explaining how it increases

tension. To encourage a more positive atmosphere, you may wish to help them rephrase some of their statements. The reframing questions in the following table may prove useful for this.

CONFLICT ANTIDOTES	
Conflict Creators	Reframing Questions
You fool! (and other insults)	What do you need? How can it be fixed?
I'm right. You (or they) are wrong.	How would you say your point of view differs from theirs?
I won't ...	What would make you willing?
It's a failure.	How could it work? What would make it better?
He (she) is hopeless!	What are they doing that's okay?
I (they) should/ought/must/ have to ...	Would you (they) choose to take up that option?
They always ...	Always? Are there any circumstances in which they don't?
I don't want ...	What do you want to happen?
I can't ...	You can't? Or you just can't see a way to? What happens if you do?
He (she) would never ...	How can we find ways for it to happen?
It's impossible.	If it *were* possible, what would it take?

If the situation lends itself to meeting separately after an initial session, you may be able to help them vent their tension and coach them on how to reframe some of their remarks.

Problem: Someone storms out of the mediation.
Tip: You might call a tea break, then find the person and say something like, 'We all have strong reactions sometimes. Can we come back and try again?' You might repeat it at the start of the next session so they feel less out on a limb.

Normalise experiences that others seem to regard as extraordinary or outrageous. For example, one participant might accuse the other, 'You wouldn't even speak to me!' and you can explain, 'It is not uncommon in this type of argument to need a cooling-off period in which the parties don't speak to each other'.

Problem: Your protagonists have no empathy for each other.
Tip: Ask the protagonists to picture a scenario that puts them in the other person's shoes or in a 'What if …' situation. Pose questions about what it would be like; invite them to reassess rigid or limited attitudes. 'What would it be like for you if you were criticised in front of your team?'

Help create new perspectives. For example: to an ex-husband who is not doing much for his children, 'What if you went to court and custody of your children was awarded to you? What would life be like for you?'

> Looking from the opposite point of view breaks down rigid thinking

Problem: Significant differences appear to divide the participants.
Tip: Do they really matter? Clarify and validate differences in values, personal styles and points of view. For example, 'To you, Jane, dress codes are very important, but John needs to express his individuality through his clothes'; 'It's quite understandable that after dinner, Mary's first priority is to do the dishes while yours, Peter, is to relax'; or 'You're naturally reserved, Alison, and Sarah likes to be upfront. You probably could both stretch your styles a bit so that you can meet halfway.'

> Respect individual differences

Problem: The mediation is dragging on, people are distressed and agreements aren't close.
Tip: Offer breaks. When emotions run high, it is good to call a cooling-off period of perhaps ten or fifteen minutes so that each person can get out of the room or at least stop talking for a while. Whatever the emotional climate, if you've been meeting for more than an hour and a half, then you will all really appreciate a little time out from the process. After the break, you might focus on them regaining their commitment to resolve. You might remind them that resolving is in their best interests and is what they have said they want.

Problem: It's a no-win situation.

Tip: Balance their dissatisfaction. Sometimes (as in a difficult divorce) by the time a mediator is called in, there is high animosity. Neither party wants the other to win; in fact, each wants the other party to be punished. The most the mediator can hope for is to end up with both parties equally dissatisfied with the settlement. Such outcomes may not provide much fulfilment for the mediator, but as a last resort they may settle the problem and give both parties a chance to get on with their lives.

At the End

Problem: The mediation requires more than one session. There is danger of momentum being lost.

Tip: You might set homework tasks. One clever mediator/family therapist, who was working with a dysfunctional family, including a withdrawn teenage girl, asked the girl to log the day, time and topic of each of her parents' arguments. The parents had their own tasks, but they knew that they were being observed by their daughter. The task encouraged the girl to move out of her isolation and participate in the solution. By carrying out the task, she indicated that she was prepared to take part in the therapy.

Problem: The agreements the participants are coming up with are wishy-washy — they don't seem to tackle the real underlying issues or cannot be assessed objectively. They may be generalities such as: 'You'll be nicer'; 'You'll show more respect'; 'I'll keep things tidier'; 'We'll go out more'.

Tip: Where possible make sure the agreements are specific, achievable and measurable. They could, for example, describe behaviours to be used in the future: 'You both will say "hello" when you arrive in the morning'; 'You both will allow each other to finish speaking'; 'You won't leave anything lying on the floor'. Compliance or non-compliance is then clear. To get there you can ask questions like:

- 'How will you know when the agreement is being kept?'

- 'What specifically would demonstrate to you that they are being more respectful?'

You might ask them to set up a yardstick to measure effective change: how many disagreements have occurred during the week; how much time has been needed to complete a job; the number of family outings in a month.

Mediation is not a mysterious process, but as you can see, there are extra skills needed in serious conflicts that may be beyond the scope of the amateur. There will be times when *you* are in conflict, emotions are highly charged and your own problem-solving reaches an impasse. At these times bringing in a professional mediator may be your most constructive approach to the conflict.

Professional Mediation Services

Mediation, where the decision-making rests with the participants, is a viable alternative to legal and other traditional methods of dealing with disputes. Mediation services are now widely offered around the world. Professional mediators provide individuals and industry with a faster, more equitable and much cheaper alternative to traditional courtroom methods.

A growing number of community-care organisations, counselling centres and private legal practices have mediation available as part of their service. In Australia, funded organisations with a number of branches include: Community Justice Centres, Unifam's Family Mediation Centres; Centrecare and Relationships Australia. They commonly deal with personal, family and neighbourhood disputes. If you need a professional mediator or conflict counsellor, start by consulting the 'Mediators' listing in your telephone directory or contact Conflict Resolution Network.[2]

Many of these professional organisations will offer a team of two or more mediators, chosen for their expertise in the problem area or for their compatibility with the clients. The Australian Government has also introduced schemes whereby 'grievance officers' are appointed and trained as mediators to deal with inequality, harassment and other conflicts within government departments. The role of Equal Employment Opportunity and Affirmative Action Officers is most frequently one of mediation, too. The Family Law Courts in Australia often require that couples use their mediation service before the court formalises any arrangements.

Mediation Training for Young People

Mediation can be a very simple process. Children as young as seven years of age are being taught about it in schools. Teenagers have been taught to use it very effectively to resolve problems with peers. Many schools have found a significant boost in morale and a corresponding drop in disciplinary problems and bullying by introducing a mediation programme. An interested teacher or counsellor, equipped with suitable training course materials, usually acts as coordinator.[3]

There are many situations where a skilled non-professional person has much to offer. First, they are on the scene! Do not underestimate the power of good intentions: holding the space so that two people can work out their difficulties in the presence of a caring third person can work miracles! Once it has been set up, the process will sometimes flow without you needing to intervene much at all.

The skills of conflict resolution will be invaluable for the mediating interventions needed. One or two good questions that turn the energy around may be exactly what's needed for the participants to move beyond their previous impasse. Understanding the basic moves of mediation and a little basic troubleshooting can turn you into a helpful force for positive change in your workplace and among your family and friends. Just know when to leave the really heavy stuff to the professionals.

EXERCISE: a conflict-resolving intervention

You live in a municipality where there is a very high level of unemployment. The outcome is a community in conflict, with much tension, dissatisfaction, ill heath, drug and alcohol abuse and violence. You are a concerned resident with an interest in this situation.

Your mayor has called a public meeting to canvass views on what she sees as necessary crisis intervention. You have accepted her invitation to speak for ninety seconds only.

You are determined to make a *conflict-resolving intervention*. List up to five points you will make to move the dialogue forward. Use this chapter in particular, and the book in general, for generating ideas for the talk on how a conflict-resolving approach could be applied. (If you really have a speech to make, a meeting to attend, or an article to write on difficult issues that need to be resolved, you may prefer to work on that in the same way rather than use this example. You could use the Conflict Toolkit in the Introduction as another starting place for your thinking.)

SUMMARY

A mediator helps both parties achieve what they need. The process demonstrates how conflict resolution skills provide a better way to manage differences.

Steps in Mediation

In the beginning: Arrange seating, the recording of the meeting and the timing. Clarify your role: you steer the process, the participants are in charge of the content. Discuss commitments, 'I' statements, focus and equal participation.

During the process: State the singular, simply stated purpose for the mediation. Develop an agenda of issues that works towards this purpose. Use mapping, summarising and silences. Define common ground. Make suggestions as options and not as directions. Allow opportunities for breaks. Maintain future, positive and action orientations. Use questions to reframe conflict-creating statements. Normalise experiences. Create new perspectives by asking participants to speak from opposite points of view to their own. Validate differences. Where outcomes are perceived as satisfactory to the parties, satisfaction is balanced; however, where it is obvious that the parties only wish to punish each other, balanced dissatisfaction may be the only reasonable outcome. Look for and acknowledge any signs or areas of agreement. Ask questions that direct the conversation to agreements.

At the end: Capture agreements. Write them down. How will they measure effective change? Ask them to make a time when they will review progress. Acknowledge participation and celebrate — you've earned it! Mediation turns opponents into problem-solving partners.

Notes

1 For an in-depth understanding of the mediation process read:

Miryana Nesic and Laurence Boulle, *Mediation: Principles Process Practise* (Australia: Butterworths, 2000)

Robert A Baruch Bush and Joseph P Folger, *The Promise of Mediation: Responding to Conflict through Empowerment and Recognition* (USA: Jossey-Bass Inc., 1994)

Ruth Charlton and Micheline Dewdney, *The Mediator's Handbook* (Australia: The Law Book Co, 1995)

Andrew Floyer Acland, *A Sudden Outbreak of Commonsense* (UK: Random House, 1990)

Andrew Floyer Acland, *Resolving Disputes without Going to Court* (UK: Century, 1995)

John M Haynes, *Mediating Divorce* (USA: Jossey-Bass, 1989)

Christopher W Moore, *The Mediation Process* (USA: Jossey-Bass, 1986)

John Winslade and Gerald Monk, *Narrative Mediation: A New Approach to Conflict Resolution* (USA: Jossey-Bass, 2000)

2 Contact Conflict Resolution Network on 61 2 9419 8500 or Shoshana Faire, Professional Facilitators International, directly on 61 2 9960 4615

3 *References for teaching mediation to children*

Fran Schmidt, Alice Friedman and Jean Marvel, *Mediation for Kids: Kids in Dispute Settlement Grades 4–7*, Student handbook and Teachers' Guide (USA: Peaceworks, 1992)

Fiona Macbeth and Nic Fine, *Playing With Fire: Creative Conflict Resolution for Young Adults* (USA: New Society, 1995)

Kenneth E Powell, Lois Muir-McClain and Lakshmi Halasyamani, 'A Review of Selected School-based Conflict Resolution and Peer Mediation Projects', an article from: *Journal of School Health* (1 Dec 1995)

Aline M Stomfay-Stitz, 'Conflict Resolution and Peer Mediation: Pathways To Safer Schools', an article from: *Childhood Education* (1 Jan 1994)

Clare Heaton and Maureen Lynch, *Managing Conflict with Confidence* (Australia: Pearson Education, 2003)

CHAPTER 12

Broadening Perspectives

Can I put this issue into perspective?

Am I including my 'heart' as well as my intellect?

Sometimes it all matters so much — you're too embroiled in the conflict, too attached to its outcome, too needful of other people behaving in a particular way — a whole toolkit of skills doesn't seem to be enough. You can find yourself so hooked by the conflict that you just can't let go. There's one tool left in the box: perhaps you need a new view.

Imagine for a moment that you're a traveller about to climb a mountain. At the foot of the mountain, when you turn around all you can see is what's directly in front of you: a few trees, a peak, a stream, a rocky track. As you climb, you can turn around and see that the few trees are in fact part of a larger forested area. A little higher you can see the farmland beyond the forest. Higher still, your view becomes more expansive — a township in the distance, a broad river — and when you reach the top, you have a full 360-degree view. *Broadening perspectives* is like climbing a mountain to see more of the scene.

As you claw your way upwards, you begin to:

• see the conflict from a different perspective

• understand another person's viewpoint

• become aware that the whole picture is much bigger than any single person's perspective.

You're not denying the problem; you couldn't if you tried. You fully accept that it's still there, but higher on the mountain, you are not so immersed in the finer details. Can you try to look at yourself objectively, even for a moment, and begin to witness your embroiled state from a little distance?

A useful exercise is the one of seeing yourself from three different levels. Think of a problem you are dealing with right now.

What would you say is your issue?

What would the *other person* in the conflict say is your issue?

How would a thoughtful and compassionate *outsider* looking at you describe the issue?

Become Observer as Well as Participant

If you can see an overview of the problem, immediately you're less immersed. Soon you might see that frustration is not your only option. This is self-awareness, one of the pillars of emotional intelligence.[1] Ron Heifetz in *Leadership Without Easy Answers*[2] calls this being on the balcony rather than on the dance floor: on the dance floor you are engrossed in your immediate situation; from the balcony your broader perspective throws up new insights. The real trick is to frequent both places. The view from the balcony might suggest that you would do better if you were to hold some of your beliefs more lightly. If you defend your opinions too rigidly, you're on the way to unresolvable conflict.

As well as living life in the thick of things, you need time out to check if you are defending outdated mindsets or habits. Are you, for example, waiting for the other person or the situation to change before you can move forward?

What Can You and Can't You Change?

Time out (on the mountain top or the balcony — whichever image you prefer) is not for fretting — it's for a change of perspective. Consider what you can and can't change. Is it time to move on now? If you've tried long enough and hard enough and skilfully enough, you might just need to know that this issue will never shift through your efforts alone.

Sometimes when you hold onto a desired outcome too strongly, any outcome at all appears to elude you. The problem is that it matters too much to you. This is when it can be useful to detach a little and take a step back. You might envisage your passionate, meaningful relationship where your partner behaves exactly as you wish, you may make a perfect business plan or work towards your

ideal holiday, yet nothing seems to go your way. Perhaps there are obstacles you can't seem to get around, people disagree with your point of view, or the timing is off and everything is dragging on. In times like these, you are not in the flow, your dream feels like it is out of reach and the harder you try to grab it, the more conflict you seem to create. You need to believe that, now you have done your part, the rest is out of your hands. Visualise a shift in attitude — from holding your outcome tightly in a clenched fist to holding it lightly in the palm of your hand. This is not to say you should do nothing; it is just that after your work, you let go, with the intention that the best possible outcome for all involved will happen. Stop expecting your desired outcome and instead observe how others respond when you stop struggling. Often they will sense your shift in energy and naturally move closer to you. Allow some magic in the mix, for things to come to you, rather than fighting for them. It may take longer or come in a slightly different form, but it is surprising; sometimes the outcome is even better than you imagined.

LISA

In preparation for starting a family, Peter and Lisa decided to move from the city to the country. They would move as soon as the details of Peter's new internet business were finalised. This business would give him work that was not dependent on location, and that seemed like a good idea. But every day Peter became more remote and despondent. There seemed to be problems involved in the set-up and Lisa could not get a date from him for their move.

She felt she had her whole life on hold, waiting for him to handle all the issues with his company before they could depart. They'd decided to rent before they bought and she'd have loved to be looking for houses. They also needed to get a bigger car, but was it too soon? She'd had enough of her job, but didn't know if she'd be quitting it in a month or was it three months? She worried that Peter might not get his act together until next year. If that was the case, she needed to look for somewhere else to work right now.

She hated with a passion the strain of being on the edge of a new life but not quite plunging in. She was becoming short-tempered and frustrated, and particularly so with Peter. She couldn't make Peter's business work for him, but she was totally dependent on that happening.

Lisa went to the mountain top. From there she could see she was stuck, she'd put her life on hold, she was waiting for Peter and the business plan. What could she do *now* that would give her back a sense of control, a sense of her life moving forward under her own direction?

She knew she wanted to have a big clean-out of junk before their move. She could start on that immediately. She'd dreamt of doing silk-screen printing once she moved. She enrolled in a local college for a course that would start in a few weeks.

She thought of something she could address at work that would make it feel a bit better.

Although she was only two steps further forward, she was on the road again and no longer felt trapped by their difficulties. She couldn't really help Peter, but she found she was pestering him less about their plans. Within a day or so, she noticed their relationship improving. He seemed less withdrawn and she felt it might have been because she wasn't so urgent about finding answers to his difficult business issues.

Find the Path with Heart

To stand up for what you want, you need to inject *heart* into a situation. You need to peel back the layers of your demand for change to locate a deeper level of compassion than you have so far brought to the situation. Trying to build empathy by active listening and other methods may not help when you're stretched to your limit. On the mountain top there is another level of empathy to consider. First, you can notice if you have closed off to the other person energetically. Have you contracted in your chest (around your heart) to protect yourself? When you're angry, or you dislike someone intensely, or they have hurt you, it is very natural to do this. Your emotional state can drive you into such a tightness that you can't find any way forward. From a place beyond emotions and contraction, you can summon compassion that you can feel towards all beings — particularly those in pain. Notice their pain and fears, even if well hidden. Sense the damage that past hurts, mental imbalance or limited life opportunities must have caused them. Let a little compassionate energy flow towards them. Do it because it serves you — it may also serve to ease the conflict.

Choosing the path with heart is always the wise choice. Focus on putting heart into even your most difficult interactions and hold to it no matter what happens. Try never to fall out of integrity with that part of yourself. It doesn't mean letting your teenage son get away with stealing or drug-taking, or your boss getting away with sexual harassment. The path with heart can crack down like a ton of bricks if that's what's needed. No matter what they've done, no matter what punishment they deserve or that you might impose, you can wish them, in their essence, well. If you must be tough, be tough with heart, not without it. Remember to include compassion for yourself as well.

If you're at a crossroads and don't know which way to turn, sense which option has more heart — it will be the better one. You may first need to work through your turbulent emotions before you clearly sense in which direction your heart is leading you.

Consider the Context

Sometimes your broader perspective is to notice that you are seeing only part of the problem, not the whole. Your issue won't resolve itself because it lies in the context of a bigger problem;

for example, you want a pay rise; you know you deserve it; but your pay rise must occur in the context of everyone's pay in the organisation. That doesn't mean you shouldn't go on pushing for what you believe you deserve, but, in fact, you might be fighting a bigger battle than you first thought. When considering the context, think about conditions, culture, customs, social and legal factors.

Consider this example: you have been treated badly by a former employer. You believe you have the right to sue them through the courts. Will you go that route? Will justice be served, or will you end up paying out all your savings to the lawyers and probably get nowhere? How can you know this before you start? You may not, but at least climb to the mountain top and have a good look. Do you know anyone who has won a case like this? What compensation could you realistically expect to achieve through the courts? Would that make a difference? Would you get your old job reinstated? After the whole situation, would you want it back anyway?

Watch the Ripples

If you are dealing with a child's behavioural problems at home, you probably should also be considering the effect of that on circumstances at school. Step back, look around. Where are the ripples? Something wrong in one work area may be affecting other parts of the organisation. Inequalities or unfair treatment in one section of society may soon be causing major problems in other areas.

If you are considering making a significant intervention in a conflict, can you see if that is likely to create change in other areas? Is that what you want? Inquiring may show you a reason to pursue the conflict resolution process with more vigour because it will have such a widespread effect. One group of employees asking for a better deal can affect the whole industry — over a few years there may even be ripples that affect the whole nation.

If you keep tracing the ripples outwards, you may see that everything and everyone is interconnected. We need each other to survive and flourish, we're bound together in a web of mutuality. The actions of one individual are interconnected with every other.

Sense the Transformational Shift

When your perspectives broaden, there may be a sudden shift in your thinking — a transformation — something clicks and suddenly you see things differently.

- Instead of seeing the other person as the enemy, you see them as your teacher.

- The other person tells you something about their past that makes their behaviour much more understandable to you.

- You notice your own Rescuing behaviours and now you can see what is needed from you and what is not.

Respect and Value Differences

We need to commit ourselves to the knowledge that we are all unique and special, with distinctive yet equally valid viewpoints. You may have heard the story of the blind people and the elephant: each person took hold of a different part of the elephant. The one holding the tusk concluded the animal was a car; the one holding the leg thought it was a tree; the one holding the tail was convinced it was a rope; and the one touching the elephant's side claimed it was a wall. Each assumed that their experience was the true representation of this thing called 'elephant', and could not understand why the others were describing something which sounded very different.

Each person's viewpoint is a part of the whole. Only if we all share information do we get a reasonably accurate picture of what we are dealing with. Someone who has a totally different set of priorities to you is telling you about another piece of the full story.

Understanding the truth of that in the complex situation you are facing may be your transformational shift.

Make Space for Synergy

Can you make a space for the miracle of synergy? Synergy is the ability to perform something together that you could never achieve alone. It can arise through a combination of unique perspectives as a result of the combined power for change of people cooperating. It can come about because solving this particular problem demands a higher order of solution, a better combination of all the factors, than you've managed before.

EXERCISE: moving beneath the problem

To find your new perspective, you may need to plunge so deep inside that you arrive at a place *below* where you have the problem. Take a moment for some quiet reflection. Think about a problem you are facing right now.

Ask yourself:	What do I need?
Ask more carefully:	What do I really need?
And inquire deeply and slowly for a third time:	What do I really, really need?

Were you able to deepen your perspective, bring in a new element, and perhaps understand the problem in the context of your core values? Conflict can be about becoming more conscious of what's going on around you and using the situation to bring you messages about yourself.

Include a Long-term Perspective

A long-term perspective must sometimes be included. Are you supporting or resisting inevitable forces for change and growth? Where are you heading in the evolution of ideas? Transforming forces are always at work below the surface. If you don't take the time to sense them, you may feel disheartened.

There are things worth fighting for, changes you need that won't come quickly. You need an inner fortitude for your long, hard campaigns, so that you can continue them for decades, if that's what's needed. Perhaps you can create a picture of the problem finally solved. How far ahead must you jump to find it? Sense what that is like. Use the vision to keep your impetus for continuing action.

LONG-TERM PERSPECTIVE

This is a story about IBM in the US. One middle executive made a tactical error that cost the company $9 million. The following week the executive was called into the chairman's office. He was sure he was about to be fired, but the chairman started discussing plans for a huge new project he wanted the executive to direct. After a certain point, the executive, squirming in his seat, had to interrupt the chairman's train of thought.

'Excuse me, sir. You know, I'm amazed. Last week I cost us $9 million. How come you are putting me in charge of this new project and not firing me?'

The chairman smiled: 'Fire you? Young man, I've just invested $9 million in your education. You are now one of my most valuable assets.'

Here was a chairman who valued above all else the willingness to risk and learn. He knew it was an essential ingredient in any executive. He trusted completely his long-term perspective.

VISION OF FUTURE SUCCESS

Thomas Edison 'failed' over 10,000 times before producing a working light bulb. When asked how he could persist after 9,999 failures, he replied simply: 'I did not fail 9,999 times. I succeeded 9,999 times in learning how *not* to build a light bulb'. He could only have kept going that long with a vision of success to sustain him.

Don't underestimate the deeply held desires of thousands of people. Ultimately they can shape major world events. Our actions can have a wider meaning and multiply their effects when we cooperate with others. Unite your heartfelt wishes with others who want the same. Millions of us already want such things as a cure for pandemic diseases, non-violent resolution of conflict, an end to the factors that encourage terrorism, the sustainable use of the planet's resources. Perhaps you might want to use your conflict resolution skills to join discussions on issues you care about and swell the forces that will drive these long-term changes. Start right where you are. How could you influence your organisation? Perhaps you'd like to see its important decisions made with more emphasis on social justice and ecologically sustainable approaches.[3]

Some of the issues we lobby for at the Conflict Resolution Network include: employment for all who need it and particularly in countries recovering from war; the continuing peacetime training and use of the military as emergency response teams; the Bilateral Peace Treaties Proposal — a network of one-to-one relationships between nations.[4]

SUMMARY

- Become an observer, as well as a participant.
- What can you and can't you change?
- Find the path with heart.
- Consider the context.
- Watch the ripples.
- Sense the transformational shift.
- Respect and value differences.
- Make space for synergy.
- Include a long-term perspective.

Broadening your perspective is like climbing higher up a mountain to see further horizons. Only from this higher vantage point can you find meaning in distressing events and seemingly unconnected circumstances. From this higher perspective, you can learn to behave as a part of cooperative global community. From the higher perspective, you can begin to envisage a world where everyone can win, a world that works for everyone.

Notes

1 Daniel Goleman, *Emotional Intelligence*, op. cit.

2 Ronald A Heifetz, *Leadership Without Easy Answers* (USA: Belknap Press, 1994)

3 Triple bottom-line management: 1. Profitable. 2. Sustainable. 3. Committed to social justice.
    Further reading:
    Andrew Savitz and Karl Weber *The Triple Bottom Line: How Today's Best-run Companies Are Achieving Economic, Social and Environmental Success — And How You Can Too* (USA: Pfeiffer Wiley, 2006)

4 The Bilateral Peace Treaty contains two proposals: 1. We will settle all disputes between us by negotiation or other peaceful means. 2. We will never be the first to resort to force, violence or war on each other or another

APPENDIX I

CONFLICT CLUES: WHAT TO DO ABOUT THEM

DISCOMFORT

Act to get comfortable. Say something. Ask a question. Check how the other person is. Are they concerned about something? It may work better to phrase your question neutrally. 'How are things going?' rather than 'What's wrong?' or say what you want rather than point out what is not quite right. Try some small talk. Get more information. The situation hasn't escalated to being a big deal at this stage. If it's not about you, stay out of it!

INCIDENT

Talk it over as soon as is acceptable to both parties. Encourage good dialogue and objective statements. Actively listen to their explanation. Emphasise that it is a small thing and that your motive is to ensure that the relationship continues well. Express respect and good will to put the situation to rest.

MISUNDERSTANDING

Have a longer, deeper talk about the situation. Make it relaxed and unrushed. Don't assume you understand. Clarify frequently. Check assumptions, conclusions, inaccurate interpretations and the meaning we put on others' behaviour. Consider an alternative, less judgemental interpretation of what has gone on. Use a neutral third party, if needed, to help you understand each other or get to the bottom of the problem. Attribute no blame!

TENSION

It has taken time to get this bad. It will take time to sort it out. Focus on the good reasons to fix the issues. All parties have to want it fixed. Deal with your own tension first. Be prepared: you will need a strategy with a range of actions, which attend to the relationship as well as the substantive issues. Involve all the parties and work through it over time together. You may need neutral help.

CRISIS

External control with authority may well be needed here. The communication of information that is clear and simple needs to be managed by someone with a cool head. Individuals may need support and practical help. Deal with the immediate issues and then work on the long-term outcomes.

Thanks to conflict resolution seminar leader, facilitator and mediator Christine James, Conflict Resolution Services P/L, for permission to adapt her material for this appendix

APPENDIX II

CONFRONTING PEOPLE IN AUTHORITY
Keep Your Focus on a Collaborative Approach

1. **Think of ways to help them trust you** — for example, talk to them more frequently; tell them what's important to you.

2. **When you talk to them about an issue be very clear about your purpose and direction** — Remember:

   a. You want everyone's needs to be considered.

   b. Use objective yardsticks to judge what is fair rather than engage in a clash of wills.

   c. Aim for a joint problem-solving approach rather than issuing ultimatums.

3. **Change tack if necessary** — for instance, if they are using their authority to be totally obstructive, but the issue is important to you. Are there appropriate incentives that might persuade them? If all else fails you may have to, without threatening, clearly outline the consequences of non-agreement. In such a case you may even have to consider legal rights and procedures.

4. **Don't verbally attack power-hungry people** — people who misuse power are out to prove they are powerful. If you don't want to be their target, feed them with positive reinforcement.

5. **Discover their specific needs** — use active listening (see Chapter 3, Empathy).

6. **What are their needs and concerns?** Explore what is behind the rhetoric being used. Ask questions to shift the focus from anger or put-downs to exploring the issues; for example: 'Is your real concern that we have to keep these goods you don't want?' Acknowledge their needs and concerns before you explain yours. It's often wise to wait until the worst of their anger has subsided before you justify your actions. Consider your next step. Would it be best to make an 'I' statement, take time out if you or they are out of control, address fears or develop options together?

7. **Work out your alternatives** — how will you make the best of it if they don't see it your way? It's important not to seem too desperate (see Best Alternatives, page 184). Needing something too badly weakens your power and might bring a pleading quality into your approach. That can turn you into a target for a serious Persecutor.

8. **Find some supporters** — the backup of others who think as you do can be persuasive.

9. **Use questions and reframes to improve the agenda** — in response to 'I don't have time ...' ask, 'When will you have time?' In response to 'You're always late ...' reply, 'No, not always, and this time what happened was ...'

10. **Redirect the energy** — opposition can be reframed.

   a. Reframe an attack on you as an attack on the problem; for example, 'You stupid idiot!' can be countered with 'What aspect of the problem haven't I taken into account?'

   b. Avoid directly opposing the other person. Instead of saying, 'You're dead wrong', ask, 'Have we considered everyone's needs here?' or 'Others see it differently. Could we look at what they see?'

   c. Present their opposition or solution as if it is just one of several options; for example, reframe 'You'll do it my way' by replying, 'That is certainly one alternative — are there any other ways that could be just as good or even better in the right circumstances?'

   d. Find out what makes them choose that option; for example: 'You say you'd like to use plan X. Tell me why you consider it the best option.'

   e. Welcome their opposing viewpoint as a contribution towards solution: 'I'm so glad you brought that up ... We must include the point you are making.' Let them discover themselves to be on your side. Let their contribution unite with yours to provide a broader focus on the problem.

   f. Bring other people's needs and values to their attention: 'I think we should include Brian's need for more room.'

11. **Decide which issues are worth fighting about and which are not** — sometimes the cost of fighting a powerful person is just too high; on the other hand, sometimes you feel so strongly about the misuse of power, it's worth it to stake everything on your opposition.

(See also Chapter 5, Cooperative Power, Confronting Powerful People, pages 118–19.)

INDEX

Actions or objects, focus on 66
Active listening 45–53, 86, 92, 136, 200
Activities, sharing 42
Adrenaline 10
Adversarial approach 24, 26
Affiliation, sense of 139
Aggression
  handling 94
  persecuting behaviour, in 103
Agreement 66
  assessing 208
  climate of, setting up 200
  confirming 208
  emphasising areas of 204–5
  separating people from problem 204
Aikido 15–17
Amygdala 9–11
Anger 142
  communicating 130
  destructive force 131
  indirect 149
Appreciation, expressing 139
Arbitration 214
Assertiveness
  appropriate 73, 95, 200
  guidelines for 75–6
  personal history on 73
  premises behind 74
Authority
  confronting people in 118–19, 244
  positions of 98
  respecting 118
Autonomy 65, 66, 139

BATNA 184
'Beginner's Mind' 20

Best alternatives 184
Bilateral Peace Treaties Proposal 242
Blame 54
Body
  changing reaction to response 15–19
  fight, flight or freeze 11–12
Body shift 126–7
Bodymind 122–3
Brainstorming 181–2
Breathing 15, 199
Bridges, building 42–3

Centring 15–16, 18, 199
Changing 234–5
Choice, operating from 113
Chunking 185–6
Circumstances 154
Closing negotiation 208
Cognitive dissonance 68
Collaborative approach 24–5
  challenges in 25–6
  key ingredients 29–33
  power, to 117–20
  shifting mindset to 38
Collaborative language 31
Collective power 99
Collins, Dianne 41
Commitment 37
Communication
  communication killers 43–5
  feelings, of 124, 130–1, 133–4
  keep communicating 35
  process 17
  warming 40–1
Competition 200
  agreement vs 66
  using 34

Compromise 26
Conciliation 214
Conditioning 25
Conflict
    clues 21, 23, 243
    emotional responses to 131–2
    hanging onto, pay-off for 141–2
    incidents 3
    mapping 160–1
    opportunity, as 38, 190
    reacting to 6–7
    responding to 1–2, 6
    secondary gains from 141–2
Conflict counselling 214, 215
Conflict resolution
    conflict-resolving interventions
        230–1
    others' unwillingness to resolve
        156–8
    pay-off for 142
    practical solutions 183
    procedures 214
    willingness to resolve 141
Confrontations
    consequences, about 91–2, 184–5
    powerful people, with 118–19,
        244
Connecting 18–19
Conscientious people 60
Consequence confrontations 91–2,
    184–5
Context, considering 237–8
Contributions 54
Control issues 116–17
Conversation topics 42
Cooperation 37, 138
Cooperative power 97
Court system 214
Creativity 138
    creating options 179
Crises 4, 57
Criticism 138

Crum, Thomas 15
Currencies 184, 193

Defensiveness under attack 26
Dialoguing 69–71
Differences, respecting and valuing
    239–40
Direct Influencing Stabilising
    Conscientious (DISC) 58–64, 193
Direct people 60
DISC model 58–64, 193
Discomfort 2, 79
Discovery, attitude of 20, 190, 200
Disempowering language 112
Dowrick, Stephanie 145
Dreams 124
Dreikurs, Rudolf 137

Emotional blackmail 137
Emotional intelligence 2, 138, 234
Emotional release 123, 124–5
Emotions see also Feelings
    changing reaction to response 19
    communication of 124, 130–1,
        133–4
    containing 124
    fight, flight or freeze 12
    handling difficult emotions in
        others 134–8
    managing 122
    positive 138–9
    suppressing 124
Empathy 40, 41, 57–8
Employment, lobbying for 242
Empowerment 107–8, 112
Energy flows 123
Equal power relationships 120
Equality 66
Ethical, what is 187
Expert appraisal 214
Expertise 98
Extraversion 58

Facilitation 214
Fairness 187
Fascination 21
Fate 154–6
Fears
    communicating 130
    parties to conflict, of 164–8
Feelings 66
    communication of 124, 130–1,
        133–4
    good, being source of
        138–9
    pent-up, releasing 124
Felt sense 125–6
Festinger, Leon 68
Fight, flight and freeze 7–14
Fisher, Roger 184
Flow, concept of 16–17, 27
Focusing 124, 125–9
    process of 127–9
    steps to 128
Forgiveness 144–6
Frank, Milo 197
Frustration 21, 131

Gendlin, Eugene 125
Goals, shared 33
Goleman, Daniel 2, 11
Good intention 68
Goodwill 37
Guilt, communicating 130

Harvard Negotiation Project
    184
Heart, choosing path with 237
Heated argument 4
Heifetz, Ron 234
Henderson, Dr Julie 125
Hostility 131
Hurt 142
    communicating 130
Hypothalamus 10

'I' statements 80–8
    sample conversations based on
        89–91, 96
Inappropriate behaviour 35
Incidents 3
Influencers 60
Intention
    good, locating 68
    your own, checking 87
Interaction
    negotiation, during 199–208
Interdependence 65, 66
Introversion 58
Intuition, trusting 79
Irritation 147

Judgement 57
Jung, Dr Carl 58, 148, 154

Language
    collaborative 31
    disempowering 112
    non-adversarial 32
    proactive and reactive 76
Law, power of 99
Legal rights 187
Listening
    active 45–53, 86, 92, 136, 200
    purposes 50

Manipulation 99–101
Maps
    benefits of 176
    creating 161–9
    difficult people, mapping 168–9
    issue 161
    making 191
    mapping the conflict 160–1
    mediation, in 221
    needs and fears of parties 162–8
    parties 161–2
    reading 169–72

time for making 172–4
Martial arts 15–17
Mediation 214
   common ground, defining 221
   completion 222
   conflict mapping 221
   definition 211
   informal 216–18
   issues, establishing 220
   mediators 212, 218
   mirroring 221
   opening 219
   preparation 219
   professional services 229–30
   steps in 219–22, 231
   training for young people 230
   troubleshooting 223–9
Meditation 124
Mirroring 221
Misunderstanding 3, 57
Motivation, understanding 145–6
Mutual respect 37
Mutuality, web of 238

Nagging 138
Needs
   core, nourishing 138–9
   parties to conflict, of 162–8
   reaffirming 118
   responding to 34, 35
   suppressed 150
   unmet 137
Negotiation 189, 214
   acknowledging points of view 204
   areas of agreement, emphasising 204
   bottom line, knowing 205
   closing 208
   conflict-resolving counter-tactics 206
   cultural differences in parties 2–6

   flexibility 205
   goal, maintaining 206
   interaction 199–208
   irritants, avoiding 204
   note taking 207
   objective 190
   opening statement 197–8
   other person's case, working on 195–6
   preparation 190–8
   questions steering 202–3
   separating people from problem 204
   skills 26
   steps in 199
   taking breaks 207
   unrealistic expectations 205
   your own case, working on 192–3
'No', saying 93

Observer, becoming 234
Observer-created reality 25
Opposing priorities 65
Options
   better 37
   brainstorming 181–2
   chosen, acting on 187–8
   creating 179–81
   designing 179
   most suitable, choosing 186–7
Outcomes of negotiation 192
   win/lose 200
Outgoing people 58–9

Parents
   authoritarian 105
   empathy breakdown 42
People/task continuum 58–9
Persecuting behaviour 103
   stepping out of 115–17
Persona 148

Personal design 154–6
Perspectives
    broadening 233
    changing 200
    long-term 240–2
Persuasiveness 99
Positions of authority 98
    confronting people in 118–19,
        244
Positive outcome, redefining 34
Power
    collaborative approach to 117–20
    collective 99
    cooperative 97
    equal power relationships 120
    law, of 99
    power bases 98
    power tactics 101–2
    relationships 97, 103
    sources of 98
Power games 103–17
    moving out of 107–17
Power struggles 137
Powerful people, confronting
    118–19
Practical solutions 183
Preparation
    mediation, for 219
    negotiation, for 190–8
Proactive language 76–9
Proactive mindset 21–2
Problem
    separating people from 204
Projection 147–9
    unconscious 147
Psychological threat 10
Punishment 98
Put-downs, handling 94–5

Questions
    asking 21
    negotiation, steering 202–3

redirecting 136
using 182

Raising difficulties with others 80–5
Reacting to conflict 6–7
    moving out of reaction 14–22
Reactive language 76–9
Reflective dialogue 70
Regret, communicating 131
Relationships, valued 98
Requests, refusing 92–3
Rescuing behaviour 103, 104
    stepping out of 108–11
Resentment 131, 142–3
Reserved people 58–9
Resolution of conflict see Conflict
    resolution
Respect 57
    authority, for 118
    differences, for 239
Responding to conflict 1–2, 6
Retaliation 138
Revenge 138
Reward 98, 137
Ripples, watching 238
Roles 139

Self-awareness 214
Self-discovery 151–4
Self-empowerment 107, 112
Self-esteem
    blows to 143
    building 114
Selling yourself 201
Shadow 148
Shuttle diplomacy 214
Skill, lack of 25–6
Somatic psychologists 125
Stabilisers 60
Stating your views 79–80
Status 66, 139
Style, adapting 87

Suggestions, offering 118
Suppressed needs 150
Synergy 240

Task/people continuum 58–9
Tension 3–4, 57
Thoughts
    changing reaction to response 20
    fight, flight or freeze 12–14
Timing 42
Transactional analysis 103
Transformational shifts 239
Trustworthiness 138

Unacceptable qualities or
    characteristics 150–1
Unconsciousness 148–9
Unresolved personal history 150

Value clashes 64–8
Victim-offender reconciliations 70

Victims
    real 104
    stepping out of role of 112–15
    victim behaviour 103, 104–5,
        110–11
Violence 4

Walking away 35
Weaknesses
    strengths, turning into 197
Willingness to resolve 141
Win/lose outcomes 200
Win/win approach 27–9
    challenges to 33–7
Wounds, healing 145

Zen 20

If you would like to know more about our lobby programmes or would like more information or training materials on Conflict Resolution, contact us at:

CONFLICT RESOLUTION NETWORK

PO Box 1016
Chatswood NSW 2057 Australia

phone: **61 2 9419 8500** · fax: **61 2 9413 1148**
email: **crn@crnhq.org** · website: **www.crnhq.org**

If you would like to run a program in your organisation contact:

PROFESSIONAL FACILITATORS INTERNATIONAL

phone: **61 2 9960 4615** · fax: **61 2 9968 1660**
email: **shoshana@facilitators.net**
website: **www.facilitators.net**